Constance Battersea

The History And Literature of the Israelites

Constance Battersea

The History And Literature of the Israelites

ISBN/EAN: 9783744717977

Printed in Europe, USA, Canada, Australia, Japan

Cover: Foto ©ninafisch / pixelio.de

More available books at **www.hansebooks.com**

THE
HISTORY AND LITERATURE
OF THE ISRAELITES.

THE HISTORY AND LITERATURE

OF THE ISRAELITES,

ACCORDING TO THE

OLD TESTAMENT AND THE APOCRYPHA.

Lucia Anna Maria Rothes — Trelawny

VOLUME II.

THE PROPHETIC AND POETICAL WRITINGS.

LONDON:
LONGMANS, GREEN, READER, AND DYER.
1870.

CONTENTS.

I. THE PROPHETS.

A. INTRODUCTION:

                                                                            Page

    The History and General Character of the Prophets ... 1

B. THE THREE GREATER PROPHETS:

    Isaiah (759 to about 700) 24
    The Second Isaiah (about 540) 49
    Jeremiah (627 to about 580) 59
    Ezekiel (595 to about 570) 91

C. THE MINOR PROPHETS 106

    I. Joel (about 810) 107
    II. Jonah (about 800) 117
    III. Amos (790) 125
    IV. Hosea (785—725) 134
    V. Micah (730) 140
    VI. Nahum (710) 148
    VII. Zephaniah (640) 154
    VIII. Habakkuk (610) 159
    IX. Obadiah (about 580) 166
    X. Haggai (520) 169
    XI. Zechariah (520) 172
    XII. Malachi (about 430) 187

D. THE BOOK OF DANIEL (about 160) 193

II. THE POETICAL WORKS.

		Page
A.	GENERAL SURVEY	219
B.	THE PSALMS	221
C.	THE PROVERBS	247
D.	THE BOOK OF JOB	259
E.	ECCLESIASTES	298
F.	THE SONG OF SOLOMON	314
G.	THE WISDOM OF JESUS THE SON OF SIRACH, OR ECCLESIASTICUS	318
H.	THE WISDOM OF SOLOMON	326

I. THE PROPHETS.

A. INTRODUCTION.

THE HISTORY AND GENERAL CHARACTER OF THE PROPHETS.

The moral truths bequeathed to us by the Hebrews, are not only embodied in the lives of their great men, or enforced by the doctrines of the Law; but they have been handed down from generation to generation in another and, if possible, even a more enduring form — by a literature remarkably rich and varied. While seeming to appeal merely to our imagination and our emotions, the Hebrew poets and prophets impress upon our minds with singular distinctness the greatness and mercy of God, and the duties of rectitude and benevolence. Their beautiful and sublime utterances reveal to us the intellectual life of the Israelites, their spiritual aspirations, and their lofty aims. Through them we seem to be carried into a brighter atmosphere, we seem to inhale a purer air. The din and turmoil of the world are heard in distant echoes, and the harmony of peace and truth falls gently and soothingly upon the ear. Hebrew poetry, not coloured by special doctrines, speaks the universal language of human sentiment and passion, and has, therefore, been readily accepted by nations of all climes and of all ages. It glorifies the ruling sovereignty of God; it expresses joy and sorrow, gratitude and supplication, in songs of rich yet measured imagery; it enshrines the moral and practical lessons of the wise and the thoughtful; and it has thus become the solace of the suffering and the guide of the erring.

But Hebrew poetry reaches its greatest power and sublimity in the writings of the prophets, of those great men who lived and toiled for the happiness of their people, who exhorted and denounced, reproved and comforted, according to the ever varying conditions of the times. The influence of the prophets was powerful and commanding; for they addressed themselves to their hearers at once as members of the political and of the religious community. They appealed to men in their various relations of life: by directing the policy of the citizen, they promoted the interests of his faith; and by enlightening his creed, they ensured his safety and prosperity. They were no enthusiasts; although pointing to heaven, they never lost sight of the world and its claims. Hence their productions are of the utmost importance and of singular interest. We may well admire the unequalled grandeur of their style and the lofty strains of their eloquence; but these must not let us forget their historical value; for they throw a flood of light upon the contemporary events of the nation. The prophets themselves appear as statesmen and noble patriots, and are the worthiest types of all that was great in their race. It is interesting to examine the origin and growth of their power, and for this purpose it will be necessary to recall to mind a few features of the inner and religious life of the Hebrew people.

The basis and guide of the commonwealth was the Law. Upon it all institutions were founded, and it was regarded as the absolute rule of conduct. It was unchangeable in its teaching and final in its directions. It was reverenced both as a moral and a penal code, and it was deemed sufficient for individual and for national happiness. It rigidly enforced personal duties and domestic obligations, and it provided for the weak and the helpless by fostering and strengthening feelings of humanity. It not only moulded the minds of the people, but also their habits and customs, and entered into the details of daily and private life. And as the Law itself was received as Divine, thus every duty which it enjoined was invested with religious solemnity. If the Hebrew committed any illegal act, it was an offence not only against the statutes of the community or the enactments of men, but against God.

Those who pre-eminently studied and taught the Law, and who in fact acted as mediators between God and the people, were the *priests*. Everything was done to imbue the nation thoroughly with the idea that God is the invisible Ruler or Monarch, that is, to strengthen the *theocracy*. The people might temporarily rebel against the accepted organisation; they might desire and even establish a monarchy with a human and visible chief, in order to give unity to their constitution; but they never strayed long from the notions which pervade the Pentateuch. Hence the priests, God's ministers, were endowed with great dignity and influence, and they gradually became a body of very considerable importance. They represented the holy aspirations of the people and their obedience to a Divine Law, and they became the public teachers, advisers, and judges.

But the priests were scarcely free agents; their individual judgment had little scope; they were hardly more than ministers and instruments. Fettered by the unalterable precepts of a Divine legislation, they could do no more than expound and enforce them, and demand passive obedience and strict adherence to the eternal precepts inherited from their fathers. But notwithstanding the authority and the diffusion of the Law, the history of almost every age since Moses proves that its teaching was neglected or defied, and that the nation sank into every heathen error, and was degraded by every immoral excess.

To quell this rebellion against the Law, a voice more powerful and more inspired than that of the priests was required. Stronger hands were necessary to uphold and to direct a struggling and a falling nation. Many events and circumstances happened which had not been foreseen and provided for by the Law, and discussions and questions were raised which could not be decided by the written precept. The affairs of the people became frequently complicated and critical. Happily, in such times, men arose who, equal to the emergency, not only delivered but strengthened the nation. They did not confine their attention to the doctrinal points of the Law, nor limit their influence to the political condition of the community; but they sought to lay the foundation of a far nobler national greatness by insisting upon the spirit of their religion; and they endeavoured to build up a powerful state upon a pure and enlightened faith. It was owing to the *prophets* that religion, refined and spiritualised, became the shield of the Israelites in battle and their guide in council, and success or defeat attended them, according as they obeyed or disregarded its voice. It was the prophets who at the same time most decidedly separated the Hebrews from the heathens, and yet upheld that common sympathy between both, which they predicted would one day result in one universal creed of love. They represented the intellectual members of the community who aspired to pass beyond the limits of tradition, who rejected the supreme rule of forms and customs, who saw in their holy legislation something more than ordinances of religious rites, and who venerated the spirit, while the mass blindly clung to the letter.

The priests and the prophets thus exercised distinct functions in the moral education of the people. It was the province of the priests to uphold the ancient doctrines, and to enforce the absolute authority of the Mosaic code in every age and under every change of political condition; but it was the mission of the prophets to take advantage of the passing events, to employ the moment itself for the illustration of religious truths, and to teach the people from actual life rather than by doctrine. But the prophets were not moral teachers alone, they were patriots as well, and came forward as leaders in all political movements. From the time of Samuel, whose influence aided in establishing the monarchy, down to the decay of the commonwealth, their voices were heard in the public councils, now stimulating king or people to some righteous and honourable war, now denouncing a hasty or impolitic treaty, passing their withering verdict on some act of cowardice or rebellion, or extolling with glowing enthusiasm the glory of a peaceful reign destined to shed its serene lustre on a virtuous and happy generation. The words which we chiefly admire for the sublimity and the fervour of their eloquence, were words spoken with an immediate and practical purpose. These orations, at once profound in thought and soaring in expression, were designed to guide the hearers to wise and useful acts, and to force their stubbornness into obedience. They often proved ineffectual to move a refractory race; but long after the events that occasioned them had passed away, they were remembered and meditated upon, recalling the greatness of men unequalled for elevation of mind and soul, and they have since become the heirloom of mankind.

For we must not forget that politics and religion were inseparably united in the commonwealth of the Hebrews. As the legislation possessed Divine authority, and God was considered as the owner of the land and the invisible King who ruled and guided the nation, the life of the community as well as that of every individual was marked by a religious sanctity unlike that of any other people. It was, therefore, impossible for the great statesmen to separate the interests of their religion and of their country; to extend and establish the one was to promote the welfare of the other. Everything depended upon and originated in God; therefore, obedience to His precepts and His commands was at once a political and religious duty. Thus the prophets necessarily exercised a double function; they were the counsellors alike of the citizens and of the members of the theocracy, the promoters of worldly success and religious zeal. They exhorted the people to avert the stroke of adversity, and even when unheeded, assisted them to bear it; for their stern and inflexible morality was tempered by hopefulness and mercy. Therefore, as great leaders both in the religious and political sphere, the prophets claim our earnest attention, and if we desire duly to appreciate them, we must carefully study the time in which they lived and worked.

The prophetic instincts manifested themselves in the nation at an early period; though then only in isolated instances. Some great calamity, some sacrilegious crime would call forth the counsel or the reproof of a voice that had till then been silent; and the "man of God", armed with a greater authority than the judge or the priest, would step forward when other means failed to rouse the irresolute and to strengthen the weak. One of the first who encouraged or threatened the Israelites by prophetic admonition was Moses, who combined the functions of leader, lawgiver, and prophet. The dark and troubled period which followed the settlement in Canaan; was replete with dangers and calamities; but these very dangers seemed to call forth men filled with the spirit of God, who, appearing at different intervals, held out hope or warning, and wrought deliverance. Gifted with the powers of expounding the Divine will, the poetess Deborah exhorted her people to piety and zeal; "a man of God" incited Gideon to action, and inspired him to free the Israelites from a foreign yoke; and later, when the sons of Eli desecrated their holy office, a prophet came forward and unfolded to them their own punishment and the fate of their descendants. Thus prophets were heard occasionally among the people, menacing or encouraging. But they had no wide-spread influence. They were considered as diviners and as advisers, who disclosed the future, and gave those who sought them the benefit of their knowledge and wisdom. They lent their aid to release men from worldly cares and difficulties; but their power was limited to individuals, it did not reach the nation as a whole. The people was as yet incapable of receiving their sublime teaching, and a long tuition was required to educate the multitude. In due time, a man arose — Samuel — singularly fitted for this great mission by rare energy, a comprehensive mind, intense perseverance, and above all, by fervent devotion to his people. He contributed to raise prophecy to the lofty eminence it was destined to occupy, and he laid the foundation for its great and lasting influence. From his time, it appeared no more in scattered rays, but in unbroken splendour; and the rights of the prophets were soon as firmly established among the people as those of the priest and the judge, the king and the general.

Samuel combined in himself nearly all the chief offices of the state: he was ruler, judge, priest, and prophet. In genius and force of character, he was only equalled by Moses. He was roused into activity by the condition of his time and country. For during the period which preceded his birth, the nation had sunk into the lowest depth of degeneracy. The Mosaic Law, designed to live in the hearts of the people and to stimulate them to righteousness and zeal, lay unheeded in the hands of the priests. The unity which the legislation was intended to effect, became, for want of a guiding hand, a dream and an impossibility. Instead of one place of assembly, hallowed for sacrifice and worship, numberless altars rose on heights and in valleys, where horrible rites were practised, and where the idols of neighbouring tribes were honoured with incense and offerings. Hence the Law, so far from raising the Hebrews above other nations, was powerless even to unite them among themselves; for their interests were divided and their sympathies conflicting. In other towns, besides Shiloh, congregations worshipped, and heathen images often disgraced the hearth of the rich man's house.

Thus estranged from each other in spiritual matters, they could hardly be expected to form a political brotherhood. In this respect their condition was indeed deplorable. Perpetual strife set tribe against tribe, and made them an easy prey to less powerful neighbours. Instead of combining to prostrate their external foes, so undaunted and so vigilant, they exhausted their energies in miserable internal feuds and petty jealousies. Their political life during that unhappy epoch did not present the spectacle of kindred races conscious of a holy mission among the nations of the earth, but of wild and ruthless outlaws recoiling from no crime, and shunning no deed of revolting horror. They appointed separate judges, commanders, and chiefs, regardless alike of their honour and their safety. Occasionally, indeed, when some great danger threatened from without, they united their councils and their forces, and rallied round some bold and patriotic leader; but the bond of union was broken when the danger ceased; and then every tribe pursued again its own selfish ends. Justice was a stranger in the land; the strong oppressed the weak without fear and mercy: "every one did as it appeared good in his eyes." Force and violence were the only arbitrators; cunning and treachery stood for prudence and wisdom. Thus the heroic grandeur and the intrepid zeal of a Deborah, a Samson, or a Gideon, would for a while illumine the gloomy darkness of the time, but they exercised no lasting influence; the lustre of their deeds lived in the traditions of an admiring posterity, but it was unable to cement that unity, and to call forth those institutions, which it was the object of the Mosaic Law to establish.

It was in this degenerate state that Samuel found the people; and because he loved them and loved the faith of his ancestors, he laboured to raise them to their appointed place among nations. His holy zeal soon caused him to be recognised as a man filled with the spirit of God, and chosen to receive Divine communications. He was throughout the land honoured as a true prophet. He used his authority for enlarging the political resources, improving the social condition, and extending the religious instruction of the people. He encouraged them when renewed invasions of the Philistines threatened their safety, and led them to victory. He made an annual circuit through the principal towns of the land, in order to administer justice and to remove that state of lawless violence which for centuries had disturbed all notions of right and wrong. But his greatest creation was the establishment of "schools of prophets", from which knowledge, purity, and zeal were to be diffused among the people.

These institutions were of course expected to do no more than to train genius. An inward mission and fitness for the propagation of Divine truth could never result from even the most careful or incessant tuition; but the spiritual ardour might be roused, the dormant powers might be awakened, cultivated, and led to a sphere of active usefulness. Besides this chief object, the schools of prophets aimed at developing the eloquence and mastery of language indispensable to the public orator. They taught the disciple the past and present history of the nation, and made him acquainted with the world in which he had to work. They promoted a deeper study of the Law among the gifted and the thoughtful. They softened the warlike and barbarous impulses of the nation, and helped to strengthen in the popular character that spiritual element by which the Hebrews were to gain dominion in the world. Thus their chief merit lay in diffusing gentler influences, in piercing through the intellectual darkness and confusion which had prevailed during the period of the Judges, and especially in stimulating to nobler aims not only chosen individuals, but the bulk of the people.

The towns selected were mostly those hallowed of old by some sacred association or reminiscence, as Ramah, Bethel, and Jericho. Here the disciples lived as members of a common order or brotherhood. In due time, they went abroad among their brethren, to fulfil the various religious missions for which they believed they were fitted or destined. In later ages, the prophet was forced upon a rough and thorny path. Then he became oftener the stern rebuker than the peaceful teacher. He had to assail the despot and his insolence and tyranny, to inveigh against a weak and ignorant, or a credulous and superstitious people, and to put to shame a priesthood often narrow-minded, bigoted, and venal. But Samuel's immediate disciples were neither destined to such toil nor to such greatness, they shed around their contemporaries the light of their religion, and then retired into obscurity. Yet prophetic teaching was not limited to men trained in special institutions. Inspiration, the free gift of Divine favour, might fall upon any member of the Hebrew community, however humble and secluded, upon the child-like shepherd or the simple-minded husbandman; it might grace and elevate even women, who were listened to with respect and deference when they disclosed the ways of God and His truths. A vision or a mysterious voice would arouse the latent faculty, and confer the power and authority of expounding Divine decrees. But the schools of prophets, intended as they were to give human aid to Divine endowments, permanently nourished in Israel the holy fire by which prophetic enthusiasm might be kindled whenever it might be required by the plans of Providence.

Samuel derived his power not only from his moral greatness, but also from the political influence which he knew how to gain and to exercise. When the tribes desired a stronger rule and a more lasting bond, they turned to him with their petition. They made him elect a king who should govern over them, lead them in their battles, and judge and decide their quarrels; for they longed for a political organisation similar to that of other nations. Yet when the prayer was reluctantly granted, and Saul was invested with royal power and dignity, the word of the prophet remained still paramount in the land. Though he apparently withdrew from the scenes of his usual activity, his interest in public affairs remained as keen as ever. We see him in his retirement at Ramah censuring or approving the actions of the king he had elected. We see his anger kindled by what he considered a dangerous and unwarrantable assumption of independence on the part of Saul; till at last he transferred the newly founded throne to the humble shepherd's son, whose courage and faith were the germs of his future distinction. Shortly before Saul's death on the battle-field of Gilboa, the great prophet expired in his calm retreat at Ramah. He had rescued his people from an abyss of religious and political degeneracy; he had given them new interests and new sympathies; he had led them to worldly success, and taught them to look to a pure faith as the only guarantee for national independence and prosperity. Thus having sown the seeds of their welfare, he patiently waited that they might take root, but he was called away before they appeared in their bright maturity during the reign of David.

The spirit of Samuel lived in the king he had chosen; for David was not merely the military chief of his people, his object was to elevate their thoughts and their feelings, and not merely to extend his own dominions. They should glory in him as their victorious leader, but they should also join in his fervent though humble songs of thanksgiving and penitence. The warfare which he carried on to quell the sedition of rebellious tribes, gave full scope to his martial talents and his personal courage. But great as were his triumphs on the battle-field, the period of tranquillity which they happily secured was far more important. Like Samuel, he felt that the strength of the country depended chiefly upon the strict adherence to a better faith, and he neglected no opportunity for refining and raising the religious tone of the nation.

In this respect the most important event of his reign was the solemn transport of the Ark of the Covenant to Jerusalem. Priestly functions were carefully revised or established. Poetry and song were turned to high and sacred thoughts, awakening the hitherto slumbering genius of the people, and diffusing the most ennobling influence on their lives and actions. In such a time, when the chief administration mainly aimed at consolidating the new kingdom from without and within, when David absorbed and combined all the powers of the state, there was no need for present advisers or for interpreters of the future: the prophets, unsought and uncalled for, all but retired from the scene. The schools originated by Samuel, were probably following their quiet avocations, patiently discussing and instilling their cherished doctrines; but no political or religious offence on the part of the nation called forth their reproving voice. But all the more necessary was that voice of guidance and warning for him in whose hands the national well-being solely rested, and nobly did the prophets Nathan and Gad fulfil that difficult and often ungracious office. They were David's faithful spiritual advisers, and announced to him unsparingly the Divine judgment on his personal trespasses. Nathan possessed all the peculiarities of a great prophet. He fearlessly pleaded for justice, rose against the oppressor, and protected the oppressed. Fortified by his noble mission, he directed his blow steadily and unswervingly against the most powerful sovereign of Israel; and he found a ready echo in a heart equally open to temptation and repentance. A stern monitor and rebuker, he brought the king to a humble sense of his moral failings, and caused him to pour out, in strains of thrilling pathos, his passionate grief and deep contrition.

The main part of Solomon's reign was still less calculated to call forth the spiritual guides of Israel. For Solomon himself was an admirable type of the Israelite's peculiar greatness. His prayer had been for wisdom, and it was the chief object of his life to give due thanks and glory to the Bestower of the priceless gift. His power as a monarch was absolute. He almost eclipsed the Highpriest, who shrank into comparative insignificance. He superintended the structure of the Temple; still more, he himself consecrated it, extended his hands over the worshipping people, blessed them, and implored God's benediction on the all-important work of his life. Endowed with supreme knowledge and wisdom, he diffused the noblest doctrines of the prophets, and gave a powerful impulse to the aspirations of genius and intellect. Poetry and philosophy, directed to the highest aims of life, could not fail to produce the most elevating and beneficent effects. Their influence upon the nation is not described in the Scriptures, but it may be best inferred from the utter silence of the prophetic voice, which never failed to make itself heard when censure was needed or encouragement required.

The decline of Solomon's reign is a melancholy foreshadowing of the subsequent decay of the Hebrew nation. The great enemy of Judaism, idolatry with all its accompanying rites and customs, was gradually allowed to enter the precincts of the palace and even the Temple, and once again to take its dangerous hold on the hearts and the imagination of the people. The later parts of Solomon's life, a painful foil to its former brilliancy, heralded in a long series of disasters; indeed it was the beginning of Israel's downfall. The culminating point of Hebrew greatness was passed; with fitful intervals of regained peace and splendour, the commonwealth sank step by step into a hopeless state of degeneracy.

The new era of Hebrew history that began with the disruption of the tribes, was no less a new era in the history of the prophets. Saul indeed may have been in some measure the creature and the tool of Samuel; but the commanding and fertile mind of a David and a Solomon had but sparingly required assistance or admonition to strengthen their motives or their efforts. The position was different under their successors. These had neither the energy nor the talent to cement the organisation of the monarchy, or to shield the belief of the people from corruption. They were too often the most eager to desert the faith of their ancestors, and to set to their willing subjects the evil example of worshipping at the altars of heathen gods. King and people alike stood in need of a Divine monitor.

These were the times when the prophets appeared in

their true greatness and importance. In a severe and humble attire, consisting in a long and coarse garment, the flowing folds of which were held together by a common leather girdle, the man of God would come among the people on the Sabbath, the Day of the New Moon, or on the Festivals. He would take his stand in the open places, in the streets, in the gates of the towns, in the Courts of the Temple — wherever business or religion brought together an assemblage. But if his mission lay among the nobles of the land, he would enter their palaces, in spite of mockery, danger, and persecution, an unbidden and often an unwelcome guest. Though his behests were rarely obeyed, though his advice was often met with contempt or derision, his office was acknowledged as legitimate, and was even reluctantly respected. The esteem in which the prophets were held, deepened into awe and veneration among the virtuous few, and not seldom changed into fear among the host of scorners who trembled while they scorned. They were allowed to take an active part in public affairs, and they exercised an unmistakeable influence on subsequent events. Free from the fetters of party, neither blinded by the ritualism of priesthood nor the ambition of royalty, they examined and judged with unbiassed discernment.

Their culture and learning made them still more honoured. Their orations, so practical in their tendency, were poetical productions of the highest order; and not only were the prophets absolute masters of their language, but in many cases, of all the science and knowledge of their age. Their writings evince especially a deep study of history, and their powers of healing were far-famed, so that the kings who in prosperity turned away from their advice, sought their aid in illness or adversity.

But as the surrounding atmosphere became more and more distasteful to their lofty minds, the opposition which they had to encounter became greater and greater. The actors in those troubled times were too short-sighted to comprehend the consequences of their infatuation, too much absorbed by the pleasures of the moment to follow the exalted inspirations of their advisers, too callous to carry out the energetic measures that alone could save them. It was neither an easy nor a grateful task to appear before the despot, to proclaim his errors, sins, and misdeeds, and to foretell the doom which awaited him. Some miraculous sign of the mercy or wrath of God would perhaps turn the monarch's obduracy into a momentary remorse; but this repentance proved generally the mere effect of fear, and vanished with the cause of the alarm. Even the priest was a formidable antagonist of the prophet. By the very nature of his calling, his sympathies and interests were engrossed in the ceremonies of his religion, in the strict adherence to those outward forms, the exaggeration or lifeless monotony of which formed a constant theme of prophetic eloquence and reproof. The priests, acting merely as agents or ministering officers, often transferred their services to idolatrous creeds which, in their perversity, they befriended rather than opposed. They followed the bent of their age or flattered the disposition of their king. At one season, they performed the pure rites of the Mosaic Law; at another, they offered incense at the altars of Baal; but at no time were they instrumental in diffusing the patriotic enthusiasm of the prophets. In fact, their bigotry and their thraldom to a minute formalism, materially retarded the growth of an enlightened faith. Hence the idolatrous priests of the empire of Ephraim were hardly greater objects of the prophets' indignation than the sacerdotal order of the kingdom of Judah, whose narrow zeal was devoted merely to the external rites of their own religion.

Under such influences the people could advance neither

in morality nor in knowledge. They gave way to the follies of luxury and the vices of sensuality. Successful wars brought ample spoils; and the wealth which was neither the effect nor the reward of industry, produced the usual evils — licentiousness, indolence, and oppression of the poor and the weak. Such was the vitiated and uncongenial atmosphere in which lay the scene of the prophets' toil. They vainly endeavoured to arrest the moral decay of the nation. The change did not immediately follow the disunion of the monarchy; but it grew slowly and steadily, as in every new reign idolatry spread farther and took deeper root. The prophets' labour became more arduous and more unpromising, even more so in the northern kingdom than in the empire of Judah. But their power seemed to increase with the difficulty or hopelessness of their mission. They felt that their path lay no more among willing auditors or anxious suppliants, and they had thenceforth to combine the tasks of opponent and teacher. Their efforts were no longer limited to the grateful duties of explaining the public law, or of dispensing the consolations of religion. They had to face a people who fancied they had outgrown the years of training, and could act for themselves, but who fell incessantly into sin. Thus the prophet appeared as the man's stern monitor instead of the child's patient instructor. The pure faith of monotheism was in danger of being lost and corrupted, and the prophet rose, not to proclaim but to defend it. He was the champion of God's unity and God's dominion, and his exalted mission required the rarest courage and devotion. But as the faith of the Hebrews and their history were closely blended, the affections of the prophet were equally twined round his religion and his country: hence his mission not only as religious guide but as statesman and patriot; hence his eager encouragement or his indignant opposition in moments of political importance or danger

The school of prophets, in later periods, is seldom mentioned as an organized band; but from their number arose in every emergency some Divinely gifted man, who seemed to speak with the weight of his whole order.

Such was, in rough outline, the prophetic office; such were the labours allotted to it. If we follow the current of history, its work and influence will appear in greater distinctness and individuality.

It made itself felt during the very first reigns of the kings of Israel, when also the fierce warfare between king and prophet commenced. We will therefore begin by giving a brief sketch of the general influence exercised in their own kingdom by the prophets of Israel.

At the time of the disruption of the tribes, a prophet came forward and promised God's protection to the new kingdom. But immediately afterwards another man of God arose as the messenger of Divine anger, because the Mosaic creed had been grievously violated, and golden images of the Egyptian Apis had been erected on the altars of Bethel and Dan. Jeroboam's successors, continuing in the same evil path, roused the wrath of the prophet Jehu, who announced the extirpation of their whole race. The peaceful days of Omri were followed by the eventful reign of Ahab, which was chiefly notorious by the fanatical hatred of Jezebel, his Phoenician queen, and her relentless persecution of God's faithful servants and their dauntless leaders. The grand figure of Elijah towers above all. His words were few but pithy; his presence was awe-inspiring; his sudden and mysterious appearance generally foreboded some event appalling to his idolatrous foes, encouraging to his few devoted followers. He had the daring courage of a hero. The hand of man seemed in vain to be raised against him, and his life was miraculously saved from a thousand snares and dangers. Inexorable to the wicked, but comforting to the pious, he came forward at every crisis with inexhaustible resources to punish or to help.

The life of his successor Elisha happily proved, that the prophets were not always instruments of God's displeasure. His path was less rugged; he enjoyed the respect of the people; and his councils were eagerly coveted. With the lofty spirit of prophecy bequeathed to him by his great master, he combined a gentle spirit of charity and forbearance. His sympathies were not limited to his own people; his fame reached neighbouring nations, who equally listened to his oracles and felt his beneficent power. Succeeding prophets exercised a similar influence over surrounding countries. They pointed out the course of events, they advised, they admonished, or encouraged Syria and Damascus, the enemies of their nation, among whom they often met with more veneration and readier obedience than among the Israelites themselves. Divine messages were even sent to distant lands — to the idolatrous people of Babylon, and to the sinning but penitent multitude of Nineveh. Yet the prophets' duty lay especially among their own people. Whenever a danger threatened, they proclaimed their Master's favour or wrath. Their voices were continually heard, whether to chastise the impetuous zeal of Jehu, to predict the certainty of Jezebel's doom, or to exalt the peaceful and glorious days of the virtuous Jeroboam.

The happy relief afforded by the reign of the last-named king, after a long period of fierce persecution and warfare, inaugurated a new phase of prophetic activity. The fatal effects engendered by the indifference or wickedness of preceding kings were irreparable. Therefore, the praiseworthy and energetic efforts of Jeroboam for the restoration of a pure faith produced merely superficial results. Entire generations ignored not only the ritual worship of the Mosaic Law, but all the civil and social virtues which it enjoins. Charity and self-denial were strangers among them. Whilst the poor were oppressed and neglected, the rich nourished their pride by accumulating land and wealth, and indulged in every sensual pleasure. Therefore, the prophets now directed their shafts against the mass of their degenerate countrymen; they raised their voices, not to check some perilous step of an erring king, but to rebuke the daily life of the people. They knew how vain was even the restitution of the Divine worship, and how bootless the pious endeavours of Jeroboam, if Samaria's luxurious plains and stately cities remained the scenes of impious revelry and gross immorality. Amos, the shepherd prophet, was one of the first to denounce the sins of the people. On his lonely hills, surrounded by all the purity of nature, the wickedness of his countrymen reached his ears, and he came among them to speak of God's displeasure and of the terrible retribution they were bringing upon themselves. With forcible words, with similes furnished by nature itself, which he knew and loved so well, Amos laid bare to them their irreligion and its inevitable results. But his auditors were intoxicated by the love of pleasure and the pomp of wealth; they cared not for the morrow, and would not listen, still less repent.

This moral debasement was the forerunner of speedy outward decay. While the chiefs and nobles sank deeper and deeper into licentiousness, the succeeding kings were engaged in continual struggles with some wily and ambitious usurper, and their names are associated only with ignoble lives and violent deaths. The internal strength of the monarchy was spending itself, whilst the external dangers became daily more imminent. The Assyrian conquerors were drawing nearer and nearer, and the Israelites, effeminate and wilfully blind, were ill prepared to oppose them. Gilead first succumbed to the overwhelming armies; and as one stronghold after another surrendered, the enemy poured into the districts of the Lebanon, and "the Sea of Galilee was made dark with his hosts." Internal feuds aided in hastening the catastrophe; and the last gleam of hope, kindled by the vain endeavours of Hoshea to restore his fallen people, was extinguished by the capture of the unfortunate monarch himself. And now commenced the terrible siege of Samaria, accompanied by all the misery and barbarity, which have been the special scourges of sieges in all ages. When after three years of endurance and famine and warfare, the Samaritans submitted to the enemy, and the surviving population was led away captive to the Assyrian dominions; then, among the cries and the lamentations of the distressed, the voice of Israel's last prophets was heard, no more stern and relentless, but pitying, sorrowing, and soothing with promises of future peace and greatness.

Having thus followed the prophets of Israel, as far as they were linked with the political events of the nation, we now turn to the neighbouring empire of Judah, to trace the operation of the same Divine force.

The first kings of Judah enjoyed peaceful and prosperous reigns, owing to their moderate policy, their more faithful adherence to Mosaism, and the active zeal of their priesthood. Idolatry flourished, it is true, but it existed side by side with the old faith, and not upon its ruins. The public worship remained intact; the sacrifices and ceremonies were restored under Jehoshaphat. The sacerdotal order acquired greater political importance; the priests came forth victorious from the fierce struggle with idolatry during the rule of Queen Athaliah, and exercised for the first time their political strength in the enthronement of the true scion and heir of David. Ardent, energetic, and devoted, they fulfilled in some measure the mission achieved by the contemporary prophets in Israel.

But the influence of the priests was by no means wholly beneficial. They were useful instruments for preserving the distinctive peculiarities of the nation, but they were incompetent to effect any lasting good. Unlike the prophets, their sympathies were contracted, not universal; their teachings doctrinal, not moral; their labours contributed to secure the establishment of their religion, but they failed to plant it in the hearts of the people. Absorbed by external ceremonies, they did little for the spiritual education of their countrymen. The growth of their political power was looked upon by the nobles with displeasure and envy, which the narrowness of their opinions and their self-sufficiency were ill adapted to conciliate. The prophetic influence was necessary to counteract the dangerous ascendency of the sacerdotal caste; and true to its great objects, it now rose to check priestly ceremonialism, and to replace it by a loftier and yet simpler code. The political aid of the prophet had not been required during the first tranquil years after the restoration of the hereditary kings of Judah. The successors of Joash were virtuous princes who "walked in the path of the Lord." The reign of Uriah was a brilliant series of successful wars and of still more beneficial reforms in the internal administration of the kingdom. A few words of praise form, in our records, the only account of the equally happy rule of his son Joram. But it is in this reign that the moral depravity contrasted most painfully with the blessings of prosperity and wealth which the nation enjoyed. Fortresses towered on every hill; the vines bent under the weight of luscious grapes; and ships came home laden with the costliest articles of trade. But the people succumbed to the temptations of wealth; the priests had failed to arm them with a healthy morality; and corruption, almost equalling that of neighbouring Israel, proclaimed the approaching decay of the commonwealth. A terrible locust plague and a destructive earthquake startled the people from their heedlessness; the plains were deserted, the vineyards lay waste, the cattle perished. And now thoughtless levity gave way to unmanly dejection and despair. Prophets came forward and declared the catastrophe to be a scourge of the Almighty: they were anxious to hold up the distress as a warning, and thus to bring back the people to the God whom they had forsaken. Inspired with Divine indignation, full of sorrowing love for their country, and gifted with an eloquence which should have pierced through the mists of ignorance and stubbornness, the prophets of Judah rose to a sublime greatness unequalled among the prophets of Israel.

Although statesmen and public orators, they directed their weapons not only against the political offender, but against the whole multitude, whose sins were those common to all demoralized ages and to all degenerate nations. But their addresses, though replete with warnings and reproof, were not without bright promises of consolation. Perceiving too clearly the danger and the wickedness of the time in which they lived, they looked far beyond it to a period of universal peace, justice, and knowledge, which they considered to be the true goal not only of God's chosen people, but of all mankind. By their fervent descriptions of that glorious future, they sought to bring the nation nearer to their own ideal, and to connect it with the whole human race.

B. THE THREE GREATER PROPHETS.

ISAIAH (759 to about 700).
[ISAI. I—XXXIX.]

Among the prophets Isaiah was the most profound in his teachings and the most exalted in his conceptions. With a natural acknowledgment of his superiority, the Bible places his writings at the head of the prophetic works. He will, therefore, first claim our attention, not as the earliest of the prophets, but as the greatest — the greatest with respect to the mission he had to fulfil, the influence his orations exercised not only during his life-time but ever afterwards, the ardour of his sympathies, and the loftiness of his ideas.

Isaiah is familiar to us less through historical accounts than through his own writings. These contain all that we know of his life and work; and from them alone can we trace an intelligible outline of the events which called forth his Divine powers.

The scanty information we possess of his life may be briefly told. He was the son of Amoz, a man of Judah, and seems to have been called to his high mission when still a youth. He himself describes the scene when he was first endowed with the gift of prophecy, which took place in the year of king Uzziah's death (B. C. 759). Nothing can be grander than the few verses in which he relates his earliest vision, and no introduction could better prepare us for his subsequent orations. The natural diffidence of a young man in accepting so exalted a charge is well marked in the trembling hesitation with which he delayed to answer the Divine summons. Like his great predecessor Moses, he doubted his competency to perform the grave duties entrusted to him.

"In the year that king Uzziah died", he relates, "I saw the Lord sitting upon a throne, high and lifted up, and His train filled the Temple. Before him stood Seraphims; each one had six wings, with two he covered his face, and with two he covered his feet, and with two he did fly. And one cried to another and said, Holy, holy, holy is the Lord of hosts; the whole earth is full of His glory. And the posts of the door shook at the voice of those that cried, and the House was filled with smoke. — Then said I, Woe is me! for I am undone; because I am a man of unclean lips, and I dwell in the midst of a people of unclean lips: for my eyes have seen the King, the Lord of hosts. Then flew one of the Seraphims to me with a live coal in his hand, which he had taken with the tongues from the altar; and he laid it upon my mouth and said, Behold, this has touched thy lips; and thy iniquity is taken away, and thy sin is purged. And I heard the voice of the Lord, saying, Whom shall I send, and who will go for us? Then said I, Here am I, send me. And He said, Go and tell this people, you shall hear indeed, but not understand; and you shall see indeed, but not perceive. Harden the heart of this people, and make their ears heavy, and shut their eyes, lest they see with their eyes, and hear with their ears, and understand with their hearts, and turn, and be healed. Then said I, Lord, how long? And He answered, Until the cities be wasted without an inhabitant, and the houses without a man, and the land be utterly desolate; and the Lord will remove men far away, and there will be a great dreariness in the land. Yet there shall remain in it a tenth, and that shall in its turn be consumed, but as a terebinth and an oak which keep their root when they are cut down — a holy seed shall be their root."

Thereupon Isaiah went forth unflinchingly to obey God's behest. His mission lay first in the very midst of that people whose uncleanness he had lamented. The depravity was great during the reign of Joram; it had increased with the prosperity, the wealth, and the security, which were monopolized by a powerful class.

The "elders of the houses and their chiefs", the very leaders of the nation, were the offenders who roused the prophet's bitterest indignation. "For you have eaten up the vineyard, the spoil of the poor is in your houses: what do you mean that you make my people poor?" cried the prophet to all the great, the honoured, and the gifted of the land. The humbler classes looked to them in vain for help and support, for advice and example. The wives and mothers of the great and wealthy were equally tainted with the sins of pride and the worst effects of opulence. The daughters of Zion exercised no softening influence; they surrounded the domestic hearth with no genial charm. Isaiah, well knowing that they were in no slight degree the cause of the general perversion, pursued their worldly vanities with the sharpest ridicule; he denounced them with equal anger and derision because "they walked with stretched forth necks, and wanton eyes, mincing as they went, and tinkling with their feet." Instead of a desire for modest retirement, they evinced by their manners and their garments an inordinate love of display and finery; frivolity turned their thoughts to the multiplicity of their ornaments, to their hoods and their veils, to their bracelets and their rings; and the constant changing of apparel seemed to be the one object of their lives. But their doom was also to come, and as the men should suffer in that which they deemed most precious, in their wealth and their grandeur, so the women should be humbled in their pride and their vanity — their gorgeous attire should be turned into tatters and sackcloth, and their beauty into repulsiveness.

The inevitable effects of unbridled luxury proved baneful to the whole community, and were closely followed by ingratitude to God, irreligious indifference, and cruel injustice to the poor. In a beautiful parable, Isaiah proclaimed the degeneracy of the people and their unworthiness of the Divine blessings: "Now will I sing to My well-beloved a song of My beloved about his vineyard. My well-beloved had a vineyard in a very fruitful hill. And he fenced it, and gathered out the stones thereof, and planted it with the choicest vine, and built a tower in the midst of it, and also made a winepress therein: and he hoped that it should bring forth grapes, and it brought forth wild grapes. And now, O inhabitants of Jerusalem and men of Judah, judge, I pray you, between Me and My vineyard. What could have been done more to My vineyard, that I have not done in it? Wherefore then, when I hoped that it should bring forth grapes, did it bring forth wild grapes? And now come, I will tell you what I will do to My vineyard: I will take away the hedge thereof, and it shall be eaten up; and break down the wall thereof, and it shall be trodden down. And I will lay it waste; it shall not be pruned, nor digged, but there shall come up briers and thorns; I will also command the clouds that they rain no rain upon it. For the vineyard of the Lord of hosts is the house of Israel, and the men of Judah the plant of His delight; and He looked for judgment, but behold oppression; for righteousness, but behold a cry."

Gross neglect of the poor had now become disgracefully common among that very people whose fairest virtue was intended to be charity towards the helpless. The rich proprietors ignored or utterly disregarded the Mosaic injunctions concerning the equal distribution of the land, the inalienable right of possession, and the effectual provisions made for the poor. "Woe to them", cried the stern rebuker, "that join house to house, that lay field to field", thus usurping the poor man's allotted property. Their excessive and unlawfully gotten wealth, was spent in constant revelry and feasting. Day and night were equally devoted to pleasure and carousals. The sound of the timbrel was tuned to perpetual orgies; and the giddy enjoyment of the moment seemed the only object of their existence. Blinded alike to censure and counsel, they were too eager to confide in their own strength; and "they were very wise in their own eyes."

Among such a people lay Isaiah's path of duty; it was his mission to show them, if possible, the folly of their ways and to give to their thoughts a higher direction; or if earnest teaching should prove unavailing, to announce to them the Divine wrath calling devastating nations from afar to invade their unhappy land.

He appears, for the first time, to have taken a part in political events during the reign of Ahaz, when a war broke out between Judah and the combined forces of Rezin, king of Syria, and of Pekah, the son of Remaliah, king of Israel. Ahaz, panic-stricken, was awaiting the enemy at the conduit of the upper pool, in the highway of the fuller's field, intending probably to turn off the springs into the city at the first approach of the enemy. At that moment Isaiah appeared before him. The prophet was accompanied by his son Shear-jashub — significantly meaning "the remnant will return". He spoke reassuring words: "Take heed, and be quiet; fear not, nor be fainthearted on account of the two tails of these smoking firebrands, the fierce anger of Rezin with Syria, and the son of Remaliah .... Thus says the Lord God, It shall not stand, nor shall it come to pass." He comforted the terrified monarch in vain; in vain did he announce the destruction of Syria and Damascus, in vain did he beseech the king to trust in the Lord. "If your faith is not strong, you will indeed not be strengthened." "Ask any sign of the Lord thy God", continued the prophet: but the desponding king remained in hopeless dejection; he said, he durst not tempt the Lord. Indignant at such a want of confidence and belief, Isaiah declared that God would yet give him a sign. This sign was to be the birth of a son by the prophet's young wife; and before that child would know good from evil, the land would indeed be freed from their present enemies, but would be struck with unparalleled calamities wrought by the approach of Assyrian invaders. The child was to be called Immanuel, or "God is with us". The sympathies of the prophet were so closely entwined with the affairs of the nation, that they became manifest even in his domestic life; he named his children according to the political events which happened at their birth, or according to the ideas which these events suggested to him. His eldest son Sheariashub embodied the fondest hopes for the future of the pious remnant of his erring countrymen; while Immanuel was meant to symbolise the conviction which he fondly cherished, that the Lord was the only strength of the Hebrews, who required no allies, and must seek none among foreign nations. Some time later, "the prophetess", that is, the prophet's wife, bore another son, to whom the father gave the no less significant name Maher-shalal-hashbaz, "Plunder hastens, booty comes speedily"; and when addressing king Ahaz who was still terrified by the Syrian armies, he declared: "Before the child shall have knowledge to cry, My father and My mother, the riches of Damascus and the spoil of Samaria shall be taken away before the king of Assyria." For this new scourge, destined to be fatal to so many great nations, was proclaimed by Isaiah to be drawing near with terrible speed; and viewing from afar the coming storm, he called the newborn infant, who was to verify his words, by the strange name of "Plunder hastens, booty comes speedily". Heartrending to the prophet must have been the headstrong wilfulness of the king. The latter, instead of waiting and trusting, as he had been bidden, sought the alliance of the Assyrian monarch, an alliance which, in return for momentary succour, exacted from Judah a permanent and heavy tribute. This act of imprudence and disobedience roused at last the prophet's indignation hitherto subdued by his longsuffering love for his people. "Unless they speak according to this word," he exclaimed, "there is no dawn of light for them; and they pass through the land oppressed and hungry, and if they are hungry, they fret themselves, and curse their king and their God; and they look upward, and they look down to the earth, and behold distress and darkness, and trouble, dimness, and anguish; for they are thrust away."

Ahaz was near the termination of his life; but he had a son, Hezekiah, of such rare virtue, that even his early youth promised the glad fulfilment of the patriot's fairest hopes. Therefore Isaiah announced and described that son in the most enthusiastic terms: "For to us a child is born, to us a son is given; and the government shall be upon his shoulder; and his name shall be called Wonderful, Counsellor, the mighty Hero, the everlasting Father, Prince of Peace, for the increase of power and for peace without end upon the throne of David and upon his kingdom, to establish and to strengthen it with judgment and with justice from henceforth and for ever. The zeal of the Lord of hosts will perform this." And again: "There shall come forth a rod out of the stem of Jesse, and a branch shall grow out of his roots; and the spirit of the Lord shall rest upon him, the spirit of wisdom and understanding, the spirit of counsel and might, the spirit of knowledge and of the fear of the Lord; and he shall have his delight in the fear of the Lord; and he shall not judge after the sight of his eyes, nor reprove after the hearing of his ears; but with righteousness shall he judge the poor, and decide with equity for the lowly of the earth; and he shall smite the earth with the rod of his mouth, and with the breath of his lips shall he slay the wicked. And righteousness shall be the girdle of his loins, and faithfulness the girdle of his reins." — Many and various have been the explanations suggested by these allusions to the wonderful child. But Hezekiah, whose piety formed so striking a contrast to the self-will and short-sightedness of Ahaz, was not wholly undeserving of the glowing epithets by which the prophet distinguished him in all the redundant imagery of the East. Recognizing such singular qualities in the future chief of the land, Isaiah foresaw years of prosperity and hitherto unequalled happiness. And then, the poet's imagination mingling with the patriot's ardour, he drew a soaring picture of universal peace and good-will, of friendship and amity, the picture of a glorious time when the strong shall cease to do injustice, and the weak to live in fear, and when, above all, piety and knowledge shall be spread over the whole earth: "The wolf shall dwell with the lamb, and the leopard shall lie down with the kid, and the calf and the young lion and the fatling together; and a little child shall lead them. And the cow and the bear shall feed; their young ones shall lie down together; and the lion shall eat straw like the ox. And the sucking infant shall play on the hole of the asp, and the weaned child shall put his hand on the cockatrice's den. They shall do no evil nor destroy in all My holy mountain: for the earth shall be full of the knowledge of the Lord, as the waters cover the sea."

The incomplete fulfilment, in Hezekiah's time, of this glowing prophecy has caused many to suppose that it portrays the Messianic age, which lies in the far-distant future; and indeed such a period is pictured in every thinking mind, as the golden reward for the toils and struggles of many generations, or perhaps the symbol of humanity in its highest and purest forms. Such an ideal was doubtless in Isaiah's thoughts, when the bright promise of Hezekiah's youth roused a hope of its possible realization: is it surprising that, in the description of that ideal, the prophet should almost unconsciously have employed colours more vivid than the conditions of his time strictly warranted? And this reign of happiness was not held out as a light illuminating the remote future, to inspire and rejoice the pious few; the men then living were to behold it; those whose thoughts and pursuits were absorbed by the confusion and wickedness of their time, would learn the brief rule of their levity; while those who bore oppression and misery with silent humility, were within their own generation promised justice and release. Encouragement and hope were the burden of that ardent prophecy. Full of gratitude for the coming change, the prophet mingled with his ardent anticipations the following exalted strains of thankfulness: "And in that day thou shalt say, O Lord, I will praise Thee: for though Thou wast angry with me, Thy anger turned away, and Thou didst comfort me. Behold, God is my salvation; I will trust and will not be afraid; for the Lord Jehovah is my strength and my song, and He has become my salvation; and with joy you draw water out of the wells of salvation. And in that day you shall say, Praise the Lord call upon His name, declare His deeds among the nations, proclaim that His name is exalted. Sing to the Lord; for He has done great things: this is known in all the earth. Exclaim and shout, thou inhabitant of Zion; for great is the Holy One of Israel in the midst of thee."

Although the beneficent reign of Hezekiah secured comparative repose to the kingdom of Judah, a storm was hanging heavily over the political horizon. It proved fatal to the neighbouring countries, and though still at a distance, threatened the safety of Judea herself. Isaiah's all-grasping mind would not be entirely engrossed in the affairs of his own people. The doom of surrounding nations also engaged his attention, and called forth emphatic comments, now inspired by pity, now by indignation. The Assyrians were considered by the prophet as the instruments of Divine justice; the fatal blow which they dealt to all the southern nations appeared to him the irrevocable result of depravity, presumptuousness, or idolatry; and he thus shadowed forth the fate which awaited them:

"Lift ye up a banner upon the bare mountain, raise the voice to them, wave the hand, that they may enter the gates of the nobles. I have commanded My sanctified ones, I have called My mighty ones for My anger, even My proudly exulting armies. The noise of a multitude in the mountains, like as of a great people; a tumultous noise of the kingdoms of assembled nations: the Lord of hosts musters the host of the battle. They come from a far country, from the end of heaven, from the Lord, as the weapons of His indignation, to destroy the whole earth. —

"Howl ye, for the day of the Lord is at hand; it comes as a destruction from the Almighty. Therefore shall all hands be faint, and every man's heart shall melt. And they shall be afraid; pangs and sorrows shall take hold of them; they shall be in pain as a woman that travails; they shall be amazed one at another; their faces shall be as flames.

"Behold, the day of the Lord comes, pitiless and with wrath and fierce anger, to lay the land desolate, and that He might destroy the sinners out of it. For the stars of heaven and the constellations thereof shall not give their light; the sun shall be darkened in his rising, and the moon shall not cause her light to shine. And I will punish the world for its evil, and the wicked for their iniquity; and I will make the arrogance of the proud cease, and I will lay low the haughtiness of the tyrants. I will make a man more rare than fine gold, yea a man more rare than the treasures of Ophir. Therefore, I will shake the heavens, and the earth shall remove out of its place, in the wrath of the Lord of hosts, and in the day of His fierce anger. And it shall be as the chased roe, and as a sheep that no man takes up: so every man shall turn to his own people, and flee everyone into his own land. Everyone that is found, shall be pierced through; and everyone that is seized shall fall by the sword; and their children shall be dashed to pieces before their eyes; their houses shall be spoilt, and their wives ill-treated.

"Behold, I will stir up the Medes against them, who do not regard silver, and have no delight in gold. And their bows also shall dash the young men to the ground; and they shall have no pity on the fruit of the womb; their eye shall not spare children. — And Babylon, the glory of kingdoms, the beauty of the Chaldees' pride, shall be as when God overthrew Sodom and Gomorrah. It shall never be inhabited, nor shall it be dwelt in from generation to generation; nor shall the Arabian pitch his tent there, nor shall the shepherds make their fold near it. But wild beasts of the desert shall lie there, and their houses shall be full of horn-owls, and ostriches shall dwell there, and satyrs shall dance upon it. And jackals shall cry in their palaces, and wild foxes in their gorgeous mansions. And her time is near to come, and her days shall not be prolonged." (XIII. 2—22.)

The Philistines, those ancient and restless enemies of the Hebrews, had been subjected to Judah since the days of Uzziah. But the troubles of that kingdom were favourable to them. During the wars of Israel and Syria against the empire of Judah, they threw off the hated yoke; and now they rejoiced in their newly acquired freedom. Their exultation was rebuked by the prophet, who foresaw that they were speedily to fall victims to the Assyrians, and bade them stay their ill-timed songs of triumph. "Rejoice not thou, whole land of the Philistines, because the rod that smote thee is broken: for out of the serpent's root shall come forth a cockatrice, and its fruit shall be a fiery flying serpent. And the firstborn of the poor shall feed in peace, and the needy shall lie down in safety: and I will kill thy root with famine, and he shall slay thy remnant. Howl, O gate; cry, O city; thou, whole land of the Philistines, art in despair: for there shall come forth from the north a smoke, and there is no straggler in their host. What shall we then answer the messengers of the nation? That the Lord supports Zion, and the poor of His people find a refuge in it." (XIV. 29—32.)

Unlike the Philistines, the Moabites are described as fallen and distressed. They had been proud and cruel, and their haughtiness had provoked the hatred of other nations. Both Judah and Edom refused to grant the help and shelter which they now humbly implored. They bewailed especially the destruction of their vineyards, the chief object of their pride and a principal source of their wealth, as even now the region between Ramoth and Heshbon is remarkable for the luxuriant growth of the vine: "We have heard of the pride of the Moabite — he is exceedingly proud — of his haughtiness, and his pride, and his wrath, of the emptiness of his talk. Therefore shall Moab howl for Moab, everyone shall howl; for the ruins of Kir-hareseth shall you mourn, utterly stricken. For the fields of Heshbon are withered, and the vine of Sibmah, whose noble grapes have intoxicated the chiefs of the nations; they reached to Jazer, they were spread through the wilderness; its branches were stretched out, they went beyond the sea. — Therefore, I wail like the wailing of Jazer about the vine of Sibmah; I water thee with my tears, O Heshbon and Elealeh: for into the gathering of thy fruits and of thy harvest the war-cry has fallen. And gladness and joy are taken away from the plentiful field; and in the vineyards there is no singing and no shouting; no treaders tread wine in their presses: I have made their vintage-shouting to cease. Therefore my bowels mourn like a harp for Moab, and my heart for Kir-hares. — And it shall come to pass, when Moab appears and wearies himself on the high place, and comes to his sanctuary to pray, he shall not prevail.

"This is the word that the Lord has spoken concerning Moab in former times. But now the Lord speaks, saying, Within three years, as the years of a hireling, the glory of Moab shall be despised and all the great multitude; and the remnant shall be very small, not great." (XVI. 6—14.)

Then rising with his theme, the prophet turned his sorrowing eye to Damascus, the glory of Syria, now a prey to the conqueror's wrath, an unsightly heap of ruins. But with yet greater grief his foreboding mind dwelt on Israel led away into dreary captivity: their idolatry and their faithlessness had prepared their doom, and they suffered for the sins and wilfulness of generations.

Another nation of great power and closely connected with Judah by very old associations, was destined to feel the might of the invincible Assyrians. The alarm which their rapid progress had spread over all the territories south and west of the Tigris, had reached the regions of the Nile; and "the heart of Egypt melted in the midst of it". This country, so far from being prepared to oppose the advancing foe, was weakened by internal dissensions. Civil disputes were raging among its various castes. Typical of the greatest disaster that could fall upon Egypt, Isaiah described the sacred Nile as being dried up, and failing to dispense its annual blessings. He commented on these calamities with sorrowful sympathy. His heart was not shut against the distress of the strange people; and, in the midst of their trial, he comforted them by pointing to God's goodness, which was not confined to one nation, nor to the boundaries of one land; true, the Egyptians should feel His wrath — "The Lord shall smite Egypt", but "He shall heal it". From the idols that could not help, and the charmers that could not advise, they should turn for guidance and wisdom to the living God. Egypt and Assyria, at peace with each other, should revere the Lord together, and Israel was to share, not to monopolize, the knowledge of the Lord. "In that day shall Israel be the third with Egypt and with Assyria, even a blessing in the midst of the earth, when the Lord of hosts shall bless, saying, Blessed be Egypt My people, and Assyria the work of My hands, and Israel My inheritance!"

Welcome indeed must have been this ray of consolation; for only a short time later, Isaiah was bidden by God to appear among the people barefoot and with loosened girdle, to symbolize the downfall of Egypt and its prostration before the northern conquerors.

When the invasion of Syria by Sennacherib naturally aroused the terror of the Edomites, they also sought the prophet's council in the dangerous emergency. The anxious people cried to him: "Watchman, what of the night, what of the night?" The night had far advanced, he told them, there was a gleam of morning — there would be changing intervals of war and peace, of danger and safety. Yet Edom fell a victim to the conquerors, who then easily subjected the neighbouring Dedanites, scattered hordes of Bedouins.

Now the eyes of Judah were turned more anxiously than ever towards the northern enemy. A large part of Palestine had become the scene of devastation; Samaria had succumbed, and the prophet, watching her fall from the sister city, viewed it with distress and grief. Deeper still than his pity was the indignation he felt at the sins which had preceded Israel's doom; and in a beautiful oration replete with the purest and loftiest thoughts, he dwelt upon her moral decay. Licentiousness had reigned supreme in every class. The priest had been wanting in piety, the warrior in valour, and the statesman in judgment and patriotism. All moral laws had been defied; religion had exercised no hallowing influence; no shelter had been given to the weary, no help to the needy suppliant. Mere formalism had superseded the observance of God's eternal decrees; and the ordinances of the Law were multiplied and analysed with scrupulous minutcness. Expressing with striking vehemence the subtle ceremonialism of the Samaritan priesthood, the prophet exclaimed: "Line upon line, line upon line, precept upon precept, precept upon precept!" And this spiritual hollowness naturally engendered internal weakness — a warning for all subsequent ages to keep aloof from slavish obedience to the letter, sure to produce disbelief on the one hand, and narrow-minded fanaticism on the other.

From this sad picture Isaiah turned to his own fellow-citizens, the people of Judah, who, alas! deserved and called forth the same remonstrances and invectives: "Forasmuch as this people draw near Me with their mouth, and with their lips do honour Me, but have removed their heart far from Me, and their fear toward Me is taught by the precept of men: therefore, behold, I will proceed to do a marvellous work among this people, indeed a marvellous work and a wonder; for the wisdom of their wise men shall perish, and the understanding of their prudent men shall be hidden;" and bursting forth into one of the noblest effusions of sacred literature, he exclaimed:

"Hear, O heavens, and give ear, O earth, for the Lord speaks; I have reared and brought up children, and they have rebelled against Me. The ox knows his owner, and the ass his master's crib: but Israel does not know, My people has no understanding. Oh sinful nation, people laden with iniquity, seed of evildoers, corrupted men! They have forsaken the Lord, they have blasphemed the Holy One of Israel, they are gone astray backward.

"Where can you be stricken any more, if you add to your revolt? The whole head is sick, and the whole heart faint. From the sole of the foot even to the head there is no soundness in it, but wounds and bruises and putrifying sores; they have not been closed, nor bound up, nor softened with ointment. Your country is desolate, your cities are burnt with fire, your land, strangers devour it in your presence, and it is desolate, overthrown by strangers. And the daughter of Zion is left as a cottage in a vineyard, as a lodge in a garden of cucumbers, as a besieged city. Unless the Lord of hosts had left us a very small remnant, we should be as Sodom, we should be like Gomorrah.

"Hear the word of the Lord, you rich men of Sodom,

lend your ear to the Lord our God, O people of Gomorrah. To what purpose is the multitude of your sacrifices to Me? says the Lord: I am satisfied with burnt-offerings of rams, and the fat of fed beasts; and I delight not in the blood of bullocks, or of lambs, or of he-goats. When you come to appear before Me, who requires it at your hand, to tread My courts? Bring no more vain oblations; incense is an abomination to Me; the Newmoons and Sabbaths, the calling of assemblies — I cannot bear iniquity and solemn meeting. My soul hates your Newmoons and your appointed feasts; they are a burden to Me; I am weary to bear them. And when you spread forth your hands, I hide My eyes from you; yea, when you multiply prayers, I do not hear: your hands are full of blood.

"Wash yourselves, make yourselves clean; put away your evil doings from before My eyes; cease to do evil. Learn to do well, seek judgment, relieve the oppressed, judge the fatherless, plead for the widow.

"Come now, and let us reason together, says the Lord: if your sins are as scarlet, shall they be as white as snow? if they are red like crimson, shall they be as wool? If you are willing and obedient, you shall eat the good of the land; but if you refuse and rebel, you shall be devoured by the sword; for the mouth of the Lord has spoken it.

"How has the faithful city become depraved! It was full of judgment, righteousness lodged in it, but now murderers. Thy silver has become dross, thy wine is mixed with water; Thy princes are rebels, and a gang of thieves; everyone loves bribes, and follows after rewards; they judge not the fatherless, nor does the cause of the widow come before them. Therefore says the Lord, the Lord of hosts, the mighty One of Israel, Ah, I will retaliate upon My adversaries, and avenge Myself of My enemies. And I will turn My hand upon thee, and purge away thy dross, and take away all thy tin. And I will restore thy judges as at first, and thy counsellers as at the beginning: afterwards thou shalt be called, The city of righteousness, the faithful city. Zion shall be redeemed with judgment, and her penitent men with righteousness. — And the destruction of the trespassers and of the sinners shall come together, and they that forsake the Lord shall perish. For they shall be ashamed of the oaks which you have desired, and you shall blush for the gardens that you have chosen. For you shall be as an oak whose leaf fades, and as a garden that has no water. And the strong shall be as tow, and the maker of it as a spark, and they shall both burn together, and none shall quench them." (I. 2—31.)

A pious king was reigning, it is true, but there existed a faction of irreligious and selfsufficient nobles, who caused serious political confusion. As the Assyrians drew nearer, the Hebrews made warlike preparations to oppose them; "the scourge shall pass through us, and not come to us", they said in ill-founded security. In vain the prophet displayed all his energy and counselled confidence without idle presumption; in vain he bade them trust in their faith, and promised help and safety to those who acted righteously.

In the year 714, or seven years after the first great blow which Canaan had received, the long-dreaded event took place. Sennacherib entered Judah, and the siege of Jerusalem was anticipated as the next step of the invader. By utterly disregarding Isaiah's remonstrances, the nobles acted in a refractory spirit and provoked the wrath of the enemy. They refused to pay any longer the hated tribute, and not only did they themselves prepare for war, but they called upon Egypt to conclude with them an alliance against the common foe. This most impolitic act aroused the indignation of the prophet. "Woe to them", he exclaimed, "that go down to Egypt for help, and rely on horses and trust in chariots because they are many, and on horsemen because they are strong"; but "the Egyptians are men and not God, their horses flesh and not spirit". Egypt would prove a faithless ally; her help would be dearly bought; the riches and treasures of Judah would be required in return for her slender aid — the condign punishment for the disgraceful alliance. In vain Isaiah assured them that the fall of the Assyrians was near, and that Jehovah alone would save His people. Many and strong were the unpalatable words with which the courageous prophet endeavoured to convince the "rebellious people". They listened not, and, like all who ask advice merely to have their own views confirmed, they turned to prophets and seers whose predictions accorded with their wishes.

The danger advanced steadily, and at last the Assyrian general, at the head of his redoubtable army, flushed by the glory of many conquests, stood before the gates of Jerusalem, and haughtily called upon the people to surrender. With pardonable irony he asked if they, small in number and insignificant in strength, hoped to withstand the force which had brought mighty nations low; and he taunted them for their reliance on Egypt — a broken reed which could give no support.

The king Hezekiah, more pious and thoughtful than his nobles, sought comfort in the House of God, and advice from His prophet. The latter, unchanging in his counsel, proclaimed once again the necessity of patient trust, and announced God's anger at the unbelieving spirit of the multitude, and His merciful forgiveness to those who sought His protection.

While Hezekiah was still mourning in sackcloth and dust, while the nobles were still resting on the fallacious hope of aid from Egypt, and Isaiah, serene in his unalterable faith, was still cherishing his brave confidence, all the eager machinations of the foe were suddenly scattered to the winds. One single night saw the gorgeous pride of the Assyrian army a pitiful ruin, crushed by no mortal hand, the victim of a fearful plague. Saved by no efforts of their own, the inhabitants of the holy city could not fail to recognize in the fatal breath of that pestilence their own impotence and insufficiency, and to revere a Power in whose hands all earthly foes are as nought.

This was the last great national event which called forth the exalted gifts and the strenuous efforts of Isaiah. Henceforth he appeared only as the friend and adviser of the pious king, who ever since the awe-striking and instantaneous overthrow of the Assyrians, placed unreserved trust in him.

A short time afterwards the king fell ill. But a touching prayer, suggested by a pious longing to live in the service of God, was not left unanswered; and Isaiah, the bearer of the good tidings, proved also to be endowed with the human means of effecting the cure. Hezekiah's life was prolonged, and was no more disturbed by the dangers of warfare. It was marked, however, by another historical event, which, though not of immediate importance, was a significant introduction to the vicissitudes of succeeding reigns. The Babylonians, at that time under the dominion of the Assyrians, aspired to regain their independence. They sent out embassies to other nations to discover how far they might count upon their aid or sympathy; perhaps they were also anxious to learn the resources of other countries, in order to shape their plans accordingly. They deemed Hezekiah's sickness and recovery a favourable opportunity for a friendly approach to the Hebrews; and their chief, Morodach Baladan, sent letters and presents to express joy at the king of Judah's restoration to health. Hezekiah, in the confiding simplicity of his nature, never suspected the honesty of his guests. He cordially welcomed them and showed them his store-houses, his silver and gold, his spices and precious ointment, his treasury and arsenal; in fact, he initiated them into every department of his kingdom. Very unlike the monarch in his short-sighted credulity, the aged prophet heard with no little indignation of this act of imprudence, and once again all the feelings of the patriot and the statesman were roused within him. He knew well the ulterior object of the Babylonian messengers' long journey, and he understood the danger which awaited Judah, and which the king himself had now unwittingly accelerated. He declared that no good would spring from any connection of the Hebrews with Babylon; and that in laying bare its resources, the weaker kingdom was pointing out to the stronger one the way to conquer it.

These sad words of remonstrance are the last records of the great prophet. Whether death shortly afterwards silenced that truth-loving and admonitory voice, or whether it was heard henceforth only in moral exhortations, it is vain to conjecture. Tradition relates that he survived the pious king Hezekiah, and during the reign of the impious Manasseh stood more than ever isolated in his strenuous warfare against wickedness and idolatry; that the people at last grew impatient and incensed under his perpetual accusations, and forced him to escape from Judea, till nature, kinder than his fellow-men, saved him, an aged tree extending its twining arms and opening its hollow trunk to shelter him in his flight and weariness. But even here his fierce pursuers are said to have left him no peace, and the legend, encircling the prophet with the glory of the martyr, describes the cruel stroke of the hatchet which destroyed the hospitable tree, and terminated the existence of the great Isaiah. How far these traditions are based upon reality, is immaterial. No romantic invention can heighten the interest which surrounds the prophet's life; no martyrdom can render more pathetic or more exalted the zealous efforts and the manly struggles which he carried on alone against the moral decay of a thankless people.

But if his death be shrouded in mystery, the tenour of his life lies distinctly before us. Throughout his long career, his counsels and actions were guided by one idea — trust, faithful and unflinching trust, in God. One duty always remained paramount among his varied efforts — a willing and unwavering submission to the Lord, to whose service he had pledged himself. To Him he ascribed the oracular gift and the counsellor's wisdom. But though he attributed his actions to a higher source, though he uttered his orations as the mouthpiece of Divine behests, the personal character of Isaiah was not lost to the reverential admiration of future ages. The veil of obedience with which he surrounded his own deeds and thoughts, beautifies and softens, without concealing, one of the most sublime figures in all sacred history. His peculiar greatness lifts him beyond that common and humble path which he cared not to leave, and his glowing eloquence betrays the intensity of his own individual feelings. What can be more evident than the profound patriotism which warmed his heart, which made his love more lasting than his anger, his consolation more readily proffered than his rebuke, his endurance stronger than the disbelief and obstinacy with which it was met? The ardour of his sympathies was not understood by the mass; for his mind grasped the whole world and all its manifold interests. Though the nation among which his lot was cast had the strongest claims upon his feelings, his heart was open to the struggles and sorrows of all mankind. The horizon of his affections was wide and clear, yet in the comprehensiveness of his views no detail was lost. Grand and sublime as were his visions of the future, he never forgot that the present moment had more pressing claims. He knew that no good result could be secured without prompt and decisive action. He saw the path distinct, when others were blinded by the confusion of the times. He shared the eager interest, but never the excited alarm of his countrymen, and he consequently stood calm among them, with a firm hand and a clear eye. A true statesman, he endeavoured by practical means to bring his people nearer to the standard of his moral ideal. In pursuing this object, he spared no efforts; he wielded his powerful instruments of derision and persuasion to uproot the errors which served as a clog to the attainment of his noble aims. But though an idealist in his ardent aspirations, he advocated energy and activity both in important national events and in the small details of domestic existence.

Wherever men acted and toiled, there lay the prophet's task to encourage, to censure, or to forewarn. Nothing can exceed the purity and loftiness of the principles which he proclaimed not only to his countrymen but to all mankind. His code of laws taught adherence to active virtue, to charity, and thoughtfulness, self-denial without self-castigation, pious trust without apathy. He preached no impossible doctrines; he desired to improve both the thoughts and the deeds of men. The purifying spark was wanting in that "unclean nation," tainted by the sins of ambition and egotism. It was this spark which worked so powerfully in Isaiah, and bade him free his people from the fetters of formularies and worldliness, and strive to bring them nearer to that distant goal which, however rarely attained, did not appear to him beyond the human reach.

The marvellous language in which his orations were delivered, proved a worthy and effectual medium for impressing his ideas upon his contemporaries, and for perpetuating them among subsequent generations: Isaiah was a poet and philosopher as well as a patriot and a moralist; and his works are, therefore, as great an addition to the literature as to the history and the ethics of Scripture. His diction is vigorous and energetic, remarkable for an intensity and variety which accorded with the boundless wealth of his ideas. His warnings and denunciations derive their peculiar force from condensed thought, fitness of words, and vividness of colouring; such a style, without being obscure, naturally offers many difficulties to the interpreter. The concise and pointed expressions must have fallen upon his hearers with equal power and distinctness, though the reader of the present day sometimes labours to understand the allusions to those rapidly succeeding events which a few verses vaguely point at, rather than describe.

For it should not be forgotten that these works which to us are lasting truths written for all ages, were in fact orations intended to produce an instantaneous effect. They are adorned with all the skilful ornaments which rhetoric suggests, and contain all those varied metaphors, similes, figures of speech, and even alliterations and conceits, which excite the feelings and arrest the attention of the listener; and the genius of Isaiah knew well how to adapt the Hebrew language to all the purposes of art, and to render it pliable for the expression of all emotions. His style is singularly free from artificial playfulness; it is noble and grand, yet not overcharged with Oriental imagery. The most concise language and the pithiest address are generally devoted to the delineation of the most important events. But when in times of comparative tranquillity, the prophet's mind dwells upon some spiritual theme, then his words flow in greater profusion, his eloquence is formed in a softer mould, and all the rich poetry of his genius bursts forth to exalt God's love and mercy, or to throw its own radiance round the picture of a glorious future. He always adapts the expression to the thought, whether he pours out praise and thanksgiving, or whether he describes that ideal happiness which the hope of the patriot suggested.

But he gave no undue predominance to the style of his orations, the form being merely intended to enhance the force of his thoughts, and these indeed its beauty helped to perpetuate. All the varied powers with which the prophet was endowed, were combined to further the great end which he had in view. The enthusiasm of the poet gave effect to the teaching of the moralist, and the genius of the orator established the influence of the statesman.

THE SECOND ISAIAH. (About 540.)
[Isai. XL—LXVI.]

About a century and a half after the time of Hezekiah, when the changes foretold by Isaiah had come to pass, and when the vicissitudes, from which he had vainly endeavoured to save his erring contemporaries, had actually befallen their descendants, another prophet arose, whose orations have long been attributed to the same great prophet of Judah, and whose writings accordingly form the concluding part of the book of Isaiah. There are indeed many similarities between the earlier and the later work, sufficient to account for this view. They are both characterised by the same lofty patriotism, the same earnest desire to promote the moral and material well-being of the people, and the same unobtrusiveness of personal identity; they are, in fact, effusions of kindred minds; yet they cannot be the creations of the same author. The later prophet, whose name is unknown to us, proves his individuality by salient differences both in the subject and style of his orations. The change is perceptible in the very opening sentences, and continues to be manifest to the last words of the Book.

We are suddenly transported from tumultuous scenes of warfare, from victories and reverses, from national strife and domestic confusion to a state of patient submission and endurance; leaving behind a time when the passing moment is all-important, we are introduced to an age, in one respect more sad, in another more soothing, when political action has become impossible, excitement lies in the past, and comfort is only to be found in the future. Instead of seeing before us the hills of Judea, we are surrounded by the plains of Babylon. The names of Hezekiah and Ahaz no longer call forth ardent rejoicings or sorrowing remonstrances; for the figure of Cyrus towers above all others, and we witness the triumphant march of the young Persian monarch, which proved so eventful to the captive nation.

For in their long and dreary exile, the Hebrews had not lost their nationality, and were as much distinguished as ever for their attachment to their peculiar doctrines, and their ardent love for the land of their inheritance. The very sins and delinquencies for which they had formerly suffered, still clung to them, and the courageous monitor who desired to combat irreligion or immorality, found as large a sphere of action as would have been offered to him in the days of their comparative prosperity. The mission of the earlier prophet was more difficult and varied; for his path lay among stirring events, and his noble patriotism placed him at the helm of a state, which might at any moment have been wrecked. But at the time of the later author, it was unavailing to devise political measures; for the people's fate lay in strange hands. Yet no humble task was allotted to the prophet during the captivity; and the very absence of political excitement peculiarly adapted this time for the counsel and admonition of the spiritual leader. He toiled to raise his fellow-sufferers from their dejection, and to improve the tenour of their lives; for a great work was in store for them — the establishment of a new and more Godfearing kingdom, which it would require the utmost energy to found, and the greatest self-denial to preserve.

He felt that the despondency of the people rendered them equally unfit to bear their present sorrows and to meet their impending labours, and he therefore again and again repeated his conviction that the days of their captivity were numbered, and attempted to pour refreshing gladness into their mourning hearts. "Comfort ye, comfort ye My people, says your God. Speak consolingly to Jerusalem, and cry to her that her warfare is accomplished, that her iniquity is pardoned; for she has received of the Lord's hand double for all her sins."

These joyful tidings were not suggested by vague and unfounded hope, but by an event which had actually taken place, and which was indeed the harbinger of the blessings announced by the prophet.

The Assyrian monarchy had, in its turn, experienced the decline which inevitably befell the colossal empires of the East, and the rapidity of which was in proportion to the rapidity of their growth. Persia was in the ascendant, and the same invincible power which the kings of Assyria and Babylon had wielded before, now belonged to Cyrus. But his uplifted arm, a terror to the surrounding countries, proved a protecting shield to the exiled Jews. The conquest of Babylon loosened their fetters; for the victorious hero cherished no ill-feeling towards the captives of his enemy, and he knew that his approach was as eagerly hailed by the desponding Hebrews, as it was dreaded by the prosperous Babylonians. It is not surprising that the prophet's description of this glorious approach breathes the most ardent enthusiasm. Great indeed must have been the astonishment and admiration which greeted the rapid progress of Cyrus, signalised by so many brilliant victories. The heathen nations cried to their deities, and in bitter humiliation moulded anew the brazen and silver images which the sword of the conqueror had laid low. But all was in vain, for "he passed over princes as mortar, and as the potter treads the clay".

As the warrior advanced and freedom seemed to be dawning on the horizon of the Hebrews, the exuberance of Oriental phraseology was devoted to the description of the hero and deliverer. He is the favoured one of the Almighty, whom He has chosen for His great work, and has endowed with power to carry out His designs. "Thus says the Lord God to His anointed, to Cyrus, whom I hold by his right hand, to subdue nations before him, and that I may unloosen the loin of kings, and open before him gates, and that doors may not be closed. I will go before thee, and make the crooked places straight; and will break in pieces the gates of brass, and cut asunder the bars of iron ... The produce of Egypt and the gain of Ethiopia and of the Sabeans, men of high stature, shall pass over to thee, and shall be thine: they shall come after thee, in chains shall they pass over, and they shall fall down before thee; and they shall make supplication to thee." And this great prince was not unworthy of his mission. "I have raised him up in righteousness, and I will make even all his ways, he shall build My city and he shall release My captives, not for price nor reward, saith the Lord of hosts." Though blind to the clearer light of the faith of the Hebrews, he was beloved by God who sent him to curb the pride of nations. The ravagers of many generations in their turn became victims, and the great and proud Babylon fell a prey to the conqueror. The former glory and the final ruin of the vast city were graphically depicted. "Come down, and sit in the dust, O virgin daughter of Babylon; sit on the ground; there is no throne, O daughter of the Chaldeans, for thou shalt no more be called tender and delicate ... Sit thou silent, and get thee into darkness, O daughter of the Chaldeans, for thou shalt no more be called The Lady of Kingdoms." With bitter irony the prophet then turned to the useless supplications which the terrified Chaldeans addressed to their numerous deities. Magical arts and sorcery had always flourished in their race, and their soothsayers and astrologers stood in high repute; but now their counsels were at fault, and their oracles fell upon unbelieving ears. In this stormy period which brought destruction to mighty kingdoms, the Hebrew exiles alone were to be safe and prosperous. They saw a prospect of returning to that cherished country, to which their hearts clung in spite of their long separation from it, and the prophet delighted in painting the new home that was awaiting them with all the glowing colours of patriotism. The land was to be large and fertile, crowded with walled cities and numerous inhabitants. Free from the attacks of strangers, a new and glorious capital should arise, and the joyful people should themselves transform the wastes into gardens, the dreary wilderness into an Eden. Those destined to share these blessings should enjoy a calm and peaceful existence, and the length and undisturbed happiness of their lives should recall the old patriarchal times. Fired by a noble patriotism, the inspired orator rose to the most sublime eloquence in describing that land, where all nations should meet in peace, and where the riches and industry of many countries should rear a second splendid Temple, in which all should come and worship Jehovah together. And the God of Israel alone was the Bestower of all this happiness; and the people were bidden to extol their Divine Deliverer in strains of fervent gratitude.

But the outward blessings of peace and prosperity which they were to receive through the mercy of a forgiving God, were not to be the only features of the new commonwealth. The true faith was to keep the land pure and untainted. Nor was the foreigner to be excluded from this joyful inheritance. "The sons of strangers that join themselves the to Lord, to serve Him, and to love the name of the

Lord, to be His servants, every one that keeps the Sabbath from polluting it and holds fast to My covenant, these will I bring to My holy mountain, and make them joyful in My House of prayer; their burnt-offerings and their sacrifices shall be accepted upon My altar, for My House shall be called a House of prayer for all the nations."

These days were indeed to bring release and happiness to the sin-laden Israelites, whose iniquities were now pardoned; but in a far greater degree were they destined to bestow a glorious recompense upon those pious men who had toiled and suffered for the people.

The torch of truth would many a time have been extinguished but for the unwearied efforts of the prophets. These had revived the latent spark which had feebly glimmered before the captivity, and which was in danger of being entirely quenched during the exile. How cruelly their endeavours had often been foiled, is manifest from the orations of this, one of their later fellow-labourers. Many an eloquent page is devoted to the praise of the great band of martyrs, and we see vividly before us their lives embittered by persecution but made glorious by self-sacrifice. "He is despised and rejected of men, a man of sorrows and acquainted with grief, and we hid indeed our faces from him; he was despised and we esteemed him not, surely he has borne our griefs and carried our sorrows, yet we deemed him stricken, smitten of God and afflicted .... He was taken from prison and from judgment, and who shall declare his generation? .... He had his grave given him with the wicked, and with the impious he lay in his death, although he had done no violence, nor was there any deceit in his mouth."

But thenceforth the earnest teachers, for ever safe from persecution and hatred, should enjoy the highest esteem and reverence. Their duties should comprise a larger field, and in the new kingdom all nations should come and listen to their teaching. No more should the burden of their grievances be, "I have laboured in vain, I have consumed my strength for nought and to no purpose"; for great was to be the reward allotted to them: "Is it a small thing that thou shouldst be My servant to raise up the tribes of Jacob, and to restore the preserved of Israel? And I will make thee a light to the nations, and thou shalt bring My salvation to the end of the earth."

However, it was not the prophet's intention to hold out to the people and their leaders unconditional promises of happiness. The glad tidings were thus tempered: "The righteous alone shall inherit the land." Righteousness and piety were the weapons indispensable for recovering and maintaining the beloved land. The visions of prosperity were, therefore, not to lull the people into indolence, but to rouse them to action, and thus render them worthy of the mercy of God.

Idolatry had, no doubt, been fostered by the surrounding atmosphere, and the prophet accused the people of having adopted, among other practices, the horrible worship of Moloch. Powerless as ever to resist temptation, the Hebrews, again and again offered unlawful sacrifices in groves and on heights. These acts provoked the stern remonstrance of the prophet; but the lack of moral and social virtue, unfortunately not less prevalent, called forth still stronger and more ardent exhortations. The people had been chastised for their misdeeds, but misfortune had not weaned them from their follies and their failings. They may have had less scope for the indulgence of their licentiousness and frivolity, but they still possessed ample opportunities for that corrupt and fraudulent conduct which painfully recalled the days of the first Isaiah. "Your hands are defiled with blood, and your fingers with iniquity; your lips have spoken lies, your tongue has muttered perverseness... None calls for justice, nor does any one plead for truth; they trust in vanity and speak lies, they conceive mischief, and bring forth iniquity."

Even more reprehensible were those evildoers, who coupled scrupulous adherence to the outward forms of their faith with sin and wickedness. The prophet's mind revolted from these shallow and perverted hypocrites, and he proclaimed with the utmost power the Divine displeasure at this mockery of religion. But he did not only rebuke his people, he desired to reform them, and he pointed out the precepts which it was most essential to observe. Piety was not to be reckoned by the number of sacrifices. The heart might be wicked and stubborn, though the head was bent low by fasting. Sackcloth and ashes, and a form emaciated by self-castigation, were looked upon by God with abhorrence, if accompanied by rancour and envy, by violence and oppression. "In the day of your fast", cried the indignant prophet, "you pursue your business and continue all your labours. Behold, you fast for strife and contention, and to smite with the wicked fist; you do not fast at present, to make your voice to be heard on high. Is it such a fast that I desire? a day for a man to afflict himself? is it to bow down his head as a bulrush, and to fall down in sackcloth and ashes? dost thou call this a fast, and an acceptable day to the Lord? Is not this the fast that I desire? to loosen the bands of wickedness, to undo the burdens of bondage, to release the oppressed, and to break every yoke? Is it not to deal thy bread to the hungry, to bring the outcast poor to thy house? when thou seest the naked that thou cover him; and that thou hide not thyself from thy own flesh? .... Then shalt thou have delight in the Lord; and I will cause thee to ride upon the heights of the earth, and make thee enjoy the inheritance of Jacob thy father."

Such was the heartstirring language that found a sympathetic chord in every human breast; such were the doctrines, so sublime and so true, and yet so obvious and so practical, that men of all nations and of all creeds can apply them in their daily life. Long and nobly had the prophets endeavoured to instil similar precepts into the minds of their people, but they had seldom succeeded in leaving so complete and impressive a picture of real piety, of piety grateful in the eyes of God, consisting in purity of thought and charity of deed, without which prayer, sacrifice, and fasting are not only lifeless symbols, but false and hateful displays.

It was thus, by exposing their failings, by exhorting them to repentance, and still more by pointing out the safe and sure path of virtue, that the prophet tried to render his countrymen worthy of their promised deliverance.

Unlike his great predecessor, he was not sent to warn and to direct the people in days of dangerous opulence, but to serve as a clear light in adversity, showing both the distant vistas of happiness and the surrounding evils and obstacles. He was not charged to proclaim God's retributive judgments. These they had long since experienced; and with earnestness and severity he urged that if their God had apparently abandoned them, it was the result of their own work, because they had knowingly and heedlessly forfeited His protection.

The condition of the captive, suffering, but still sinning people, called forth less diversity in the style of the prophet's orations than is naturally to be found in those of his predecessor. But the absence of intense excitement and varied historical interest is amply compensated for by language so poetical and beautiful, so sweet and flowing, and yet so bold and vivid, that in some respects it is unequalled throughout the Hebrew Scriptures. The struggle of former times had given way to a passive state of endurance; this change is reflected in the different style of the two prophets whose writings chance has united: energy and activity of the mind on the one hand, calmness and poetical imagery on the other. Still in spite of these dissimilarities, the thread which unites the whole brotherhood of prophets is unbroken: they both exhibit a spirit of purity and patriotism, devotion to the cause of true religion and a humble resignation of all personal claims. Therefore, the noble and sublime work of the elder Isaiah with its grand thoughts moulded in majestic words, is not unaptly supplemented by the softer and more heart winning utterances of the Isaiah of the age of Cyrus.

JEREMIAH. (627 to about 580.)

The words of the great prophet Isaiah proved as unavailing after his death as they had been unheeded during his lifetime, and the sins and abominations which he had sought to weed out, flourished apace during the reign of Manasseh. The evils were too deeply rooted to be remedied even by the zeal and devotion of king Josiah. The mild and beneficent rule of this monarch only delayed for a time the calamities which the infatuation of his people had rendered inevitable. Altars were indeed once more consecrated to a purer worship, and the Mosaic laws commanded unwonted obedience. But the reforms so piously planned and so ardently carried out, were of short duration, and created but a temporary effect. Many vices and errors had become too much a part of the national character to yield to a better influence; and they multiplied under the rule of succeeding kings, whose propensities coincided with those of their subjects, and who were ill fitted to improve the moral condition of the people by precept or example.

The prophetic warnings had met with derision and neglect; and idolatry, the fatal scourge of the Hebrews, was undermining their unity and nationality. Side by side with a wanton contempt of the spirit of a purer religion, rose an utter disregard of all moral obligations. The eloquent entreaties and fiery invectives of Isaiah left no enduring impression on his callous countrymen, who, as generation followed generation, became more and more enveloped in an atmosphere of guilt and perversion.

While licentiousness and crime were thus weakening every branch of the commonwealth, outward difficulties began to thicken, which it required the greatest vigilance and energy to encounter and to vanquish. The Hebrews lived in perilous vicinity of two powerful nations, the Babylonians and Egyptians, and constantly provoked the anger of the one or the other, and often of both, by injudicious alliances hastily formed and as hastily broken. Occasionally they were awakened to a sense of their danger by some unexpected panic, which found them helpless because they were habitually indifferent and improvident.

Yet the chosen people were not allowed to rush into destruction unwarned. The energetic appeals which had resounded for generations, and the devoted though ineffectual endeavours of inspired patriots were not wanting at this juncture. Indeed, eloquence and earnestness, which had been spent, and alas! all but wasted during the long years of prophetic toil ungrudgingly borne, and of danger fearlessly defied, were in the last days of the Jewish commonwealth more urgently needed than ever before. The attempt at regenerating the fallen people was now more arduous, but the necessity of the task more imperative, than at any previous period. To this attempt was devoted one of the noblest lives recorded in all history, noblest in action, in example, and in teaching. Later ages have looked upon his figure standing out in bright relief amidst surrounding darkness, as a proof that the race to which he belonged, though degenerate, was not hopelessly depraved, and though deserving reproach and chastisement, was not bereft of Divine love and care.

The career of Jeremiah, unlike that of his great predecessor Isaiah, is so closely connected with his writings that the one cannot be considered apart from the other. The life of Isaiah is hardly known to us in more than shadowy outline. His orations proclaim the truth and sublimity of his ideas, the aims and objects of his existence; but we are but little initiated into the conflicts of his feelings or the impressions of his heart. We regard the closely veiled author of the most lofty prophecies with profound veneration; but we turn with a keener interest and deeper sympathy to the more human Jeremiah. We follow him from his earliest years when, inexperienced and diffident, he first received the Divine commands, through a long career beset with dangers and constantly exposed to humiliations; we watch with unwavering interest his changeless purpose, his patriotic devotion, his dauntless courage, the deep sorrow which wellnigh crushed his soul, and at last the martyrdom which he suffered through the wanton cruelty, and still more through the obdurate unbelief, of his people.

In the time of Isaiah, the nation had not yet lost all its energy nor all its virtue, and his severe indignation was occasionally varied by hopeful rejoicing. But the tragedy of Judah was fast drawing to its close, when Jeremiah sought in vain to avert or to delay it. The perpetual warfare which he carried on with his countrymen, and the anguish which this warfare inflicted upon him, surround his person with unequalled interest; indeed the life of Jeremiah is an unbroken chain of deeds of self-sacrifice, and forms a grand central figure in the last struggles of a great nation.

He was born in Anathoth, a small town in the province of Benjamin. His father was the priest Hilkiah, and he was therefore from his birth connected with the most learned class of the people. It was in the fifteenth year of the reign of king Josiah (627), that the gift of prophecy was aroused in him, and he was stimulated to undertake the ungrateful mission of administering advice and rebuke to his countrymen. Like Isaiah, he received the Divine commands with fear and hesitation, and pleaded the immaturity of his years: "O Lord God, behold, I cannot speak, for I am a child." But he was comforted by Divine promises, and the modest and trembling youth felt encouraged to confront a reckless and angry multitude. He became as "a fenced city, an iron pillar, a brazen wall." Thus girt with strength, he was sent on his manifold and difficult duties, "to root out, to pull down, and to destroy, to throw down, to build, and to plant."

He was only in his twenty-first year, when this arduous and perilous task was imposed upon him. He had to impeach and to condemn all that was most revered, most powerful, and most haughty; for priest, people, and prince were alike his inveterate foes. But trust in his mission, unflinching courage, and patriotic enthusiasm were his weapons in the bitter and protracted strife. A less energetic and less zealous mind would have shrunk from the harrowing difficulties which surrounded him. It seemed indeed hopeless to raise the people from the abyss of idolatry, into which they had fallen, or to persuade the king and the elders to follow a more independent and more prudent policy. Never had the horizon borne a more threatening aspect. The clear mind of the prophet saw the kingdom hemmed in by the most fatal dangers. Palestine lies in the direct road between Egypt and Assyria, and though neither empire cared for the possession of that small country for its own sake, its independence was inconvenient to both. The Babylonian monarch, who shared the love of conquest that distinguished his race, regarded the territory of Judea as a stepping stone to the coveted regions of the West, as a suitable centre from which to levy troops and taxes. Another and still greater cause for alarm threatened the kingdom. Wild tribes, natives of the desert steppes of Curdistan, had not long since emigrated from their homes and established themselves in southern Mesopotamia, where they made themselves feared by their boldness, their rapine, and their ferocity. The eloquence of the prophet was often employed in describing the various and terrible peculiarities of this people. He compared them to the lion rising from the thicket, to the lurking leopard, to serpents and adders which defy the conjuror's art. This tribe of Chaldeans, so restless, so impetuous, and so warlike, did not tarry long to fulfil the prophet's anticipations, and to display the strength which was to procure them a new kingdom and endow them with new fame.

Judah stood unprotected in this danger. The treaty which Hezekiah had concluded with Assyria was probably still in force, but the Hebrews could expect little support from an ally who was himself in imminent peril of being crushed by the ruthless conquerors. — To the pious mind of the prophet, this sudden complication of calamities appeared as the punishment for many years of transgression, as the result of disregard to those laws which had given to the small territory of the Hebrews dignity, influence, and stability. "Just as you have forsaken Me", was the Divine answer which he proclaimed to the people, "and serve strange gods in your land, so shall you serve strangers in a land that is not yours." He was convinced that the only possibility of rescue from their trials lay in the removal of the cause in which they had originated. To effect this was his primary object; and while yet a young man he attempted, now without fear or hesitation, to remedy the great internal evils from which his people were suffering. With all the fervour of patriotism, and all the earnestness of conviction, he denounced the prevailing vices, and insisted upon repentance and reform. "Thus says the Lord of hosts, the God of Israel, amend your ways and your doings, and I will cause you to dwell in this place ..... yea, if you thoroughly amend your ways and your doings: if you indeed execute judgment between a man and his neighbour, if you oppress not the stranger, the fatherless, and the widow, and shed not innocent blood in this place, nor walk after other gods, to your own harm; then I will cause you to dwell in this place, in the land that I gave to your fathers for ever and ever."

But the people, far from following the paths pointed out to them by each successive monitor, gave themselves up to their vicious inclinations with unbridled recklessness. They desecrated the House of God by images of idols. The wickedness which stained their domestic hearth, extended to their public assemblies. The idolatrous rites which they continually practised were of the most varied forms. Every country with which they had ever come into contact, contributed to increase the number of their deities. They honoured the gods of the Egyptians and Phoenicians, of the Ammonites and the Canaanites. They adopted the Egyptian animal worship; they prayed to the gods of light and darkness; they burnt incense to the misshapen figure of Dagon, the idol of the Philistines; and they moulded images of gold and silver and placed them on costly altars. Some of these statues stood in the very Temple, side by side with the sacred vessels; and many disgraced the houses of the rich and the poor, who kept them for domestic worship. All classes indulged in the horrible rites of Moloch, at whose shrine children were mercilessly burnt; and superstition, following in the train of idolatry, gave ready access to the foreign belief in the power of demons and spectres. The magician and the soothsayer helped to pervert the minds of the people, and gorgeous processions and licentious rites corrupted alike their taste and their lives.

Jeremiah became soon aware of this deplorable condition of the country. He was deeply grieved, but not disheartened. He inveighed bitterly against the idolatry into which the people had sunk, and with the most earnest eloquence contrasted the greatness of the God they had abandoned with the nothingness of the beings to whom they were praying. He tried to make them appreciate the blessings and mercies which they were constantly receiving from their God. He was unable to understand how they could withhold their allegiance from "the everlasting living God, the King of nations, who made the earth in His power, and the world in His wisdom, to bow down before gold and silver, their own handicraft". The only excuse he could find for conduct so perverse and so fatal, was the blindness and folly of the human heart.

He saw with equal distress that the idolators, in abandoning the pure faith of their ancestors, defied also the laws of morality which that faith enjoins. He saw, how they oppressed the poor, and despoiled the weak. He sought in vain for justice among the chiefs and elders of the people, or for charity and truth among the priests and prophets. He exhorted them in vain to mend their ways and to lay aside their evil practices; and he urged in vain that faithful allegiance to God was demanded no less by gratitude than by reason. And when he could neither convince his hearers of their sins nor awe them into repentance, he described the fearful calamities which they were bringing down upon themselves, and which he said were near at hand.

The bitterness which pervades Jeremiah's indignant orations, is rendered still more manifest by the outbursts of passionate grief which occasionally interrupts them. His clear and keen-sighted mind was far above the mean and narrow spirit that ruled his countrymen; yet his sympathies were ever with them; and in his orations, his personal grief made itself felt again and again. He was pained in his inmost heart; he was hurt for the hurt of his people; he wished that his head were water, and his eyes a fountain of tears, that he could weep day and night for the slain of the daughters of his people; and his indignation could never quench his love. Even now, seen through a long vista of ages, it is impossible to appreciate too highly the compassion and charity which he exercised towards his erring countrymen, and which made him look upon their infatuation as resulting from the frailties common to mankind: "the heart", he said, "is deceitful above all things, and desperately wicked." There was but one source of wisdom and goodness — "O Lord, I know that the way of man is not in himself, it is not in man that walks to direct his steps ..... Blessed is the man that trusts in the Lord, and whose hope the Lord is." It was to his heavenly Master that he looked for solace; it was His support, that allowed him to bear with patience and humility the neglect and derision he so often received.

But he could not be long engrossed in his own sorrows, for a life of action lay before him. The task of chiding and threatening was most painful to one whose tender heart understood the failings of humanity; it was an ungrateful duty for the zealous patriot to foretell the doom of his country; but he felt that as a Divine messenger he must accomplish his mission. "My wound is grievous," he said; "truly this is grief; but I must bear it."

Like Isaiah, he extended his sympathies to the surrounding countries. Moral depravity prevailed to a fearful degree among the neighbouring tribes; and it called forth the earnest admonition of the prophet, who saw the dangers which they were hastening by their heedlessness. He warned the Philistines, and he proclaimed to the Moabites the unavoidable destruction which awaited them on account of their arrogance. He announced desolation to the flourishing valleys of Edom, and he foretold the fall of the proud Damascus. He employed no withering scorn to heighten the pictures of misery; but he truthfully portrayed the effects of the sad degeneracy which he beheld on every side. He devoted, however, the utmost fervour of his eloquence to the description of the awful calamity from which his own people was suffering. The unhappy country was visited by a terrible drought; the children of the nobles were sent to the springs and cisterns; but they found no water, and they returned with empty pitchers, ashamed and confounded; man and beast were languishing alike; for "the grass refused to grow on the ground, and the wild ass stood forlorn upon the high place." — Jeremiah pointed to these inflictions as the result of the people's own sins, and endeavoured to make the present evil an inducement to repentance and improvement.

But whilst the prophet was thus untiringly pursuing his mission, his own life was not spent in unruffled smoothness. The people of Anathoth listened with great discontent to his forebodings of evil, and to the causes which he assigned to their actual misfortunes. Among all the priests and prophets he was the only one who reviled them; why should the opinion of one man have greater weight than the views of his entire order? and why should his accusations be endured? Jeremiah knew that his life was in danger, and he felt with pain and sorrow the necessity of leaving his native country. A wider field for his patriotic endeavours presented itself in the neighbouring capital, and he consequently repaired to Jerusalem.

The leaders or the most prominent members of the community were the chiefs of the clans and families, and next to them the priests exercised a powerful and often a pernicious authority. They repudiated of course every advice detrimental to their influence or clashing with their interests, and they were disinclined to give a willing ear to the warnings and denunciations of so stern a preacher as Jeremiah. They opposed him with as much vehemence as their neighbours of Anathoth had done. Indulging in every luxury and enjoyment, they would not hear of approaching evil. The prophet announced to them the destruction of the Temple, which they believed was destined to remain for ever. He accused them of many transgressions, and censured their priests and their leaders, whose crimes he laid bare with unsparing severity. But they marvelled who was this presumptuous and intruding counsellor, who placed himself above prince and priest, and attacked the whole nation from the most honoured of the elders to the humblest artisan? His exhortations, received with contempt, called forth increased bitterness and irritation. His motives were perverted; his efforts for the safety of his country were misconstrued, and he was derided as a senseless enthusiast.

Such a complete failure might well have discouraged even Jeremiah's intrepid spirit. His life appeared to him a dreary waste, and his existence a burden. "Cursed be the day", he exclaimed in bitter despondency, "wherein I was born, let not the day wherein my mother bare me be blessed; cursed be the man who brought tidings to my father, saying, A man-child is born to thee, making him very glad." Fear for his personal safety added but little to his dejection; yet the people became more and more exasperated, and longed to still for ever the unwelcome voice. The words, "he must die! he must die!"

were shouted alike by prince, priest, and populace. He was publicly accused of high-treason, and brought before the elders of the kingdom to hear his judgment. The despair to which he had for a moment yielded was now vanquished by his usual fortitude. He felt that he was not there to uphold his own honour, but to glorify the name of God. Consequently he disclaimed all personal responsibility; the words he had uttered were the words of the Lord, who had sent him to prophesy against the city. Once again he would warn and entreat the people to mend their ways; once again he would threaten their land with desolation if they disobeyed; and he would fulfil his mission to the last. He was indifferent to the fate they might have in store for him. "As for me", he said, "do with me as seems good and right to you." His hearers were touched; his fearlessness and veracity had at length impressed and convinced them. They confessed they were in the wrong; "he does not deserve to die", they said, "for he spoke to us in the name of the Lord our God."

This unexpected change in the minds of the people induced Jeremiah to repeat his admonitions. He accordingly repaired to the valley of Hinnom to declare his detestation of the worship of Moloch on the very spot where the disgraceful sacrifices were offered. He was accompanied by a number of priests and elders; and in their presence he dashed a vessel to the ground as a symbol of the destruction the people were bringing upon themselves. At the same time, he expressed in the strongest terms his horror of their corrupt practices, and he renewed his predictions of the terrible consequences which would ensue. He was not suffered to finish his oration; for he was seized by a priest of the Temple, and placed in the stocks to be mocked and humiliated. No attempt was made upon his life; yet this new outrage filled him with deep sorrow and mortification.

Thus far Jeremiah's endeavours had been limited to moral reforms. More stirring times were drawing near, and political events began to demand his attention and anxious care.

The great Chaldean kingdom had been increasing in extent and power. In the year 606, Nebuchadnezzar succeeded his father Nabopolassar, and the new monarch gave a fresh impulse to the love of conquest which distinguished his race. A victory he gained over Necho II, king of Egypt, at Circesium, rapidly matured his schemes, and he now conceived the plan of adding the kingdom of Judah to his territories, which already almost extended from the Euphrates to the Nile.

Jeremiah, whose patriotic heart had long grieved for the degeneracy of his people, was now dismayed at the imminent danger of his country. His sorrow was not less intense because he had foreseen the disasters, the approach of which his countrymen had wilfully ignored. His alarm was heightened by the vacillation and weakness exhibited by the king Jehoiakim in all matters of importance. He knew that internal unity and a vigorous administration could alone secure the means of resistance; and once again he strenuously exhorted his fellow-citizens, while there was still time for preparation, to avert the impending calamity by resolute measures.

But such was the fatal distrust and aversion with which he was regarded, that prudence forced him to conceal himself, and to avoid for a time all intercourse with the people. In his retreat, he dictated from memory to Baruch, one of his faithful friends, the orations which he had, with unabated earnestness, delivered to the unwilling Hebrews for now twenty-three years. He requested Baruch to take the scroll to the Temple, where the assembled people might hear a part of it read. Baruch did as he was desired, and the scroll was read "in the chamber of Gemariah, the son of the scribe Shaphan, at the gate of the Lord's House, in the ears of all the people." The news of this proceeding was brought to the palace where the princes and elders had met. The scroll was taken to the king and read aloud. A few of the unpalatable lines sufficed for Jehoiakim's ear; he cut the document through with his knife, and threw it into the fire which was blazing in the room to cheer a winter's day. The words he had heard aroused neither remorse nor fear, but only wrath against the prophet, whose immediate presence together with that of his scribe the king commanded; but "the Lord had hid them." Jeremiah, nothing daunted, sent forth from his seclusion another scroll similar in contents to the first, and these addresses have probably come down to posterity among the works which bear the prophet's name.

His words were verified with alarming rapidity. The enemy's army was steadily advancing, and continued unimpeded its victorious progress. The terrified king hastened to propitiate the invader, and readily agreed to pay the heavy tribute which he demanded. For three years the people bore the humiliating tax; but in the fourth they refused to submit to it, for their spirit was not entirely broken. The danger now assumed more formidable proportions, as Nebuchadnezzar ordered the troops of adjacent countries to enter the rebellious land. About this time Jehoiakim died, leaving to his son and successor Jehoiachin an enfeebled empire and a tottering throne.

The rapidity with which events followed one another, and the almost instantaneous fulfilment of the prophet's words, dispelled all hope that might still have sustained the Hebrews. The Chaldean monarch, coveting the glory of striking the final blow at the empire of Judah, joined his army, and himself conducted the siege of Jerusalem. The new king surrendered after a short and unavailing resistance. Though the town suffered comparatively little, the deathblow had been given to the independence of the nation. The magnificent Temple was spoiled of the treasures stored up by the piety of generations. Ten thousand captives were led away, among whom were the king and the queen, the foremost statesmen and generals, and many useful artisans. The city, bereft of all the valour that could defend, and of all the wisdom that could govern it, became a refuge for those who owed their safety to their poverty or insignificance. Nebuchadnezzar installed Zedekiah, the uncle of the captive king, on the vacant throne, and invested him with a mock sovereignty over the unhappy remnant of Judah under the most humiliating conditions: he was to pay to the conqueror an annual tribute, and to follow his policy with implicit submission.

Deep indeed must have been the grief of the prophet, when he came forth from his seclusion, and beheld that destruction which he had fruitlessly laboured to avert — his beloved city spoiled of its treasures and its proud buildings; the best of his countrymen expelled from the land, and their fields and vineyards in the possession of strangers. Yet he felt that his mission was not at an end, and that the hour had not yet come for abandoning his task as hopeless. There was still a remnant, weak and slender, it is true, of the once prosperous nation; and while Jerusalem counted any of the chosen people among its inhabitants, the prophet would not desert them, but would continue to point the way to duty and righteousness, perhaps to success and deliverance. He saw with bitter affliction that the few who had witnessed the direst calamities, and had escaped death and captivity, had not abandoned the sins and evil practices which had prevailed in happier times. The retribution and heavy chastisement which had fallen upon them, did not turn their minds to the God whom they had forsaken; nor did the dangers and sorrows they had experienced soften their hearts towards the widow and the orphan. An untiring monitor, he again raised his voice to entreat, to remonstrate, and to rebuke; but he had not only to condemn their immoral and idolatrous conduct, he had also to upbraid the spirit of rebellion and impatience by which they were agitated. He told them that their resistance would be vain, and that having lost the moment when energy might have saved them, they must now accept their self-inflicted doom with calmness, and resignation. More gratifying words flattered the ears of the people from other advisers, from men who were dishonestly seeking popular favour, who declared they had received Divine visions promising the speedy restoration of an independent Jewish commonwealth. Jeremiah's solemn voice strongly condemned these deceivers. In order to give greater impressiveness to his words, he appeared in the public places with a yoke round his neck, symbolic of that yoke which his countrymen were destined to bear. "Bring your necks under the yoke of the king of Babylon, and serve him"; such was the Divine message he brought to them; "serve him and his people, and live; hearken not to the false prophets that speak to you, You shall not serve the king of Babylon; for they prophesy a lie to you." One of these deluding predictions was uttered by Hananiah, the son of Azur, a Gibeonite, who, in the presence of a large assembly, foretold the destruction of Babylon within two years, and the consequent renewal of the freedom and glory of Judah. Jeremiah was among the auditors, and when his mendacious opponent had ceased, he exclaimed,

"Amen! the Lord do so! the Lord perform thy words which thou hast prophesied to bring back again the vessels of the Lord's House!" But he added that misfortune and God's displeasure would fall upon the prophet who spoke peace when there was war. Yet Hananiah repeated his predictions, and then broke asunder the yoke which Jeremiah was wearing. But the prophet replaced the emblem by an iron yoke to symbolise the far stronger fetters which would result from their futile resistance. Again he exhorted the refractory people to place their trust in God, to desist from all schemes of revolt, and to bear the Divine decrees with patience.

But his thoughts were not entirely engrossed by the thankless duties he performed in his native country; they accompanied the unhappy captives into the land of their misery; and upon them also his active and devoted mind tried to exercise a beneficent influence. He sent them written addresses not merely to convey to them his sympathy, but to soothe and cheer their dreary exile with hope and encouragement. Prudent and judicious as ever, he bade them trust and confide in God's promise, he advised them to turn their energies upon their immediate welfare, and he warned them against vain repining. "Build ye houses", he wrote, "and dwell in them, and plant gardens and eat the fruit of them." He felt that a hopeful tone of mind was the surest means of securing a happier future. So far from encouraging unavailing and restless discontent, he bade them pray for the peace of their new country, for thus only could they expect peace and prosperity for themselves. Their duty to the Chaldeans was passive obedience, their duty to themselves was allegiance to their God, and a faithful conformity to the moral laws they had too long defied.

But Jeremiah's remonstrances were again unheeded. In Babylon, his influence was also counteracted by false prophets, who excited feelings of dissatisfaction and roused idle hopes among the exiles. In his own country, the people disregarded his injunctions and counsels with a perversity that was the result of long years of indifference and crime. Licentiousness and cruelty prevailed among them with as much pertinacity as at any former period. The rebellious spirit, so fatal to their existence, became uncontrollable. Secret negotiations between Zedekiah and the king of Egypt brought this lamentable state of affairs to a crisis. In the ninth year of the reign of Judah's last king, the Jews refused to continue their allegiance to the Chaldeans. Nebuchadnezzar immediately sent an army to the refractory city, but alarmed by the rumour of the approach of hostile forces, withdrew his troops. This moment was one of exultation for the Hebrews; but their shortsighted delight was rebuked by Jeremiah who exclaimed: "Behold, Pharaoh's army which is come forth to help you, shall return to Egypt into their own land, and the Chaldeans shall come again, and fight against this city and burn it with fire. Thus says the Lord, Deceive not yourselves, saying, The Chaldeans will surely depart from us; for they shall not depart."

In the midst of their rejoicings, the Hebrews received these words of evil omen with intense anger. They determined to silence for ever that voice which, in war and in peace, was heard only to chide and to threaten. The great officers of the state accused him of treason, and of favouring the Chaldeans whose rule he so constantly advocated; and notwithstanding his strenuous denials, he was cast into prison.

But not long afterwards, Zedekiah, anxious in spite of the unexpected rescue, ordered the prophet to be secretly brought before him, and asked him if he had any Divine message concerning the future. Adversity had not broken

Jeremiah's courage, for he answered unhesitatingly: "Thou shalt be delivered into the hands of the king of Babylon." For one moment he remembered his own wretched fate, and added a fervent supplication that he might be restored to liberty. The request was pitilessly denied, and he was again consigned to the dreariness of his dungeon, with the spare allowance of a piece of bread a day to sustain his miserable existence.

But the ominous words he had uttered, had sunk deep into the minds of the king and the people, and it was impossible to efface their effect. This was recognised with dismay by the chiefs and elders, Jeremiah's constant and inveterate enemies, and though they saw him shut out from all power and even from all intercourse, they feared the old and helpless man in his lonely cell. They were determined to hear him no more, and to crush for ever the revival of those eloquent strains, which, in spite of all efforts, retained their hold upon the populace. "We beseech thee", they said to the king, "let this man be put to death, for thus he weakens the hands of the people in speaking such words; for this man seeks not the welfare of the people, but their hurt."

Zedekiah, a wretched tool in the hands of his chiefs, and unable to resist them, granted their request. They hastened to carry out their impious plan: "they took Jeremiah and cast him into the dungeon of Malchiah the son of Hammelech, that was in the court of the prison, and they let down Jeremiah with cords. And in the dungeon there was no water, but mire: so he sunk into the mire."

In these fearful moments, his dreary life passing before his thoughts, must have appeared to him a long course of unprofitable sufferings; for so far from having achieved any good results, he found his last faint hope suddenly destroyed by the near prospect of a horrible death. But he was destined to be spared for still greater trials.

Ebed-Melech, a foreigner in the king's service, heard of the ruthless cruelty perpetrated against the aged prophet, and entreated the king for his life. The permission to save him was granted by Zedekiah with that powerlessness of resistance which characterized him. Ebed-Melech immediately commenced his labour of mercy, and with the help of thirty men released Jeremiah from his awful position. The prophet was again conducted to his old place of confinement. He enjoyed one short moment of liberty, when Zedekiah for the second time secretly demanded his advice on the important events of the times. Adversity had not cowed his spirit, and isolation had not dimmed the clearness of his judgment. With greater decision than ever he recommended submission to the Babylonian rule which, he said, had been imposed upon Judah by the Divine will: if his advice was not followed, he predicted that the city would speedily be given into the hands of the Chaldeans, to be burnt with fire, and that the king himself would fall into their power. Fear was the mainspring of Zedekiah's actions, and apprehending the censure of his priests and generals, he was incapable of feeling for his counsellor either gratitude or reverence, and for the third time consigned him to his lonely prison.

While Zedekiah was vacillating, the catastrophe was rapidly approaching. The hope that had been aroused by the sudden disappearance of the Chaldean army proved deceptive, and the people became gradually aware of the disastrous results of their impolitic rebellion. Nebuchadnezzar, after having strongly re-inforced his troops, was once more marching towards Palestine. His army first halted at the border town of Riblah, and then went on unchecked, destroying and pillaging the country, and reducing towns and fortresses to ashes. He arrived at last before Jerusalem, where the people had hastily prepared fortifications. An obstinate siege ensued. For eighteen months the Jews refused to surrender, though every day added to their miseries. Pestilence wrought terrible havoc among those who had not succumbed to the sword or to starvation. Distress produced indifference to the most unnatural atrocities; and cruel and relentless necessity loosened all bonds of affection. All had but one thought — escape from the maddening pangs of hunger.

In this universal confusion and dismay, Jeremiah alone retained his courage and self-possession. As he had not been elated by a momentary gleam of hope, so he did not yield to despair whilst there was work to be done, energy to be revived, and courage to be inspired. He pointed out that, as the Divine punishment so long predicted was now a palpable reality, so the Divine promises of future restoration and happiness would prove equally true. In order to create among his countrymen the confidence he felt in their subsequent deliverance, he purchased in his native town of Anathoth a piece of land, which he was certain would be enjoyed by his descendants in coming generations.

It may indeed have been impossible for the people to understand and to share the hopeful views of the prophet. The feeble resources of the city were rapidly becoming exhausted. Hunger told its horrible tale in every household, and fostered crimes from which the basest would at other times have recoiled. At last all means of sustenance utterly failed, and the emaciated soldiers were unable to hold out any longer. The final attack upon the city was made in the early part of the year 588. The long and stubborn resistance and the constant rebellion of the Hebrews, had infuriated the conqueror, and when the victorious troops rushed into the unhappy city, they were commanded to show no mercy.

Zedekiah and a portion of his army attempted to escape, but they were at once pursued. The king was captured at Jericho, and brought before Nebuchadnezzar at Riblah, where a barbarous scene was enacted. All his sons were slain in his presence, and immediately afterwards, his own eyes were burnt out, so that no other impression should efface the memory of that horrible sight. He was then condemned to listen to the agonising cries of his generals who were ruthlessly massacred; and he alone remained — a sightless, childless prisoner. In this miserable condition he was led away into the land of captivity to form a part of the trophies of Nebuchadnezzar, and to end his wretched life in prison.

The commands of Nebuchadnezzar were strictly carried out by his general Nebuzaradan. The walls of the town were destroyed; heaps of ruins marked the places where the royal palace and the dwellings of the elders and princes had seen many a day of revelry and rejoicing; and the sacred edifice which had survived the faith and piety which it was intended to foster, was consigned to the flames. The sword exterminated the desperate soldiers who still attempted resistance; and many were led as captives into the strange land, whose resources they were expected to enrich by their strength and energy. Feeble indeed was the remnant of the great nation, humiliating their lot of toil and dependence.

Amidst the general destruction, however, one man was saved to whom the prison had proved a refuge. The fetters which his own countrymen had cast round Jeremiah, were loosened by the heathen king, who had spared neither prince nor statesman, but who appreciated the exalted character and the great mind of the old and sorrow-stricken prophet;

and he sent his captain Nebuzaradan to take him from his prison and to provide for his safety and comfort.

Jeremiah paid dearly for his unexpected liberty. When he left the dreary solitude of the prison walls, death and devastation met his sight on all sides. Neither cruelty nor hardship had dried up the stream of his love and patriotism. Among helpless old men and distressed women Jeremiah forgot the turbulent partisans that had sought his life. He only saw the ruins which buried the manhood and strength of Jerusalem, the city "once great among nations, once mistress among provinces". His deep anguish found utterance in those eloquent and touching strains which have come down to us in the form of his Lamentations. They speak to us of the destruction from which the city could not escape, which surrounded him everywhere, and appealed to him in the shattered walls and the drooping figures of forlorn mourners. Overwhelmed with agony, he struggled in vain for consolation. "My eye runs down with rivers of water for the destruction of the daughter of my people, my eye streams down and ceases not without any interruption. Behold, O Lord, for I am in distress, my bowels are troubled, my heart is turned within me ... for abroad the sword bereaves, and at home is death." Though he laid stress upon the sins of his people, he only felt commiseration for the result they had produced. "Jerusalem has grievously sinned, therefore she is removed", he repeated mournfully; but his mind had no thought for his own fulfilled predictions and disregarded counsels. The humility and patience which he had shown when rejected by his prosperous fellow-citizens, did not forsake him now when he saw the calamity that he had foretold, and was himself enjoying security. None of those who felt most conscious of their misdeeds could be more sorrow-stricken, more anxious for the Divine forgiveness, than this great man, so sinned against, so faithful, and so humble. In the deep love he bore to his countrymen, he identified himself with their grief, he suffered with them, and he prayed for the alleviation of their misfortunes. Firmly confiding in God's mercy, he sought to diffuse the consolations of faith and of trust. "The Lord", he said, "is good to them that wait for Him; the Lord will not cast off for ever; though He cause grief, yet He will have compassion, according to the greatness of His mercies; for He does not afflict willingly, nor grieve the children of men." With such words he endeavoured to conjure up a last ray of hope and courage; but ever and anon the power of holding out comfort failed him, and he broke forth into renewed lamentations:. "The joy of our heart has ceased; our dance is turned into mourning; the crown is fallen from our head: woe unto us that we have sinned; for this our heart is faint; for these things our eyes are dim."

While the prophet was thus bowed down with grief, he received from Nebuchadnezzar the offer of a peaceful home in Babylon, where he should live honoured and protected. "If it seem good to thee", said the heathen monarch, "to come with me to Babylon, come, and I will take care of thee there; but if it seem ill to thee to come with me to Babylon, forbear, behold, all the land is before thee, whither it seems good and convenient for thee to go thither go." Jeremiah was unwilling to leave the land in which all his interests were centred; in prosperity or in adversity, his path lay among his own people, who now, discouraged and bent low, required more than ever his guidance and teaching. Following the advice of the heathen general, he lived with Gedaliah, the son of Ahikam, whom the king of Babylon had appointed governor of Judah.

A short interval of tranquillity followed the terrible catastrophe. Gedaliah was a man of prudence, and insisted upon faithful allegiance to the conqueror. The small community prospered under his judicious rule; and the fertile land, which not even war could entirely devastate, abundantly rewarded their labours. They increased in strength and in number; and such was the extraordinary vitality of their race, that they bade fair, ere long, to regain something of their former power. But this prospect also was doomed to vanish.

The neighbouring tribe of the Ammonites saw with displeasure and jealousy that their old enemies had not been entirely crushed by the Babylonian conqueror; and they determined to destroy the possibility of their returning prosperity. During the war, many Jews had escaped into their country, and among them was a certain Ishmael, who was of royal extraction; he looked with envy upon the dignities conferred upon Gedaliah, and stirred up the enmity of the Ammonites against his own people. An attack upon Gedaliah's life was planned, and Ishmael offered to lead the undertaking. Gedaliah was warned of the conspiracy, but, generous and unsuspecting, he indignantly discarded the report. Such was his reliance on the good feeling of all his countrymen, that some months later, he hospitably entertained Ishmael with ten of his friends, who visited him in Mizpah. There, in the house of their host, they carried out their iniquitous plans. Not satisfied with the life of the virtuous governor, the assassins slew all his followers who were around him. Some travellers arriving from Shiloh and Samaria with sacrifices, were also massacred lest they should become dangerous informants. Every stranger was seized, and either put to death or laden with fetters; and among the captives were the daughters of the late king. Thus stained with bloodshed, the murderer led his unhappy captives away on the road towards Ammon. Meanwhile, however, the terrible tidings had been spread; and Johanan, the son of Kareah, and all the captains of the forces that were with him, rose to avenge the crime. They pursued Ishmael to the waters of Gibeon, where they succeeded in rescuing the captives, but not in seizing the traitor, who escaped into the land of his adoption.

The foul deed was fraught with the worst results. The murder of Gedaliah was not merely the extinction of a noble life, but the deathblow of the new commonwealth. For Gedaliah alone had by his wisdom held together the members of the feeble colony, and by his moderation had conciliated the reckless Chaldeans. And now the people asked one another with good reason, who should thenceforth propitiate the tyrant, or who should guide them in their own actions?

Their position was indeed one of the utmost danger, and they were constantly planning schemes to improve their precarious condition. Among the various proposals suggested to them was one peculiarly congenial to their restless spirit and love of change — the proposal to leave the land of their misery and trials, to emigrate to Egypt, and to sojourn there under the protection of the powerful king, who would gladly shield them against their common enemy, the Chaldeans. The question was difficult and important, and called forth different opinions among the principal members of the community. Perplexed and uncertain, the people remembered the clear mind, which had never refused them advice in spite of contempt and persecution. All the people, "from the least even to the greatest", turned to Jeremiah, and eagerly implored his aid. They promised faithfully to follow his counsel, saying, "Whether it be good or whether it will be evil, we will obey the voice of God."

Once more Jeremiah appeared in all the greatness of his earlier days. Regret or lament no longer mingled in his words. Anxious to avert the fatal step, he declared the message of his Master with dignity and firmness. "Thus", he answered to them, "says the Lord God of Israel to whom you sent me to present my supplication before Him: if you still abide in this land, then will I build you and not pull you down, and I will plant you and not uproot you; for I repent of the evil that I have done to you, and I will show mercies to you, that he may have mercy upon you, and cause you to return to your own land." But "if you indeed set your faces to enter into Egypt, and go to sojourn there, then it shall come to pass, that the sword which you feared shall overtake you, and the famine whereof you were afraid, shall follow close after you there in Egypt, and there you shall die." Painfully familiar with the effect which his words usually produced, and anticipating again the same unfavourable reception, he concluded by saying: "You have dissembled in your hearts, when you sent me to the Lord your God, saying, Pray for us to the Lord your God, and according to all that the Lord our God shall say, so declare to us, so shall we do."

Jeremiah had divined the truth; the people had unalterably fixed their purpose; and they had come to him to obtain his sanction, and not his advice. His determined opposition to their plans aroused their anger. Having no reason or argument to bring forward, they had recourse to denunciation and abuse. "Thou speakest falsely". they said; "our God has not sent thee to say, Go not into Egypt to sojourn there; but Baruch, the son of Neriah, sets thee against us, to deliver us into the hands of the Chaldeans, that they might put us to death, and carry us away captives to Babylon." They would listen no more, but all the people, "men, women, children, the king's daughters, and every person that Nebuzaradan, the captain of the guard, had left with Gedaliah", all turned from the home of their ancestors, and went to sojourn in the land which, from the earliest times, had almost constantly been hostile to them.

The unhappy prophet was forced by the infatuated and heedless emigrants to follow them; and, grown old in misery and humiliations, he had to drink this last and bitterest cup of affliction.

But compassion soon roused again his prophetic strains. As the wanderers arrived at one of the towns on the northern boundaries of Egypt, he bade them once more listen to him, and stop at the threshold of their new danger. The land itself, he told them, which they were about to enter, was doomed; the shelter they sought was vain, and the strength on which they relied was broken; for the king of Babylon was sure "to array himself with the land of Egypt, as a shepherd puts on his garment, and he shall go forth from thence in peace." Yet the headstrong people continued their march, and settled in the land where their fathers had been slaves. But even now, when their political history seemed to draw to a close, the indefatigable prophet watched eagerly over their welfare and their honour. Though by deserting their country they had apparently destroyed every possibility of recovering their ancient position, their religious duties remained as of old. He felt that it was only by a rigorous adherence to their faith, and a constant practice of the virtues it enjoined, that they could rise again, and attain that moral distinction which they had been in a fair way of winning, but had forfeited by their recklessness. Yet weak and wavering, they were unable to resist the atmosphere of idolatry which surrounded them; and they remained utterly indifferent to the prophet's indignant exhortations, which had lost none of their former vigour and earnestness. Not only were they callous to reproof, but they declared they would continue their worship as before. Their relinquishment of heathen deities, they said, had been followed by misfortunes; and they were therefore less than ever willing to accept the Divine truths which the prophet had laid before them.

The last words which the Bible records of Jeremiah reflect faithfully the ideas and principles he had endeavoured to diffuse during his long life. He pronounced the doom of those who had, with contemptible cowardice, sought a momentary security by self-banishment. He saw their degeneracy with grief and sorrow; but he had faith in the release of the Babylonian captives, and in the career for which they were eventually destined. The present was indeed full of despondency and gloom; but with hope and trust he turned to a coming time which was disclosed to his clear vision; and in contemplating the certain fulfilment of his prophetic expectations, he felt less bitterly the present wretchedness and oppression. How long he lived in an atmosphere so uncongenial to him, is unknown. According to one tradition he died during his forced exile in Egypt; according to another Nebuchadnezzar summoned him to Babylon.

It was not till long afterwards, that his life and works began to be appreciated among his countrymen. But when that earnestness of faith and energy of purpose which, in his days, he alone had evinced, became common features among a bold and striving race, the once disregarded words were read with devout veneration, and the memory of the prophet was cherished with the deepest love and respect. Succeeding ages have intensified this feeling of admiration for his noble oratory and his still nobler life. The homage accorded to the manliness and pathos of his eloquence was indeed less than the profound sympathy felt for his long career of devotion and courage. Yet his writings are among the chief treasures of Hebrew poetry. Although inferior to the utterances of Isaiah in precision and force, they are by no means wanting in impressiveness. They have a charm peculiarly their own, an eloquence which at once touches and elevates, because it owes its effect to earnestness of purpose rather than to a skilful style. Yet ever and again the poet mingles with the statesman, and devotes the language of which he is master to the praise and glorification of the Almighty; and when he enlarges upon such themes his oratory abounds in apt and striking metaphors, and attains a beauty even rivalling that of his great predecessors. As an instance may be taken his description of Nebuchadnezzar's victory over Nebo king of Egypt at Carchemish or Circesium.

"Prepare you the buckler and shield; and draw near to battle. Harness the horses, and get up, ye horsemen, and stand forth with your helmets; furbish the spears, and put on the brigandines. Wherefore do I see them dismayed and turned away backward? and why are their mighty ones beaten down, and flee apace, and do not look back? for fear was round about, says the Lord. Let not the swift flee away, nor the mighty one escape: they shall stumble, and fall towards the north by the river Euphrates. Who is it that comes up as a flood, whose waters rush like rivers? Egypt rises up like a flood, and her waters rush like rivers; and he says, I will go up, and will cover the earth; I will destroy the city and the inhabitants thereof. Come up, ye horses; and rage, ye chariots; and let the mighty men come forth; the Ethiopians and the Libyans, that handle the shield; and the Lydians, that handle and bend the bow. For this is the day of the Lord God of hosts, a day of vengeance that He may avenge Himself of His adversaries; and the sword shall devour, and it shall be satiate and made drunk with their blood; for the Lord God of hosts has a sacrifice in the northern country by the river Euphrates. Go up into Gilead, and take balm, O virgin, the daughter of Egypt; in vain hast thou multiplied medicines; for thou shalt not be cured. The nations hear of thy shame, and thy cry fills the earth, for the hero has stumbled against the hero, and they have fallen both together." Then he refers to Nebuchadnezzar's expected attack upon Egypt:

"Declare ye in Egypt, and publish in Migdol, and publish in Noph and in Tahpanhes; say ye, Stand fast, and prepare thyself; for the sword shall devour round about thee. Why are thy valiant men swept away? they stood not, because the Lord chased them away. He made many fall, yea, one fell upon his neighbour, and they said, Arise, and let us go again to our own people, and to the land of our birth, from the oppressing sword. They cried there, Pharaoh king of Egypt is lost; he has allowed the appointed time to pass. As I live, says the King, whose name is the Lord of hosts, Surely as Tabor is among the mountains, and as Carmel by the sea, so shall he come. O thou daughter dwelling in Egypt, prepare thyself to go into captivity; for Noph shall be waste and desolate without an inhabitant. Egypt is like a very fair heifer, but destruction comes; and it comes out of the north. Her hirelings also in her midst are like fatted bullocks; for they also are turned back, and flee together; they do not stand, because the day of their calamity is come upon them, and the time of their visitation. Her voice shall go like a serpent; for they shall march with the army, and come against her with axes, as hewers of wood. They shall cut down the forest, says the Lord, for is it impassable; because they are more than the locusts, and are innumerable. The daughter of Egypt shall be confounded; she shall be delivered into the hand of the northern people. The Lord of hosts, the God of Israel, says, Behold, I will punish Amon of No, and Pharaoh, and Egypt, and their gods and their kings; even Pharaoh, and all those that trust in him; and I will deliver them into the hand of those that seek their lives, and into the hand of Nebuchadnezzar, king of Babylon, and into the hand of his servants: and afterwards it shall be inhabited as in the days of old, says the Lord. — But fear not thou, O My servant Jacob, and be not dismayed, O Israel: for, behold, I will rescue thee from afar off, and thy seed from the land of captivity; and Jacob shall return, and be in rest and at ease, and none shall make him afraid. Fear thou not, O Jacob My servant, says the Lord: for I am with thee; for I will utterly destroy all the nations whither I have driven thee; but I will not utterly destroy thee, but correct thee in justice; yet will I not leave thee wholly unpunished." (XLVI. 2—28.)

Jeremiah's writings present, on the whole, little variety either in matter or expression. The shadow of grief which darkened his existence, is spread over his works. They are less often than those of Isaiah political orations, but generally utterances of a sorrowful heart. We admire the elder prophet in his soaring eloquence; we acknowledge the loftiness of his ideas and the truth of his doctrines, which are still, as they were in the days of old, powerful to guide, to comfort, and to strengthen. The object of Jeremiah's orations was indeed more immediate, and consequently less universally adapted to all ages; yet as the effects of great deeds are not limited to the time in which they take place, the life of Jeremiah with the noble example it offers is as undying as the immortal words of Isaiah. Among the great men which the Scriptures delineate, the figure of the prophet of Anathoth is, therefore, one of the most conspicuous. The loneliness of his condition surrounds him with a pathos which, at the very outset of his career, attracts our sympathies. He was alone in everything. All were opposed to him — three successive kings, a faithless and unstable priesthood, a refractory and stubborn people. He had to contend with the bitterest sorrow of a patriot, the hatred and distrust of his countrymen. Personal sufferings, though little heeded by him on their own account, added their cruel pangs to his melancholy life; he was never free from actual danger or grave apprehension; and he survived all vicissitudes to see his hopes crushed, his country destroyed, his people either pining captives or reckless emigrants.

Such a fate alone were enough to arouse commiseration and interest; but with enhanced sympathy we follow the struggles of the man who met that fate so valiantly. We admire his dauntless fortitude, which adversity could not subdue, which scorned the threats of the powerful, and disregarded the stings of ingratitude; but we admire him doubly when we see his firmness give way in witnessing the sorrows, the misery, and depravity of those that surrounded him. For he could harbour no animosity, and in return for cruelty and injury, he bestowed forgiveness, help, and comfort.

His whole existence was one great example of the noblest self-denial. He considered himself merely as the mouth-piece of a higher Wisdom; he knew but one law — obedience to God; he expounded but one doctrine — unconditional adherence to the Divine rule. To the one unselfish purpose of serving his Master and delivering his people, he devoted the great powers of his mind, the glow of his eloquence, and his long years of misery. None of the prophets reflect all the human struggles and emotions more faithfully than Jeremiah.

EZEKIEL. (595 to about 570.)

The long line of prophets who were immediately connected with political life, was broken at the death of Jeremiah. Their power and influence had co-existed with the commonwealth of whose history their efforts and labours formed a part. When the nation ceased as such, the voice of the inspired statesman was indeed not silent, but it assumed a different character. No counsel for the arrangement of internal affairs was needed; no foreign wars called forth stirring appeals to patriotism and self-sacrifice. Yet at the same time when the closing scenes of Jewish history revealed the eventful life, and gave rise to the untiring admonitions, of Jeremiah, another messenger of God, roused by holy enthusiasm, worked for the welfare of his people in a distant land. We mourn with Jeremiah over the last remnants of Jewish greatness and the final overthrow of national power; while his contemporary gives us the comforting assurance, that the seed, though transplanted, had not died, and that the spirit of prophecy, of truth, and of wisdom illuminated the dreariness of the exile.

Ezekiel, the son of Buzi, belonged, like Jeremiah, to the sacerdotal order. He himself was for some time occupied with priestly functions; and many of the similes, by which he enriched his later works, are derived from his old pursuits, to which he refers with clearness and familiarity. Many years elapsed in the calm discharge of his sacred duties, years of which his writings contain no record, but which were fraught with events of deep and fatal importance to his country. Ezekiel had passed the prime of life when Jerusalem succumbed to the conquest of the Babylonians in the reign of Jehoiakim. He shared the general fate, and was taken as a captive to the land of the invader. Here he exchanged the humbler path he had hitherto trodden for a higher and more lasting sphere of usefulness. He spent the rest of his life in the plains of the Chaboras, where a number of his countrymen had congregated together, and formed a small colony. But he did not limit his thoughts to the welfare of his fellow captives. His affections, like theirs, were bound up in the fortunes of his native land; his memory clung to the cherished associations of the past; indeed his interest turned more keenly to those who were still inhabiting the districts of Judea than to the exiles who surrounded him. Jerusalem was the sole theme of his inspirations. Every event which might contribute to the restoration of the kingdom, roused his eager sympathy, and called forth his fervent eloquence. This change from a comparatively calm and retired existence to a life of toil and difficulties, which was inseparable from the mission of a prophet, was not effected without hesitation. The unpalatable words of reproof which the monitor had incessantly to utter, rendered his task hard and thankless. Isaiah had doubted whether he possessed the moral purity necessary to fulfil the Divine commands; Jeremiah had trembled in the consciousness of his weakness and inexperience; and Ezekiel was apparently overcome by a similar fear and distrust when a new path, "one beset with thorns and briers", was opened before him. It was the duty of Ezekiel, as it had been that of each successive prophet, to oppose the multitude. But he received the Divine encouragement in the difficulties he was about to encounter. Again and again he was commanded not to be dismayed; for although the people were hard-hearted and rebellious, he would not lack the power to convince them. Their taunts and derision would fail to hurt him, for he would appear before them armed with irresistible strength.

Henceforth, the prophet gives us no account of the incidents of his private life. One event only is recorded, a domestic sorrow, and that is related merely as a symbol of momentous public changes. The Hebrew prophets associated every occurrence with the thoughts which happened to occupy them, and which were always connected with the interests of their own nation. It was thus that Isaiah gave to his children significant names emblematical of happiness. But sad and dismal events were foreboded by the death of Ezekiel's wife. The desolation of Jerusalem was reflected in the gloom of the prophet's home. He was commanded not to weep for her he had loved so well; he was to forbear from all signs and expressions of mourning; for these would be unbecoming in one who descended from the priestly line of Aaron, and who was entrusted with Divine messages. Beyond this the reader is not initiated into the prophet's personal destinies, and we seek in vain among his works for any landmarks to trace the history of his exile. Nor is the inner man more clearly disclosed to us. No outbursts of feeling remind us of the varied emotions which were so obvious in his elder contemporary. He does not appear to have taken an active part in the events which he describes, and he is consequently less able than the great Isaiah to awaken our sympathies; nor had he opportunities for rousing dormant feelings by an example of active virtue, or for awakening that pious endurance and self-abnegation of which Jeremiah was the type.

We must, therefore, look to another source as the cause of his influence and power; and we easily find it in his works. For Ezekiel was essentially the writer. The man in the white robe with the inkhorn at his side, the constantly recurring figure of his visions, represents the prophet himself, the Scribe of a Divine Master, and the faithful recorder of His words. The statesman and the moralist are both eclipsed by the author and the poet. In his earlier life, which had been one of thought and retirement, he had laid up rich stores of knowledge to be worked out and employed at a future time. He was evidently well versed in the writings of the great men of his nation, and thoroughly imbued with the poetry of the Hebrew language. The years spent in the performance of his priestly functions exercised a decided influence on his compositions. The retirement of the philosopher is evident in his contemplative style. For his writings were penned, not during a time of turmoil and excitement, but at a period when individual exertions were uncalled for, and men indulged in speculation, and tried to deduce lessons from the past. The captivity proved necessarily a period of inaction, when the patriot and poet could devote long hours either to the reproduction of earlier and more stirring scenes, or to the representation of his ideal thoughts. It was in such a time that Ezekiel composed the addresses which have perpetuated his greatness, and in which he sets forth doctrines at once humane and sublime, comprehensive and varied. His works, therefore, reveal his individuality, in spite of their want of historical interest, and in spite of the veil of obscurity thrown over his life; but they deserve also to be studied on account of their own intrinsic value, apart from any consideration of authorship.

The prophet specifies the date of his orations with great exactness, and this is the more welcome as they contain no allusions to striking events by which the reader might be guided.

The exiles naturally looked upon the loss of their independence as a new era, from which they counted the years; and Ezekiel relates that his first vision took place in the fifth year of king Jehoiakim's captivity. At this period, the public calamities, terrible as they had been, began already to fade away from the fickle memories of the Hebrews. Indeed those who had seen their country fall a prey to the horrors of warfare, were rapidly returning to the very evils in which their destruction had originated. While Jeremiah was, in Palestine, indignantly preaching against the depravity of the people, the same admonitions were pronounced by Ezekiel at the waters of Babylon. The latter, turning to the ancient home of his countrymen, sought also to avert the doom which they were calling down upon themselves. He proclaimed a fearful vengeance for their disobedience, and threatened them with desolation so complete and terrible that it defied all ordinary modes of description, and could only be brought home to the mind by typical illustrations. For thus sounded the Divine command: "Thou son of man, take thee a sharp knife, take thee a barber's razor, and cause it to pass upon thy head and upon thy beard; then take the balances, to weigh, and divide the hair: thou shalt burn with fire the third part in the midst of the city, when the days of the siege are fulfilled; and thou shalt take a third part, and smite about it with a knife; and a third part thou shalt scatter in the wind, and I will draw out a sword after them." It was easy to find the interpretation of this symbol and to understand its intensity: "A third part of thee shall die with the pestilence, and with famine shall they be consumed in the midst of thee; and a third part shall fall by the sword round about thee; and I will scatter a third part to all the winds, and I will draw out a sword after them."

The wickedness of the Hebrews, their distrust in God's promises, and the fearful results of their iniquity, were generally the themes which for generations past had awakened the eloquence of their prophets. But it was in the treatment of these all-engrossing subjects that Ezekiel showed the peculiarity which distinguished him from his predecessors. In him the poet predominated over the statesman: the concise and pithy outbursts of Isaiah, and the pathetic strains of Jeremiah, were replaced by the use of metaphors and symbols unequalled in freedom and extent. The Hebrews, like all Eastern nations, delighting in poetical narrative, had always been eager admirers of parables. Their exuberant imagination, combined with elevation of thought and of feeling, had ever made them adepts in the art of inventing and interpreting ingenious comparisons and riddles. A parable roused dormant interest, because it endowed the subject with a reality and lifelike force unattainable by argument alone. Consequently, in moments of solemnity and importance, the public teachers often resorted to that most effectual mode of conveying their thoughts. All the terrible events which befell the doomed city, were described symbolically: the people could read their whole history in the changing fortunes of a child — at first unclothed and uncared for, and then, through God's love and protection, cleansed and anointed, dressed in embroidered work and girt with pure linen, decked with ornaments and wearing a beautiful crown, prosperous and renowned. Another time, Babylon, the conquering city, was represented as an eagle taking the seed of the land of Israel and planting it in his own soil where it grew and became a flourishing vine.

The prophet's advice and reproof were not limited to the morals of the people; their political errors also excited his indignation and sorrow. He looked with particular disapproval upon their foolish trust in Egypt. In the tenth year after his acceptance of the prophetic mission, he began to raise his voice against Pharaoh, who in his impotent pride had declared, "My river is my own, and I have made it for myself." During three successive years he told of the doom of that mighty empire, which was now certain to become the spoil of the king of Babylon; once a lion among nations, a whale in the wide ocean, and a terror to all mankind, it was destined to fall into the pits dug by the Chaldeans.

The prophet's attention was also directed to the calamities which threatened to overwhelm Tyre, where a commerce of unparalleled extent and prosperity, and a dazzling accumulation of wealth had created as much pomp and presumption as existed among the Pharaohs themselves. When Tyre succumbed to the irresistible conquerors, fear seized all surrounding nations. "Shall not the isles shake at the sound of thy fall", cried the prophet, "when the wounded cry, when the slaughter is made in the midst of thee?" He described this catastrophe in his own characteristic language, and he dwelt upon the fearful overthrow caused by arrogance and overweening pride: "O Tyre, thou hast said, I am of perfect beauty; thy borders are in the middle of the seas, thy builders have perfected thy beauty!" — All the world had contributed to her greatness; the treasures of every land had helped to pile up the stores of her merchandise. The prophet is bound to acknowledge, "Thou wast very glorious in the midst of the seas;" but he is compelled to add, "Thy rowers have brought thee into great waters; the eastwind has broken thee in the midst of the seas; thy riches and thy fairs, thy merchandise, thy mariners, and thy pilots, thy calkers and the occupiers of thy merchandise, and all thy men of war that are in thee, and all thy company which is in the midst of the seas in the day of thy ruin,... and all that handle the oar, the mariners and all the pilots of the sea, shall come down from their ships, they shall stand upon the land; ... and in their wailing they shall take up a lamentation for thee, and lament over thee, saying, What city is like Tyre, like the destroyed one in the midst of the sea!"

If the fall of the great merchant town called forth the ardent eloquence of the prophet, he did not remain silent when minor tribes, such as the Ammonites and Edomites, in common with the Jews, suffered from the Babylonian invasion. Like his predecessors, he regarded the misfortunes of the heathen races as the Divine vengeance for deeds of iniquity which they had perpetrated during many ages against the chosen people. "Thou shalt say to the Ammonites, Thus saith the Lord God — Because thou saidst Aha! against My Sanctuary when it was profaned; against the land of Israel when it was desolate, and against the house of Judah when they went into captivity: I will deliver thee to the men of the east for a possession .... I will make Rabbah a stable for camels, and the Ammonites a couching-place for flocks. Because Moab and Seir say, Behold, Judah is like all the nations, ... therefore will I execute judgment upon Moab." Nor should the Edomites and the Philistines, those constant and implacable enemies of Israel, be exempt from the general destruction: "I will execute great vengeance upon them with furious rebukes, and they shall know that I am the Lord, when I shall lay My vengeance upon them."

Many years elapsed before another date was assigned to the prophet's orations. In the meantime, the aspect of the political world had entirely changed. The fruitless struggles for independence, which the doomed tribes had attempted, were all but forgotten; the last echo of the fall of Tyre had died away; and above all, the Jews, once a powerful nation, were now no more than a small band of discouraged and hopeless exiles scattered over the vast territories of their subduers. Inaction and passive endurance were alone left to the captives.

Yet this pause in the history of the people produced no despondency in the prophet's mind. If the present had no immediate claim upon his interest, his thoughts were engrossed by a future, such as an ardent patriot might have looked and longed for. He, therefore, now employed his literary powers to sketch those ideal pictures which were suggested both by love for his country and attachment to his faith. Twenty-five years of separation had not dimmed his recollections of his native land, nor effaced the influence which his priestly functions had exercised upon his mind. Therefore, in working out his prophetic compositions, he turned to the scenes of his earlier life, not however to that Jerusalem which he had known during the last years of the monarchy, nor to those times of dissension, idolatry, and fanaticism, which had hastened, if they had not caused, his country's fall, but to a new Jerusalem which should flourish by strict allegiance to God's religious and moral ordinances.

In his vivid imagination, the holy city rises in beauty and splendour, and in the midst of it stands the Temple perfect in the smallest detail. Every court, every chamber has its own peculiar use, every stone its meaning. All the dimensions are set down with an accuracy, which point to the days when the Temple shall be erected before the eyes of an eager multitude. However, not the edifice alone is described; the worship and the ceremonies to be performed in the Sanctuary are dwelt upon with equal minuteness. Once more the priests stand in the holy place and offer sacrifices in the name of a devout people. Purified and strengthened, they never again pollute the altars confided to their charge. Their ministrations are worthy of the sanctity of the place. They themselves, their persons and their lives, are placed under rigid control. The holy seed of Aaron must be distinguished by perfect freedom from all moral and physical stains. These ordinances reflect indeed the time when the Temple was erected by the piety of Solomon, but their resemblance to those early days is less striking than the contrast in which they stand to the practice of the last years of the monarchy, when the simple worship of the pure faith had degenerated either into pomp and vaingloriousness or into the detested rites of idolatry. In Ezekiel the loftier spirit of the prophet superseded the doctrines of the priest. He declared emphatically that at the revival of the ancient worship, the ministers of religion should have other duties to perform besides those connected with sacrifices. They should guide the people in the ways of righteousness, and teach them to live so as to merit God's approval and blessing.

The community was once more destined to be strong and united, and the government, though essentially theocratic, was to be placed in the hands of a wise and humble prince, who should not merely be the chief of the state, but also the example of the people in all moral duties. The land was, in equitable proportions, assigned to the different tribes. In fact, the organization of the new state was delineated with as much care and precision as that of the Temple. These descriptions worthily conclude the Book of Ezekiel. They are the productions of a mind which, though appreciating the ancient laws and institutions, shook off the fetters of tradition and clerical presumption. They show the love of the priest for the national worship; but that love is tempered by the prudence of the statesman and patriot. The hope of the renewal, at some future time, of the greatness of the Hebrew nation, was common to all the prophets, and formed the main source of comfort which sustained them in moments of bitter trial; and it brightened above all the dreary exile of Ezekiel, and strengthened his trust in God's promises and mercy.

Such are the subjects which engaged the prophet's eloquence. But his works contain portions which neither possess any historical allusions, nor are devoted to his favourite theme, the ideal state. Some of them are intended, like the productions of his predecessors, solely to enforce doctrines of humanity, while others, peculiar to Ezekiel, are of a mystical character. Most of his compositions commence with a vision, and some are entirely devoted to the description of supernatural scenes, which are made the medium for conveying Divine commands. All the prophecies of Isaiah and Jeremiah are attributed to a Divine origin with a pious acknowledgment of an Almighty power, all-directing and all-ordaining. The familiar terms, "to him came the word of the Lord" precede most of their addresses; they simply indicate a holy inspiration; and in one solitary instance only Isaiah describes a vision. But Ezekiel alludes constantly to a direct intercourse with the Most High. He not only sees himself transported into the land with which his sympathies are entwined, and describes the distant objects with all the accuracy of an eye-witness; but his prophetic vision, not limited to earthly scenes, follows the Almighty Himself in His heavenly abode.

The chapter in which he relates the most solemn event of his life, his initiation into the prophetic order, is worked out into a minute account of the glory of God appearing in all His transcendent majesty. This personification of God was foreign to the conceptions of the enlightened Hebrews, and the detailed description of the celestial rule was contrary to the mysterious feeling of awe with which they uttered the name and the attributes of the Most High; and they felt a repugnance to an elaborate delineation of spheres which they considered to lie beyond human comprehension. It was consequently, according to Jewish tradition, a matter of long and anxious discussion, at the time when the canonical works were collected, whether the Book of Ezekiel ought to be incorporated in the sacred volume; and it is supposed that it owes its admission into it only to the wise intercession of those who, overlooking its unfamiliar and un-Hebrew notions, laid stress on the sublime moral principles it proclaims.

Many vain attempts have been made at deciphering the images which the prophet portrays; but all speculations on their meaning are gratuitous and ill-judged. Those visions show how entirely the writer had shut himself out from the objects that surrounded him; they prove that he communed with God more than with man, and that he was entirely wrapt up in the contemplation of God's majesty.

Unlike most of the prophets, Ezekiel was not burdened with any practical duties. In his small community, there was no political movement to guide, no king to counsel; there was never any immediate claim upon his activity; all his works bear, in their peculiar style, the manifest proof that they were produced in a life of seclusion, where the sounds of strife and of distress reached him only muffled and subdued. They are, therefore, less emphatic and powerful than ornate and rhetorical. They are marked with the stamp of the poet, of the man of thought and isolation, who is not devoted to worldly aims, but to a spiritual existence.

A chief cause of the somewhat fantastic imagery which abounds in his works, may be found in his long sojourn in the Chaldean kingdom. Here he was surrounded by the most extraordinary creations of art and fancy. Grotesque figures filled the public places, and all that was marvellous or mystical was readily accepted. These influences account for the changes of style and conception, which are visible in Ezekiel's orations, and stand in striking contrast to the purity and simplicity of preceding writers.

The characteristics of Ezekiel are not limited to his language and his imagination. His ideas and teachings, no less than his peculiar mode of expression, belong to a later stage of Hebrew culture. The doctrines of a life beyond the grave and of resurrection had but gradually been adopted. They had dawned upon the minds of men who, perplexed at the strange and unequal distribution of happiness on earth, questioned the justice of the dispensation which often sent sorrow to the pious and earthly blessing to the wicked. This problem, so naturally suggesting itself to every reflecting mind, remained long without a satisfactory solution. In the course of centuries, more spiritual and consolatory ideas were proposed and accepted; and in Ezekiel's time the doctrine of immortality seems to have been generally received. The prophet does not enforce it as a truth to be taught and commented upon, but it was obviously familiar to his mind, and must have been current among the people, as he employed it to illustrate, in his usual metaphorical style, the future restoration of the people of Israel. This description belongs to the finest portions of his writings.

"The hand of the Lord was upon me, and carried me out in the spirit of the Lord, and set me down in the midst of the valley which was full of bones, and caused them to pass by me round about: and behold, there were very many in the open valley; and lo, they were very dry. — And He said to me, Son of man, can these bones live? and I answered,

O Lord God, Thou knowest. Again He said to me, Prophesy upon these bones, hear the word of the Lord: thus says the Lord God to these bones, behold, I will cause breath to enter into you, and you shall live; and I will lay sinews upon you and I will bring up flesh upon you, and cover you with skin, and put breath in you, and you shall know that I am the Lord . . . . . So I prophesied as He commanded me, and the breath came into them, and they lived, and stood up upon their feet, an exceedingly great army. Then He said to me, Son of man, these bones are the whole house of Israel, behold they say, Our bones are dried and our hope is lost, we are cut off from our parts; therefore prophesy and say to them, thus says the Lord God, Behold, O My people, I will open your graves, and cause you to come up out of your graves, and bring you out into the land of Israel. And you shall know that I am the Lord, when I opened your graves, and put My spirit in you, and you shall live, and I shall place you in your own land; then shall you know that I the Lord have spoken it and performed it, says the Lord."

Ezekiel's moral teachings evince also a more advanced stage of thought. He emphatically insists upon the doctrine that each man is answerable for his own sins. The following proverb had apparently been current among the Hebrews for generations, "The fathers have eaten sour grapes, and the children's teeth are set on edge." The prophet, deeply impressed with the dangerous fallacy of this adage, opposed it with vigour and earnestness. "As I live, says the Lord God, you shall not have occasion any more to use this proverb in Israel. Behold, all souls are Mine; as the soul of the father, so also the soul of the son is Mine: the soul that sins, it shall die. But if a man be just, and do that which is lawful and right, and has not eaten upon the heights, nor lifted up his eyes to the idols of the house of Israel, nor . . . oppressed any, but has restored to the debtor his pledge, spoiled none by violence, given his bread to the hungry, and covered the naked with a garment; he that has not lent upon usury, nor taken any increase, that has withdrawn his hand from iniquity, executed true judgment between man and man, walked in My statutes and kept My judgments, to deal truly; he is just, he shall surely live, says the Lord God. — If he begets a son that is a robber, a shedder of blood, and that does like anyone of these things... shall he live? He shall not live: he has done all these abominations; he shall surely die; his blood shall be upon him. — Now, lo, if he beget a son, that sees all his father's sins which he has done, and considers, and does not such like,... he shall not die for the iniquity of his father, he shall surely live.... The soul that sins, it shall die. The son shall not bear the iniquity of the father, nor shall the father bear the iniquity of the son: the righteousness of the righteous shall be upon him, and the wickedness of the wicked shall be upon him. But if the wicked will turn from all his sins that he has committed, and keep all My statutes, and do that which is lawful and right, he shall surely live, he shall not die. All his transgressions that he has committed, they shall not be mentioned to him: in his righteousness that he has done he shall live. Have I any pleasure at all that the wicked should die? says the Lord God; and not that he should return from his ways and live?"

C. THE MINOR PROPHETS.

In addition to the writings of the three prophets Isaiah, Jeremiah, and Ezekiel, the Hebrew Scriptures contain orations and narratives of twelve other or "minor" prophets, which constitute together one of the twenty-four Books of the sacred volume. It is probable that these compositions were at first preserved by means of memory and verbal tradition, and that they are no more than fragmentary portions of works as elaborate and complete as those of the three "great" prophets. Consequently the canonical arrangement does not preserve chronological order, and the twelve Books extend over a very long period; for the earliest date from a time when the Hebrew monarchy was still strong and prosperous, while the latest were written more than a century after the end of the Babylonian exile. Hence they necessarily present very great variety in style and imagery, in conception and historical allusions; and the characteristic features of each reveal almost conclusively the age when its author wrote and worked. In eloquence, in force, and in pathos, some of them are worthy of the greatest masters of Hebrew poetry; while in the sublimity of their doctrines many of them stand unrivalled.

The works which first claim our attention, belong to the ninth century before the present era, or to a comparatively early period of Hebrew history. They mark a new epoch in the annals of public teaching. Their writers followed, after a very short interval, the prophets of the type of Elijah and Elisha, whose influence lay particularly in miraculous deeds, in their timely and unlooked for presence, in their concise and pithy sayings. The "minor prophets", though divested of such majesty and power, secured for themselves a more widespread and more lasting influence by infusing into the Hebrew character a more spiritual element, a more enlarged view of religion, and a more extended feeling of brotherhood and humanity. They changed accordingly the very scenes of their labours. They no longer regarded the king all-important and all-powerful in matters of religion; but they came forward as the friends and counsellors of the people, and appeared more frequently in the open streets and public places than in the palace. Their strenuous efforts were less directed against political offences than against the misdemeanours which were of daily occurrence amongst the people. Both monarchies had to contend with internal evils of a slow but dangerous growth; and not even the brightest example from the throne was able to counteract the baneful propensities which always prevailed in the nation, and the effects of which were at all times manifest.

I. JOEL (about 810).

The commonwealth of Judah was enjoying apparent prosperity, when Joel, probably the earliest of the minor prophets, sought to free his people from the idolatry and corruption which lay beneath the outward gloss.

The reign of Uzziah formed a decided epoch in the history of Judah. It followed after a succession of humiliating calamities, such as the defeat of Judah and the pillage of Jerusalem by the Ephraimites in the time of Amaziah; and eager efforts were made to retrieve the fallen fortunes of the nation and to restore the glories of David and Solomon. The patriotic zeal of Uzziah was crowned with success; the neighbouring tribes submitted to Judah with unparalleled loyalty; new buildings, roads, and fortifications secured prosperity and protection to numerous cities, and commerce helped to increase the general wealth and comfort. But although the activity both of the king and the people flowed in praiseworthy channels, it introduced, side by side with renewed vigour, new and dangerous evils. A more complicated machinery was required to rule the state in its larger dimensions and with its more extensive possessions; and a variety of nicely balanced authorities were introduced, whereas before a simpler form of government had sufficed. The conflicting bodies were the nobles and the priests, who shared and often eclipsed the influence of the king. Their peculiar attitude and sudden importance proved that the nation had emerged from its primitive state, and had entered a maturer phase.

The nobles had given themselves up to luxury and sensual pleasures. The priests were hardly better fitted to lead the way to a purer life; for at this period they also demanded a share in the wordly affairs of the nation. Jealous of their prerogatives and ambitious of power, their selfishness annulled the beneficial influence which their watchfulness over the observances of religion might otherwise have exercised. But between the callousness of the chiefs and the bigotry of the priests, rose the prophet's voice, calling his countrymen back to truth, to simplicity, and above all to the God whom they had heedlessly deserted. In the midst of a thriving commerce and of unwonted wealth, he sought to impress the people with a sense of humility, and to enforce the practice of those virtues and duties which were forgotten in a dazzling life of pomp and vanity. The momentary success of his endeavours shows that their depravity was as yet not irremediable, and that they were not altogether hardened against warning and remonstrance. He abstained from severe denunciations and expressions of despair; for he was not hopeless for the result of his mission, though he required great strength to brave the scorn and the menaces of an angry multitude.

Joel, the son of Pethuel, lived in the kingdom of Judah. Tradition names the small town of Thebor in the territory of Reuben as his birth-place. His writings furnish but scanty information with respect to his career; and there are no other reliable sources from which we might gather more. His frequent allusions to the priesthood, and his evident familiarity with the offerings and ceremonies of the Temple, suggest that he belonged to the priestly order. With regard to the time when he lived, his works afford a sufficient clue. He mentions as the enemies of Judah only the neighbouring tribes of Philistia and Edom, of Tyre and Sidon, the old and inveterate foes of the empire. These, and these alone disturbed, at different intervals, the calm of Uzziah's reign; whereas in the times of the next king, Jotham, the dreaded hosts of northern invaders excited the alarm of the nation and became the theme of prophetic eloquence. Joel alludes neither to the Assyrians nor to the Chaldeans, and it is consequently natural to suppose that he lived before the period when these conquerors occasioned such great changes in Palestine. Therefore, the political horizon being comparatively clear, the social condition of the people mainly engaged the prophet's attention.

The short but beautiful orations which make up the Book of Joel, are devoted to three different subjects, which, however, are in a certain manner connected with each other. They commence with a description of the Divine vengeance wrought upon the people by a fearful calamity. A plague of locusts, a dreaded scourge of eastern countries, visited Judea, and the cruel ravages which it caused are pictured with the most forcible eloquence. The next part of the Book is an earnest appeal to the people to acknowledge the Divine punishment as fully merited; the prophet endeavoured to move them to repentance by menace and rebuke, and he tries thus not only to secure a return of their former prosperity, but to lead them, cleansed by suffering, to religion and virtue. Rejoiced at the apparent success of his words, and at the cessation of the plague, he closes with a sublime and ideal description of a pure theocracy, and of the ultimate glory and triumph of the Hebrews.

The first section delineates the terrible visitation, which was so exceptional in its severity that the prophet declared, generation would relate of it to generation, and its horrors would for ever be kept fresh in the recollection of the people. Travellers of all ages bear witness to the alarming numbers and destructive power of locusts. As they move onwards, darkening the sky, they are the precursors of desolation and pestilence. In one night they alter the aspect of the landscape; the trees are stripped bare, the fields laid waste, and gardens changed into deserts. No form of rhetoric could axaggerate the terrors of the reality, and it is not surprising that the conscience-stricken Hebrews saw in the fearful distress the vengeance of an offended God and the approach of the final day of judgment. The prosperity which they owed to the rich products of their soil was suddenly checked; for the vineyards stood bereft of their beauty, and the countless herds and flocks were starving on parched meadows; and the husbandman saw his wealth perish with the withering olive-trees or the blighted corn-fields. Within the very walls of the

Temple the dread calamity made itself felt; for empty altars told of the desolation abroad. Death and decay took the place of the smiling plenty of former years, and the sufferers looked vainly around for relief. The prophet thus describes the horrors of the plague:

"Hear this, old men, and give ear, all inhabitants of the land. Has this been in your days, or even in the days of your fathers? Tell your children of it, and let your children tell their children, and their children another generation. That which the palmerworm has left the locust has eaten, and that which the locust has left the cankerworm has eaten, and that which the cankerworm has left the caterpillar has eaten. Awake, drunkards, and weep, and howl, all drinkers of wine, because of the new wine, for it is cut off from your mouth. For a nation is come up upon my land, strong and without number, whose teeth are the teeth of a lion, and whose cheek-teeth are those of a great lion. He has laid my vine waste, and barked my fig-tree, he has made it all bare, and cast it away; its branches are made white.

"Lament like a young wife girt with sackcloth for the husband of her youth. The meat-offering and the drink-offering are cut off from the House of the Lord; the priests, the Lord's ministers, mourn. The field is wasted, the land mourns; for the corn is wasted, the new wine is dried up, the oil languishes. Be ashamed, O husbandmen; howl, O vine dressers, for the wheat and for the barley, because the harvest of the field has perished. The vine is dried up, and the fig-tree languishes; the pomegranate-tree, the palm-tree also, and the apple-tree, even all the trees of the field, are withered: indeed joy has withered away from the sons of men. . . . . . .

"The day of the Lord comes, forsooth it is nigh at hand: a day of darkness and of gloom, a day of clouds and of thick darkness, as the morning spreads upon the mountains: a great people and a strong one; there has never been the like, nor shall there be any more after it, even to the years of many generations. A fire devours before them, and behind them a flame burns: the land is as the garden of Eden before them, and behind them a desolate wilderness; yea, and nothing escapes them. Their appearance is as the appearance of horses, and as horsemen so they run. Like the noise of chariots on the tops of mountains they leap, like the noise of a flame of fire that devours the stubble, as a strong people set in battle array. Before them the people tremble, all faces lose their brightness. They run like heroes, they climb the wall like men of war, and they march every one on his way and they do not break their ranks; nor does one thrust another, they walk every one in his path, and when they fall upon the sword, they do not break their line. They move to and fro in the city, they run upon the wall, they climb up upon the houses, they enter in at the windows like a thief. The earth quakes before them, the heavens tremble, the sun and the moon are dark, and the stars withdraw their splendour. And the Lord makes resound His thunder before His army; for His camp is exceedingly great, and strong is the executor of His word: the day of the Lord is great and very terrible, and who can abide it?"

But Joel was not merely the chronicler of troubled days, nor merely the stern rebuker who pointed out the visitation of the Lord in the dire calamity; he was also the friend and adviser of the people, zealous for their welfare, and sympathising with their misfortunes, for which he anxiously sought redress. Universal depravity had caused the misery they were lamenting. Earnest repentance, and humble prayer might bring back the Divine grace which they had forfeited. The prophet, therefore, thus exhorted his hearers: "Blow the trumpet in Zion, sanctify a fast, call a solemn assembly; gather the people, sanctify the congregation, assemble the elders, gather the children, and those that suck the breasts; let the bridegroom go forth of his chamber, and the bride out of her closet. Let the priests, the ministers of the Lord, weep between the porch and the altar, and let them say, Spare Thy people, O Lord, and give not Thy heritage to reproach, that the heathen should rule over them: wherefore should they say among the nations, Where is their God? Then will the Lord be zealous for His land, and pity His people."

And now for the first time, the theme, so often recurring in the later prophets, is introduced; in opposition to the servile observance of the ritualism so carefully fostered by the priesthood, Joel insisted upon inward purity and upon sincerity of devotion. And in this respect he rose above the great men who had preceded him: while these had merely declared the will of God, and had set forth the inevitable consequences of defiance to that will, he showed his people, how to follow the Divine behests under all circumstances, and in all emergencies of private and public life. In one short sentence he gave his hearers the keynote to all true repentance, and to the highest form of religion. "Rend your heart and not your garments!" he exclaimed, when the distressed people sought to regain the favour of God by the tattered robe, the coarse sackcloth, and the symbolic ashes. He declared that no tormenting of the flesh can atone for the callousness of the heart; that one day's or a few days' fasting and abstinence are unavailing, unless they are followed by a lasting abandonment of a selfish and purposeless existence.

Thus the first great step towards spiritualizing the religion of the people was achieved; it produced an effect which was neither derived from the formalism of the priesthood, nor from the awe-striking but transitory power hitherto wielded by prophecy; and its influence was stronger than any that had yet been felt; for it came home to every one and appealed to the noblest feelings of human nature.

Joel's injunctions were listened to with deference, and upon the sincere repentance of the people the Divine punishment was withdrawn. Then the tone of the prophet was altered: he had before described the terror caused by the locusts, he had given counsel to the suffering inhabitants; but now he dwelt upon the glorious change which they were then witnessing. "The Lord was zealous for His land, and took pity on His people." The fearful "northern army" was removed, and the products of the earth appeared again with increased plenty. Therefore, when the Hebrews beheld once more their store houses replenished, their fields waving with golden corn, and their trees laden with precious fruit, they were called upon to rejoice, and to praise their merciful Father. But the prophet saw other and even stronger reasons for gratitude and exultation; he promised in the name of the Lord spiritual blessings, far exceeding all worldly treasures in value; for he announced that the breath of Divine wisdom should pervade and raise the whole nation. Virtue should reign for ever in Zion and Jerusalem, and peace and safety be secured for all future time. Yet this glorious consummation should be preceded by additional signs of God's anger, and the storm should continue for a while, before undisturbed serenity would set in. "The day of the Lord" was appointed for the vindication of all wrongs of Judah, a day of retribution against the nations that had so cruelly vexed the chosen people. A few spirited verses tell of the impending warfare, of the multitudes that were to assemble in the "valley of decision", of the ploughshares and pruninghooks to be beaten into swords and spears, and of weak men becoming heroes ready to take part in the great combat which was to determine the fate of the heathen world.

But the Book does not end with this picture of din and turmoil. Bright gleams of concord and peace illumine the future; the newly restored beauty and verdure of the country are considered by the prophet as pledges of rest and prosperity, and of restitution to more permanent and more precious benefits. Not only, in the language of Joel, "shall it come to pass on that day that the mountains shall drop down new wine, and the hills shall flow with milk, and all the rivers of Judah shall flow with water, and a fountain shall come forth of the House of the Lord, and shall water the valley of Shittim;" but "Jerusalem shall be holy, and no strangers shall pass through it any more; Judah shall stand for ever, and Jerusalem from generation to generation; and God will remit the guilt which He has not remitted, for He will dwell in Zion." A short but vivid recital of past sorrows and trials winds up with most comforting promises — the promises of God's constant protection, and of ultimate deliverance from all worldly and spiritual evils.

The Book, though small and fragmentary, reveals the varied powers of the writer. He stands before us as the gifted poet dilating upon scenes full of terror; as the warm friend and judicious counsellor of the people, strengthening them in their endurance, and assisting them in their struggles for relief; and as the fearless and faithful messenger of God, the mouthpiece of His anger and of His mercy.

A beautiful, clear, and concise style is employed for the delineation of these manifold subjects. For the Book of Joel was written in the classic age of Hebrew literature, when the severity and sternness of earlier times had been mellowed by culture and an improved taste, but when the language had not yet been impaired by the introduction of foreign words and forms. The diction of Joel unites vigour and simplicity, but its primitive freshness is by no means devoid of beauty and grace. The description of the locust plague is most powerful; the desolation of the land and the languor oppressing all animated nature, are brought before the reader with the skill of the poet and the accuracy of the experienced observer. In the purely descriptive parts, the language is graphic and picturesque; in the earnest appeals addressed to the feelings of the multitude, and in the account of their distress and their lamentations, it combines clearness with true pathos; while it attains an almost unsurpassed force in the admonitions to repentance, and a stirring sublimity in the anticipations of the terrible day of retribution. Indeed, in the few short chapters that have been rescued from oblivion, Joel succeeds in giving worthy utterance to the highest feelings of religion in words never obscure or abrupt.

II. JONAH. (About 800.)

Among the works of the twelve minor prophets, there is one that bears a character entirely different from the rest. It is not, like most of them, connected with the history of the Hebrews; it does not, like some, propound, in poetical or admonitory language, any great doctrines, nor even directly enforce ethical truths; nor does it — and this is the most striking difference — bring before us the prophet whose name it bears, as an unerring mouthpiece of Divine wisdom, claiming our undivided veneration. This is perhaps the sole instance of a messenger of God not proclaiming words of instruction or comfort, nor shining as an example of piety and obedience. For Jonah, though gifted with the Divine power of prophecy, though chosen by God to make known His will, is throughout represented as a man sharing, to a great extent, the common failings of humanity. His conduct as set forth in the narrative of the Book, reflects those ordinary minds that bear down under the burden of vexations, and are annoyed by wounded pride and offended dignity and by grievances morbidly magnified. He is a type of men whose hearts are never warmed by a genial glow, who fail to appreciate God's bounties, and who embitter their lives by selfishness. In contrast to this human side of the picture, the Divine attributes of love and compassion stand out in bold relief. The long-suffering of God, so often dwelt upon in all parts of the sacred Volume, is illustrated in a remarkable instance of forgiveness extended equally to an offending Hebrew and to unenlightened heathens. The Scriptures are replete with descriptions of the greatness of God as opposed to the littleness of man; that greatness is indeed generally manifested by an immeasurably superior power, but often also by God's unlimited mercy which man is bidden humbly to imitate. It is these lessons which the Book of Jonah indirectly teaches; and in proving that the heathen is a worthy object of Divine care, it moreover sets forth the duty of toleration.

Once only is the name of Jonah mentioned in the historical records of the Hebrews. The Book of Kings relates, that in the reign of Jeroboam, "the coast of Israel was restored from the entering of Hamath to the sea of the plain, according to the word of the Lord God of Israel, which He spoke through His servant Jonah, the son of Amittai, the prophet who was of Gathhepher." As Jeroboam II reigned at the end of the ninth and the beginning of the eighth century (825 — 784), Jonah was the contemporary of Joel, Amos, and Hosea. But in the work which bears his name, the prophet Jonah is not connected with events so insignificant as a slight extension of royal dominions; but with the fate of one of the mightiest empires of the ancient world.

In Jonah's time, the formidable power of Assyria was steadily increasing. Relations, now of a friendly and now of a hostile nature, had long existed between the Holy Land and the distant Assyrian territory; and the Book of Jonah proves that those relations had grown into close intercourse; for it relates that a Hebrew prophet was sent with messages from his God to the remote regions of the Tigris. Yet the main interest which we feel in Jonah, does not lie in the sphere of history; for the work which bears his name was written long after his time, and throws no light upon contemporary events; the facts which tradition may have handed down from generation to generation, are not the most important part of the Book; they are only the medium for conveying doctrines of universal and human interest far outlasting the fluctuating destinies of conquerors and dynasties. These ideas, however, are all so closely blended with the narrative, that it is impossible to analyse the one without referring to the other.

Foremost in the territory of Assyria was the huge city of Nineveh remarkable for its vast extent, its large buildings, and teeming population. The rapid increase of power and wealth, combined with a complete ignorance or neglect of nobler aims, produced a state of moral depravity. But the wickedness of the people moved the compassion of God; and the prophet Jonah received the Divine command to proceed to Nineveh and to exhort the inhabitants to return from their evil ways.

Such a mandate, however, required no ordinary messenger. His path was not among his own people, where the words of his Master, even if unheeded and neglected, were at least listened to; nor even among the neighbouring tribes that often acknowledged the omnipotence, without following the laws, of Israel's God. His mission lay in a far distant land, where no echo of a purer creed had ever reached. A strong faith and uncommon intrepidity were necessary to uphold the prophet on his solitary journey, and to fortify him for the daring attempt to appear before a proud and powerful assembly, unknown and unbidden, uttering only unpalatable words of menace.

But Jonah neither possessed the simple-minded obedience which silences all hesitation, nor the noble courage which conquers all dangers. When he had received the Divine commands, he left his native land, not to execute them, but to flee, as he thought, from the Master whose behests he dreaded. At Joppa he took a ship that was about to sail westward, to Tarshish or Tartessus on the coast of Spain. But he could not escape the anger of God; for a violent storm arose, and the vessel was in imminent danger of being engulfed by the waves. The heathen sailors trembled; for they ascribed the fury of the elements to an unatoned for crime committed by one of the passengers; and they cried aloud to the several gods whom they worshipped. During this scene of terror, Jonah lay asleep in a corner of the ship, till the master of the vessel, excited and perplexed, aroused him and bade him join in the general prayers. He decided to draw lots, and thus to discover on whose account the storm was raging. When the lot fell upon Jonah, and his fellow travellers learnt that the deity whom he adored was the God of heaven and earth whom he was trying to evade, they were terrified, for they were well aware of the power of the God of Israel. — In the face of this fearful peril, the prophet and the heathens vied in generosity and zeal. Jonah promptly demanded to be thrown into the waves, for he was certain that thus only the safety of the ship could be secured; but the sailors shrank from the idea of destroying his life; they strove with all their might to reach the shore, and to land him there; but their endeavours were fruitless; the storm grew fiercer and fiercer; and at last they yielded to Jonah's pressing demand. The calm which followed instantaneously, proved to them that they had acted rightly; and they acknowledged their escape from imminent peril by thank-offerings and vows which they presented to the God of Israel.

"Now the Lord", thus the Bible narrative continues, "had prepared a great fish to swallow up Jonah: and Jonah was in the belly of the fish three days and three nights." Jonah was miraculously saved from a grave in the depth of the sea, to be entombed alive in a huge monster. Yet his deliverance from the immediate danger was so wonderful that now the prophet's voice, usually uplifted for complaint, rose in beautiful tones of praise and prayer. "For Thou hadst cast me into the deep, in the midst of the seas; and the floods compassed me about: all Thy billows and Thy waves passed over me. Then I said, I am cast out of Thy sight; yet I will look again toward Thy holy Temple. The waters compassed me about, even to the soul; the depth closed me round about, the weeds were wrapped about my head. I went down to the bottom of the mountains; the bars of the earth were over me for ever: yet Thou hast brought up my life from corruption, O Lord my God. When my soul fainted within me, I remembered the Lord, and my prayer came to Thee in Thy holy Temple. The worshippers of lying vanities forsake their Merciful Father; but I will sacrifice to Thee with the voice of thanksgiving; I will pay that which I have vowed. Salvation is of the Lord."

The unceasing goodness and compassion of God were again manifested: "And the Lord spoke to the fish and it vomited out Jonah upon the dry land" — the prophet was saved, and free to commence a new and better life. Once more he was commanded to set out upon his mission, and this time he obeyed without hesitation.

Nineveh, the ancient chronicler relates, was "the great town"; for her huge walls extended to a three days' journey in circumference. Within them lived and revelled an immense population, ignorant of the eternal truths, but, as was afterwards evinced, not unwilling to receive them. It does not appear that power, vast dominions, and unparalleled wealth, had tainted the people with pride and self-conceit. The Hebrew prophet had often to contend with trying difficulties in his native land; his counsels were rarely acted upon, and his words seldom failed to rouse the wrath of an offended monarch or a self-sufficient people. By contrast with them, the heathen inhabitants of Nineveh appear in a favourable light. A strange prophet of a strange God came before them and declared, that within forty days Nineveh should be destroyed. The announcement was implicitly believed. When it reached the royal palace, the powerful despot was abashed and conscience-stricken. He cast off the imperial purple, put on the penitential garb of sackcloth, and covered himself with ashes, and forthwith commanded a day of general humiliation. Then all the people, suddenly impressed with their depravity and the idea of an Almighty and all-righteous God, threw themselves down in prayer, to propitiate His anger and to avert their doom. The rich and the poor, the young and the old, and, according to ancient customs, even the beasts, abstained from all food. When God saw that they truly repented of their evil works, He withheld the calamity with which He had intended to chastise them.

One heart alone grieved amid the universal relief and happiness. The prophet Jonah "was very angry." He had been the bearer of a decree full of gloom and terror; and when that decree was revoked, he believed that his authority was lost, and that his prophecies would no more be regarded as unfailing. He could not endure such humiliation; and uncheered by the joy of numberless fellow-beings, he broke forth in the murmuring cry, "Oh Lord! take my soul, for I would rather die than live!" His heart was apparently closed to every feeling save a gnawing grief at the supposed failure of his mission; but God reproved him, saying, "Dost thou well to be angry?"

Then Jonah withdrew from the town in which he fancied he was despised. He went to the eastern side of the city, where he built for himself a booth, and here he watched the events, of which, instead of an active leader, he had become a dissatisfied spectator. God, however, did not forsake him in these moments of angry selfishness. He made a large gourd grow on the spot, to screen him from the scorching heat of the sun. Jonah was exceedingly rejoiced. But when the morning came, a worm had eaten of the gourd, so that it withered, and once again the prophet saw cause for complaint and repining. Physical suffering was now added to mental annoyance. The dry east-wind blew remorselessly over his unprotected head; but fiercer than the blazing sun, raged within him the mingled passions of anger and mortified pride. He repeated with greater vehemence than before, that it was better for him to die than to live; and when the Divine voice asked him if he did well to be angry about the gourd, he answered, that he did well to be angry, "even unto death."

These are the last words which are recorded from the lips of the fretful prophet, and we leave him sitting in moody gloom, brooding with vexation over that happiness in which he took no part.

But the Book does not end with this sad description of human failings; it has another lesson to teach besides the impotence of man, the narrow limits which encircle his sympathies, and the selfishness which arouses his passions. It terminates with the reverse side of the picture, and presents, with force and simplicity, an example of God's all-pervading goodness. No anger is discernible in the last Divine reproof, and the mercy which had been extended to the erring Ninevites, was not withheld from the ungenerous Hebrew; God said to him, "Thou hast had pity on the gourd for which thou hast not laboured, and which thou didst not make grow, which came up in a night and perished in a night; and should not I spare Nineveh, that great city, wherein are more than sixty thousand persons that cannot discern between their right hand and their left hand, and also much cattle?"

It is most probable that this episode in the life of Jonah was treasured for many generations in the retentive memory of the people, till an able writer, desirous to perpetuate the lofty truths and moral lessons it implies, wrote it down in its present form. The language bears unmistakeable traces of a later age, and points to a time contemporary with, if not later than the Babylonian exile. The style is so simple, and so free from all obscurity, that it would be unwarrantable to search for hidden explanations of the story. The supposition of an allegorical or typical meaning underlying the account of miraculous occurrences, is contrary to the spirit of the work, which clearly aims at impressing the all-pervading power and the inexhaustible long-suffering of God. This lesson would be weakened if Jonah's supernatural deliverance were explained away by the assumption of a vision or a dream. As a miracle it had probably been cherished by the people; as such it was accepted by the author; and as such it enhanced the interest of his narrative, and intensified the contrast between Divine omnipotence and human fallibility.

Apart from its leading ideas, the Book of Jonah bears comparison, in other points also, with some of the most sublime productions of prophecy; for it exhibits a largeness of spirit peculiar to the greatest of the sacred writers. Narrow minds often considered the chosen people alone as worthy of Divine favour, and believed that the heathens were destined to destruction, and their land to desolation. But the more comprehensive sympathies of the great prophets diffused the light and the blessings of a purer faith extending over all nations alike. The author of the Book of Jonah was even more impartial in his appreciation of an alien people. The plain and unadorned

facts he narrates, present many contrasts unfavourable to
his own nation. The pagan crew readily bow down before
the supreme will of a God whom they have not been taught
to revere, while the Hebrew prophet evades and defies His
command. The childlike trust of the Ninevites, their humility and speedy repentance, stand out in marked opposition
to the unconquerable stubbornness which the Jews evinced
during long generations. The heathens are treated with generosity; far from being held up to scorn, or looked upon as objects of God's wrath, they appear no less than the Hebrews
as recipients of His benefits and His protection. There
breathes throughout the Book a spirit of toleration rarely
surpassed in any religious work. Therefore, the Book of
Jonah, though simple and unpretending in language, occupies a worthy place by the side of grander and more ambitious writings. Few of them illustrate with so much
vigour the efficacy of ready obedience and humble repentance; few of them represent so happily the comforting side
of religion; and few have brought to our human comprehension so strongly as the Book of Jonah the God of
Israel as "a gracious God, and merciful, slow to anger, and
of great kindness, and repenting of evil", as a God showing
His omnipotence not by the terror of His punishments, but
by His love and forgiveness.

III. AMOS. (790.)

The reign of Jeroboam II (825—784) was of particular importance in the history of the empire of Israel on account of the many influences then at work in preparing subsequent calamities. For at that period, the people found more
delight in the fantastic and sensual rites of neighbouring idolators than in the stern and simple creed of their ancestors.

Indifference to their religion and worldly ambition combined to taint every class of the community, not excepting the sacred order of the priesthood. Still the voice of truth could not be checked, and it rose with increased force after every attempt that was made to silence it. Among the contending factions that were striving only for aggrandisement and wealth, the figure of Isaiah, the statesman and prophet, stood out in strong relief; somewhat earlier, the priesthood, though as a body perverted either by bigotry or callousness, had sent forth Joel armed with a loftier religion than any which public teachers had been wont to proclaim; and almost at the same period, the desire of reforming the people and averting their doom kindled the heart of a representative of a much humbler class. Whilst multitudes were listening in the gates and public places of Jerusalem to the inspiring orations of renowned prophets, Amos, far removed from those busy scenes, was enrolled among the faithful servants of God.

Belonging to the tribe of Judah, and born at Tekoa in the vicinity of Bethlehem, he was a contemporary of the prophets Joel and Hosea, and lived during the reigns of Uzziah and Jeroboam II. The moral corruption and frivolity so conspicuous at the court of the latter king, the want of justice and charity prevalent among the great and powerful, the cries of the oppressed extending far beyond the city gates, reached Amos in his simple life of seclusion, and called him to action. Unlike many of his great fellow-workers, he did not belong to a learned or distinguished caste, but was an untutored herdsman. Nature, his teacher and companion, imprinted on him her own freshness and vigour, and his love of her marvels and beauties was fostered by his pastoral occupations. While tending his flocks on the distant mountains, the echoes of men's strife and turmoil reached him with a stranger and more thrilling sound; and falling upon a mind of the greatest moral sensibility, they called forth in him a longing to abandon the quietness of his retired life, to move in the great world, and to battle against its follies and sins. He, therefore, left his native place, and went to the large and important town of Bethel in the kingdom of Israel, determined to lift up his voice where warning and reproof were so urgently needed.

But like many other Hebrew teachers, he did not limit his prophecies to his own people. The neighbouring countries were as notorious for their cruelty and rapine, as the Israelites for their heedlessness and idolatry; and the prophet deemed it his duty to announce to them the day of Divine vengeance. It was on account of pitiless and revengeful treatment of conquered enemies that the proud commonwealth of Damascus and the principal Philistine towns, as Gaza, Ashdod, and Ashkelon, were to suffer the misery which they had themselves inflicted; Tyre should be laid low for her faithlessness; and a terrible doom awaited the Ammonites and the Edomites, because they had shown mercy to no one.

Having declared the fate of these once triumphant communities, the prophet addressed himself to his own countrymen, in language more explicit and even more decided; for their transgressions had fearfully accumulated. "They sell", he exclaimed, "the righteous for silver, and the poor for a pair of shoes." They humiliated the poor, persecuted the virtuous, and profaned, by licentious revelries, the House of that God who had overwhelmed them with favours, and had humbled their powerful enemies; and with a vivid recollection of the familiar scenes he had recently left, the prophet indignantly burst forth: "Thus says the Lord, I have annihilated the Amorite before them: his height was like the height of the cedar, and he was strong like the oaks, yet I destroyed his fruit from above and his roots from beneath. And I brought you up from the land of Egypt, and also led you forty years through the wilderness, to possess the land of the Amorite. And I raised up many of your sons for prophets, and many of your young men for Nazarites. Is it not even thus, O children of Israel? says the Lord." — But a terrible time was in store for the ungrateful nation: "Behold, I am pressed under you, as a cart is pressed that is full of sheaves. Therefore the flight shall perish from the swift, and the strong shall not be strong in his vigour, nor shall the mighty deliver himself; nor shall he stand that handles the bow; and he that is swift of foot shall not deliver himself; nor shall he that rides the horse deliver himself. And he that is courageous among the mighty shall flee away naked in that day, says the Lord."

For their destruction, so Amos assured his countrymen, would not be a casual incident; it was prepared by adequate causes, which must work their inevitable result. He turned again to nature, this time to animate creation, to illustrate his meaning: "Will a lion roar in the forest when he has no prey? will a young lion cry out of his den, if he has taken nothing? Can a bird fall into a snare upon the earth, where no gin is for him? shall one take up a snare from the earth, and have taken nothing at all? Shall a trumpet be blown in the city, and the people not be afraid? shall there be evil in the city, and the Lord has not done it?"

Darkly and vaguely the prophet shadowed forth those evils which were soon to become the untiring theme of prophetic eloquence. In the adversary "who shall cover the land, bringing down the people's strength and spoiling their palaces", the Assyrian is pictured, the dreaded scourge of the Hebrews. Like some of his contemporaries, the prophet referred also to the calamities which from time to time visited the land; he bade the people look upon them as a just retribution for their sins, and for their ingratitude and unequalled callousness. "And I have given you cleanness of teeth in all your cities, and want of bread in all your places: yet have you not returned to Me, says the Lord. And I have also withheld the rain from you, when there were yet three months to the harvest; and I caused it to rain upon one city, and caused it not to rain upon another city: one piece was rained upon, and the piece whereupon it did not rain withered. So two or three cities wandered to one city to drink water, but they were not satisfied: yet have you not returned to Me, says the Lord. I have smitten you with blasting and mildew; when your gardens and your vineyards and your fig-trees and your olive-trees increased, the palmerworm devoured them: yet have you not returned to Me, says the Lord. I have sent to you the pestilence after the manner of Egypt; your young men have I slain with the sword, and have taken away your horses; and I have caused the smell of your camps to come up unto your nostrils: yet have you not returned to Me, says the Lord. I have overthrown some of you, as God overthrew Sodom and Gomorrah, and you were as a firebrand plucked out of the burning: yet have you not returned to Me, says the Lord."

But Amos did not trust to this dreary picture alone to move the hearts of his hearers. He had recourse to less menacing remonstrances, and he exhausted every form of entreaty to lead the sinners to penitence. He described God's grandeur in the following terms: "Behold, He that forms the mountains and creates the wind, and declares to me what are His thoughts, He makes morning and darkness, treads upon the high places of the earth: the Lord of hosts is His name." He implored the people to leave the altars of iniquity, not to seek Bethel and Gilgal, where Egyptian worship flourished, but to seek the Lord, "who makes the seven stars and Orion, and turns the shadow of death into morning, and makes the day dark with night, who calls for the waters of the sea, and pours them out upon the earth: the Lord is His name."

Idolatry was indeed the fatal disease that was destroying the strength of the nation, but the prophet knew well, that the depravity which prevailed in the social life of the people was not less grievous and alarming. He gave them a rigorous code of morals, commanding them not only to do good and avoid evil, but to love good and hate evil; he declared that God beheld and visited their transgressions, and that He would avenge the perversion of justice through the rich man's bribe, and the sufferings of the righteous by the rule of might and oppression. Even when the altars of God were not deserted for heathen groves, they were polluted by wicked priests who disgraced their sacred office. The meaningless devotion of the obtuse, and the more hateful worship of the hypocrites provoked the prophet's deepest detestation, to which he gave vent in strains rivalling those of Isaiah on the same theme. "I hate, I despise your feast-days, and I have no delight in your solemn assemblies. Though you offer to Me burnt offerings and your meat-offerings, I will not accept them, nor will I regard the thank-offerings of your fat beasts. Take thou away from Me the noise of thy songs, for I will not hear the melody of thy harps." The sacrifice offered with a blood-stained hand, the prayer uttered by deceitful lips, these were abominations in the eyes of the Lord, who demanded that "judgment should flow like water, and righteousness like an eternal stream." Lying upon ivory couches, drinking wine out of deep bowls, revelling to the sound of music, and mocking the solemn warnings of their teachers, the Israelites closed their eyes to their impending fate, and thus hastened its approach. Though deeply commiserating the perverseness of the people, and praying that God would stay His rod of anger, he saw that they were blindly rushing into destruction, and he announced it with unflinching firmness, declaring that "the high places of Isaac should be desolate, and the sanctuaries of Israel be laid waste, and that the Lord would rise against Jeroboam with the sword!"

The prophet's remonstrance and censure had never fallen upon a willing audience, but this last galling speech which foreshadowed the ruin of their monarchy, proved too much for their endurance, and it was not uttered with impunity. The priest Amaziah reported the alarming words to the king; yet though he feared their effect, he did not dare to do violence to the prophet; but he ordered him to repair to the land of Judah and there to speak, if speak he must: "but prophesy not any more," he commanded, "at Bethel, for it is a royal sanctuary, and it is the king's dominion." Amos possessed the courage which distinguished his order, and he combined firm trust in God with humble diffidence in his own powers. He was not a prophet, he replied, but a simple herdsman and gatherer of sycamore fruit; while following the flocks, the Lord had commanded him to prophesy against Israel, and he merely obeyed the mandates of his Master; and he finished by pronouncing a fearful doom upon the man who presumed to debar him from his sacred mission.

Though Amos deemed it necessary to act upon the caution of Amaziah, he never ceased to utter warnings against the depraved kingdom of Israel, whose dire fate he delineated with a relentless hand. "Though they dig into the lower world, thence shall My hand take them; though they climb up to heaven, thence will I bring them down; and though they hide themselves in the top of Carmel, I will search and take them out thence; and though they be hid from My side in the bottom of the sea, thence will I command the serpent, and it shall bite them; and though they go into captivity before their enemies, thence will I command the sword, and it shall slay them: and I will set My eyes upon them for evil and not for good."

Yet this terrible picture was not the last scene portrayed by the prophet. For his heart was not estranged from his countrymen, sinning and ungrateful though they were; he knew that God chastised whom He loved, and that His mercy was more enduring than His anger. Accordingly the tenor of his prophecies changes; a ray of light relieves the prevailing darkness; it dawns in the far distance, and ushers in a day, when the strength and glory of Israel, rising triumphantly above danger and degradation, shall create a new national existence: "I will not utterly annihilate the house of Jacob, says the Lord; for behold, I will command and I will sift the house of Israel among all nations, as corn is sifted in a sieve, yet shall not the least grain fall upon the earth .... In that day will I raise up the tabernacle of David that is fallen, and close up the breaches thereof; and I will raise up its ruins, and I will build it as in the days of old .... Behold, the day comes, says the Lord, that the ploughman shall overtake the reaper, and the treader of grapes him that sowes seed; and the mountains shall drop sweet wine, and all the hills shall overflow. And I will bring back the captivity of My people of Israel, and they shall build up desolate cities and inhabit them, and they shall plant vineyards and drink the wine thereof, and they shall make gardens and eat the fruit of them. And I will plant them upon their land, and they shall no more be torn out of their land which I have given them, says the Lord thy God."

Thus end the speeches of Amos, like most of the prophetic utterances, with words of peace, with glad tidings that rejoiced and upheld the pious few, and encouraged even the callous and the wicked to hope for a share in the promised glory, if they repented and reformed.

The Book of Amos is small in compass, and less varied in matter than most of the prophetic works. Its continuous and regular form suggests that it is the composition of one special period, and not a collection of orations delivered on various occasions. It does not relate to any striking event of prominent interest, and the unbroken sameness of the subject and the absence of all historical dates lead to the same conclusion.

The individuality of Amos is conspicuous in the manner, in which he accomplished his arduous task. In the warfare against the sins of his nation, he wielded weapons peculiar to himself. He did not speak with keen satire or bitter irony; but he was impressive by his great earnestness. The severity of his language reveals the thoughts of a man long used to retirement. His style bears the seal of a tranquil and reflecting mind. It is not soaring or sublime; but it is forcible without the help of bold rhetoric or studied brevity. His illustrations, chiefly taken from the spheres with which he was best acquainted, are stamped with faithfulness and truth. The noble cedar of Lebanon was to him a symbol of strength and durability; and animated nature in all its wonderful varieties suggested striking similes for describing the varieties of human life and thought. He regards the God of Israel not as the God of battles or of judgment: when he most desires to show Him to his people as the Lord to whom love and reverence are due, he speaks to them of the God who forms the mountains and creates the wind, who sends the morning dawn and gilds the lofty peaks with light, who unchains the waters of springs and seas, and pours them out upon the face of the earth; or he delineates Him as the Omnipotent Lord of the powers upon which he had learnt to look with awe. This love of nature not only opened his mind to the glory and greatness of the Author of the Universe; it not only endowed him with that freshness, purity, and vigour which he knew so well how to infuse into his orations; but it was his most efficient weapon in his fight against the dangerous condition of his people; for it lent power and effect both to threats of punishment and destruction, and to promises of deliverance and mercy.

IV. HOSEA. (785—725.)

The age of Amos was followed by a time of excitement and confusion which particularly needed prophetic admonition and guidance. Notwithstanding the depravity of the people, the condition of the country had till then caused no serious alarm; but now ensued a period of anarchy and strife which extinguished all hopes of political security and social happiness. Many vigorous efforts were made to avert the cheerless future; and the prophet Hosea was among the most zealous patriots: like Jeremiah at a later and still more tragical epoch of Hebrew history, he was an earnest teacher, a sorrowing friend, and an impartial recorder of events.

The activity of Hosea must have extended over a long period, for he prophesied during the reigns of Uzziah, Jotham, Ahaz, and Hezekiah, kings of Judah, and also in the days of Jeroboam II, the king of Israel; and these reigns encompassed more than half a century. The kingdom of Israel was during this time weakened from a variety of causes. After the death of Jeroboam followed a ten years'

Interregnum, marked by a perpetual change of government, and by deeds of violence and oppression. In those lawless days, the evils which Amos had vainly attempted to eradicate, greatly increased. The monarchy was indeed at last restored, but the new occupant of the throne enjoyed his authority only for a few short months, and was assassinated by Shallum, the son of Jabesh, who seized upon the government. But soon afterwards, Menahem, the son of Gadi, killed the usurper, and reigned in his stead. He was cruel and arbitrary, and the ten years of his despotism (773—763) caused a visible decline both in the moral and political condition of the kingdom. This degeneracy is faithfully depicted in the Book of Hosea, which traces in language all the more emphatic perhaps for a certain vagueness, the external dangers which were threatening the reckless people. During Menahem's reign the Assyrians under their king Pul invaded the country, and this disaster was followed by the imposition of a heavy tribute, and not long afterwards by the final ruin of the empire of Israel.

[The important period at which we have rapidly glanced, naturally afforded many a suggestive theme for prophetic eloquence. Of Hosea himself few details only have been preserved to us. He was the son of Beeri, and probably a citizen of the kingdom of Israel. Although he occasionally addressed Judah, Ephraim was the chief object of his solicitude; and his writings will, therefore, be best understood if viewed in connection with the history of his native country. His life does not seem to have been endangered in the cause for which many other prophets suffered, and his orations, though not inferior to those of any public teacher in candour and boldness, do not appear to have aroused the resentment of his hearers.

The Book of Hosea may be divided into two parts, which differ from each other more in their treatment than in their subjects. The first four chapters consist of symbolical illustrations of Israel's faithlessness; the remainder have a threefold object — remonstrance and warning, announcement of punishment, and lastly pathetic lamentation. But throughout the work we find dark pictures of confusion, misery, and vice; we find them in the first allegorical chapters, in the prophet's outbursts of indignation, and in his calmer but not less intense expressions of grief.

He first described in general terms the fatal sins of the people, and pointed out the origin of their depravity — their desertion of the true God. He declared that they worshipped everywhere, while the holy Temple in Jerusalem was forsaken. On hill-tops and under the shadow of oak-trees licentious rites were performed in honour of fictitious deities or of the heavenly bodies. The priests were heedless guardians of their precious charge, and the prophet protested that, "as the troop of robbers wait for a man, so the company of priests murdered in the way by consent." Religion exercised no beneficent influence on the community; morality had vanished, and the iniquity of the people was appalling. "There is no truth, and no mercy, and no knowledge of the Lord in the land", exclaimed the prophet; "swearing, lying, and killing, and stealing, and committing adultery — they break forth, and blood touches blood." It is not surprising that these words, uttered with the irresistible power of truth, struck the prophet himself with dismay, and forced him to exclaim, that "he had seen a horrible thing in Israel!"

Another grief weighed upon Hosea's mind. The unprincipled leaders succeeded neither in gaining the confidence of the people, nor in raising the position of Israel among neighbouring nations. Weakened by civil contentions and an imperfect organization, the country sought foreign help in times of distress, and concluded treaties of alliance alternately with Assyria and Egypt: "When Ephraim saw his sickness and Judah his wound, then went Ephraim to the Assyrian." The prophets had ever shown a strong aversion to Israel's reliance upon foreign help. Intercourse with the stranger had always proved fatal to the faith of the Hebrews, and very rarely conducive to their political welfare. The prophet saw that no advantage could arise from an alliance with powers to whom the land or the tribute of the Hebrews was of greater value than their friendship; and he, therefore, admonished both Israel and Judah to be cautious. He rebuked them for being faithless to a Protector who had delivered them in times of far greater peril: "Ephraim is like a silly dove without a heart: they call to Egypt, they go to Assyria. When they go, I will spread My net upon them; I will bring them down as the fowls of the heaven; I will chastise them as their congregation has heard. Woe to them! for they have fled from Me; destruction to them, because they have transgressed against Me: though I have redeemed them, yet they have spoken lies against Me. For they are gone up to Assyria, a wild ass alone by himself: Ephraim has hired lovers. Yea, though they have hired among the nations, now will I gather them, and they shall sorrow a little for the burden of the king of princes." — The prophet never ceased to dwell upon the fatal imprudence of this confederacy: "They are gone for destruction, Egypt shall gather them up, Memphis shall bury them, the pleasant places for their silver — nettles shall possess them; thorns shall be in their tabernacles." Again and again he pointed out their own wickedness as the only cause of their actual and their impending misfortunes: "They have sown the wind, and they shall reap the whirl-wind... Israel has forgotten his Maker, and builds temples, and Judah has multiplied fenced cities; but I will send a fire upon his cities, and it shall devour the palaces thereof."

Through the whole Book sounds this gloomy burden, first expressed in unadorned language, and then in the numberless metaphors of poetry and rhetoric. But often, when the prophet seems most overwhelmed by the dismal reality, he suddenly changes the current of his eloquence, and abandoning stern admonition, he gives vent to mournful lamentation. For he was deeply concerned in the events of which he was an observant spectator. He suffered all the more for being clear-sighted among the blind and heedless, and earnest among the depraved and indifferent; and at last, tired of constant rebuke, he exclaimed: "Come, let us return to the Lord, for He has torn, and He will heal us; He has smitten, and He will bind us up. After two days will He revive us; on the third day He will raise us up, and we shall live in His sight. Then shall we know, if we follow onward to know the Lord: His going forth is prepared as the morning; and He shall come unto us as the rain, as the latter and former rain upon the earth." — Then turning with evident relief to the past, he continues: "When Israel was a child I loved him, and I called My son out of Egypt." In touching terms he pictured the love which God had always shown for His people, His reluctance to punish, and His ever renewed mercy; and he declares in the name of His Divine Master: "My heart is turned within Me; My compassion is kindled altogether.... I will not execute the fierceness of My anger, I will not destroy Ephraim again." A few weighty words teach that this long-suffering is a chief attribute of the Lord, and that He is indeed a God of retribution and chastisement, but also a God of compassion and forgiveness; for He is "God and not man" — not man judging with capriciousness, and cold justice, but a God who delights in the happiness of the penitent. And thus, Hosea urged, man also should temper justice with clemency.

Moreover, he never omitted to condemn the unmeaning ceremonialism into which religion had degenerated; he declared that "God desires mercy and not sacrifice, and the knowledge of God more than burnt-offering." He recommended fervent and humble prayer: "Take with you words, and turn to the Lord; say to Him, Take away all iniquity and receive us graciously; so will we render the offerings of our lips."

It was indeed a religion of the heart, earnest, simple, and enlightened, which Hosea endeavoured to impress upon his hearers; he placed before them a code of kindness and truth; he bade them not only fear God's anger, but rely upon His inexhaustible love.

It is impossible to fix an exact date for these orations, or to arrange them in chronological order. They appear to be the result of the prophet's reflections and impressions during a lengthened period, in which, notwithstanding a variety of events, the country remained, on the whole, in the same condition. They vary according to the feelings which happened to be uppermost in the author's mind: at one moment they convey his bitter sorrow aroused by the recklessness of his countrymen, at another they give utterance to his indignation and remonstrance, and they invariably include, almost without connection or transition, regretful retrospects, gloomy views of the present, and consoling glimpses into a happier future. Thus the prophet carries his auditors from dreary desolation to smiling peace, changing the subject in rapid sequence, now painting the anger of God and now disclosing His unceasing mercy. And yet a certain unity exists in the incongruous contents of the work, and we can trace a natural progress of ideas. The prophet usually commences with remonstrance, which rises to indignant condemnation; dark forebodings follow; and the address generally concludes with expressions of pity and solace. The prophet does not appear to have been directly connected with public affairs, or to have offered his advice at any momentous crisis. His orations were, therefore, prompted by the impulse of enthusiasm rather than by practical experience. They are consequently characterised by a strong, and often by an overwhelming intensity; they are the faithful reflections of indignation in all its fervour, and of sorrow in all its depth and pathos. The language is unadorned, sometimes rugged in its stern simplicity, but always well adapted to the subject. An obscure style almost veils the gloomy predictions; and the ideas, following each other with irregular rapidity, are touched upon rather than developed. When severe thoughts are uppermost in the prophet's mind, his words are strong and powerful; but when his enthusiasm is aroused by the contemplation of God's glory and greatness, his speech flows on with gentleness; and nowhere is the God of love and mercy described more beautifully and more forcibly than in the vehement, yet occasionally soft and mellow addresses of Hosea.

V. MICAH. (730.)

The prophet Micah was a younger contemporary of Hosea, and consequently his fellow-worker during that important period of Hebrew history which witnessed at once the lowest stage of social depravity and the sublimest aspirations of patriotism. Amos, the shepherd prophet, had been followed by Hosea and Isaiah; and midway between the two last-named stands the prophet Micah, exerting himself with the same devotion for the same great cause. He lived during the reigns of Jotham, Ahaz, and Hezekiah; and it is probable that he exercised his greatest influence in the early part of Hezekiah's rule, commencing B. C. 728. Babylon is indeed mentioned, but only as a part of the great Assyrian empire, which appears as the ruling power of Asia; and the prophet's warnings are addressed not only to Judah but to the empire of Ephraim also, which still enjoyed its independence; they must, therefore, have been written before the conquest of Samaria by Shalmanassar, or before the year 722. They were called forth by the same enthusiasm which so often kindled the eloquence of prophets, and by the ardent desire of benefiting a heedless generation by rebuke and encouragement.

Micah's orations were chiefly addressed to the great and powerful leaders of the commonwealth, who were conspicuous for their want of righteousness. He appealed with particular emphasis to "the heads of Jacob and the princes of the house of Israel", and to their instruction he devoted his untiring energy; for he saw how great was their influence upon the people for good or for evil. But he felt that an equal danger menaced his country from the false prophets, who were constantly misleading the credulous multitude. Therefore he exclaimed: "Thus says the Lord concerning the prophets that lead My people astray, that bite with their teeth, and cry, peace! and who prepare war against him that puts nothing into their mouths. Therefore shall night be to you without a vision, and darkness without divination, and the sun shall go down over the prophets and the day shall be dark over them." Besides these two influential classes, a third, whose sacred office ought to have been a safeguard against national depravity, called down the prophet's severe rebuke: the priesthood were devoid of all virtue and equity, and bent only on self-aggrandisement and love of gain. "Hear this," he exclaimed, "O ye heads of the house of Jacob, and princes of Israel, that abhor judgment and pervert all justice, who build up Zion with blood, and Jerusalem with iniquity; her chiefs judge for reward, and her priests teach for hire, and her prophets divine for money."

Then turning towards the people and the statesmen, he pathetically described their base selfishness and the utter absence of all honesty and truth: "The good man has perished out of the land, and there is none upright among men; they all lie in wait for blood, they lay nets every man against his brother; they have hands for evil to do it well; the prince asks a bribe, and the judge judges for reward, and the great man utters the lust of his mind; and thus they plan it. The best of them is like a brier, the most upright is sharper than a thorn hedge.... Trust not in a friend; put no confidence in a companion; keep the gates of thy mouth shut from the wife of thy bosom." The very ties of nature were disregarded: "For the son despises the father, the daughter rises up against the mother, the daughter-in-law against her mother-in-law, a man's enemies are the men of his own house."

This picture is indeed sad enough; but it is free from those vehement denunciations which render the reproof of Hosea almost appalling. For the anger of Micah is constantly tempered by his natural buoyancy of hope and trust: "I will look to the Lord, I will wait for the God of my salvation, my God will hear me."

Nevertheless a just retribution was announced to the disobedient nation: "For, behold, the Lord comes forth out of His abode, and comes down, and treads upon the high places of the earth ... I will make Samaria as a heap of the field, and as plantings of a vineyard, and I will pour down the stones thereof into the valley, and I will lay bare the foundations thereof. Thus says the Lord, Behold, against this family do I devise an evil, from which you shall not remove your necks, nor shall you go haughtily, for that time shall be an evil one." — Like so many other prophets, he looked upon the powerful Assyrian, that terrible scourge before which all Asia trembled, as the instrument of God's punishment. He was probably informed of the enemy's alarming designs upon his ill-organised country, when he uttered the following words: "Now, why dost thou cry out aloud? is there no king in thee? or have thy counsellors perished? Tremble, O daughter of Zion, for now thou shalt go forth out of the city, and thou shalt dwell in the field, and thou shalt wander even to Babylon!" — But the announcement of desolation did not constitute the chief burden of his speeches. He desired to guide the people by hope and encouragement rather than by fear and menace; therefore, he did not dwell long upon their impending calamities; but he held out glad promises of deliverance. He foretold indeed the Assyrian conquest, but he added that even in Babylon would God save them from the hands of their enemies; and rapidly passing from a scene of distress to one of the highest felicity, he described a future rich in all worldly blessings, but more glorious still by the fulfilment of all spiritual hopes; and he declared that its effects would be visible not only in the greatness of Israel, but in the peace and love that would unite all nations: "In the last days it shall come to pass that the mountain of the House of the Lord shall be established in the top of the mountains, and it shall be exalted above the hills; and people shall flow to it. And many nations shall come and say, Come, let us go up to the mountain of the Lord, and to the House of the God of Jacob, and He will teach us His ways, and we will walk in His paths; for the Law shall go forth of Zion, and the word of the Lord from Jerusalem. And He shall judge among many people, and direct numerous nations afar off, and they shall beat their swords into ploughshares, and their spears into pruning hooks; nation shall not lift up a sword against nation; neither shall they learn war any more."

Glad tidings were especially announced to the little town Bethlehem-Ephrathah, David's birth-place, in which should be born the deliverer destined to restore, and for ever to secure Israel's power, to subdue all enemies, and to spread the greatest blessings over the whole earth: "But thou Bethlehem-Ephrathah, though thou be little among the thousands of Judah, yet out of thee shall he come forth that is to be ruler in Israel; whose origin has been from of old, from primeval days. Therefore will He give them up until the time that she who travails has brought forth: then the remnant of his brethren shall return to the children of Israel. And he shall stand and feed in the strength of the Lord, in the majesty of the name of the Lord his God; and they shall abide; for then shall he be great unto the ends of the earth. And this man shall be the peace, when the Assyrian shall come into our land; and when he shall tread in our palaces, then shall we raise against him seven shepherds, and eight chiefs. And they shall waste the land of Assyria with the sword, and the land of Nimrod in the entrances thereof: thus shall he deliver us from the Assyrian, when he comes into our land, and when he treads within our borders. And the remnant of Jacob shall be in the midst of many people as a dew from the Lord, as the showers upon the grass, that tarries not for man, nor waits for the sons of men."

But in unfolding this splendid picture of the future, the prophet showed more clearly the gulf which separated it from the dreary present, and he had recourse to a stirring form of rhetoric to urge the people to repentance: he summons the hills and mountains of the earth to listen to the appeal which the Lord was addressing to His people: "O

My people, what have I done to thee, and wherein have I wearied thee? testify against Me. For I brought thee up out of the land of Egypt, and redeemed thee out of the house of bondage; and I sent before thee Moses, Aaron, and Miriam. O, My people, remember now what Balak, king of Moab, designed, and what Balaam, the son of Beor, answered him; remember the march from Shittim to Gilgal, that you may know the mercies of the Lord."

And what do the people reply to these accusations so lenient in form, yet so emphatic? With ill-repressed irritation they exclaim: "Wherewith shall I come before the Lord, and bow down before the high God? shall I come before Him with burnt-offerings, with calves of a year old? Will the Lord be pleased with thousands of rams, or with ten thousands of rivers of oil? shall I give my firstborn for my transgression, the fruit of my body for the sin of my soul?" But the prophet answers with calmness, and propounds a universal code of religion in the following words: "He has shown thee, O man, what is good: and what does the Lord require of thee but to do justice, and to love mercy, and to walk humbly with thy God?"

How far was his heedless and ungrateful generation removed from this ideal! For "the statutes of Omri were kept, and all the works of the house of Ahab;" and righteousness and piety had vanished from the land. "Woe to me," cried the prophet, "for I am, as when they have gathered the summer fruits, as the grape-gleaning of the vintage: there is no cluster to eat, no firstripe fig for which my soul desires." He saw that the safety and happiness of the people were more and more endangered. He had little faith in their repentance; for a survey of their conduct during past ages almost extinguished every hope of their amendment; yet he did not give vent to bitter invectives or to desponding lamentations. Though he did not expect any decided change in their actions, he believed in God's unalterable mercy and compassion, upon which he dwelt with great emphasis. "Who is a God like Thee, that pardons iniquity, and passes by the transgression of the remnant of His heritage? He retains not His anger for ever, because He delights in mercy. He will again have compassion upon us; He will subdue our iniquities, and Thou wilt cast all their sins into the depth of the sea. Thou wilt show truth to Jacob, and mercy to Abraham, as Thou hast sworn our fathers from the days of old."

The individuality of Micah is more concealed from us than that of most of the prophets, and we have no records of his life and career. Though he alludes to national events of great moment, he connects them principally with the moral condition of the nation. He never offers advice to direct the troubled commonwealth or to ward off foreign danger. Even the beautiful doctrines with which his work is replete, are not set forth with the authority of a public instructor, but inobtrusively diffused over his pages.

Micah addressed special orations to the Hebrews, in which he suggested to them words of repentance and supplication. His work is chiefly composed in the form of a dialogue; and even when the subject renders that form impossible, his style is dramatic and full of vivacity and power. His writings bear a strong resemblance to those of his contemporaries Hosea and Isaiah. The rapid succession of subjects, and the sudden transitions from the present to the future, and from real life to the scenes conjured up by a fervent patriotism, remind the reader of the same peculiarities in Hosea; and a remarkable combination of energy and gentle forbearance exhibits a still greater affinity to the prophet Isaiah; not only are they akin to each other in the humane and universal principles which they enforce, but in the moral elevation of their addresses, and the consummate refinement of their style. Micah, like Isaiah, had recourse to the arts of rhetoric to lend an additional charm to his orations; nor did he disdain those conceits of sound and language which never fail to captivate the Oriental ear. The closing description of a happy future belongs to the most finished productions of Hebrew poetry, to which a translation can hardly do justice: "Therefore I will hope for the Lord; I will wait for the God of my salvation; my God will hear me. — Rejoice not against me, O my enemy: when I fall, I shall rise; when I sit in darkness, the Lord shall be my light. I will bear the indignation of the Lord, because I have sinned against Him, until He plead my cause, and execute judgment for me: He will bring me forth to the light, and I shall behold His righteousness. Then she that is my enemy shall see it, and shame shall cover her who said to me, Where is the Lord thy God? My eyes shall behold her; then shall she be trodden down as the mire of the streets. A day comes when thy walls shall be built; in that day shall the boundary be far removed: in that day they shall come to thee from Assyria and the cities of Egypt and from Egypt to the Euphrates, and from sea to sea and from mountain to mountain. But first the land shall be desolate on account of its inhabitants, for the fruit of their deeds. Feed thy people with thy rod, the flock of thy heritage, which dwells in solitude in the wood, in the midst of Carmel: let them feed in Bashan and Gilead, as in the days of old. 'As in the days of thy coming out of the land of Egypt will I show thee marvellous things.' — The nations shall see and be confounded at all their might: they shall lay their hand upon their mouth, their ears shall be deafened. They shall lick the dust like a serpent, they shall move out of their holes like worms of the earth, and tremble forth from their castles; they shall come in fear to the Lord our God, and shall be afraid of thee."

But a spirit of quiet hopefulness softens the edge of Micah's terrible predictions; and by laying down the means by which it may be attained, his ideal of a golden future is brought within reach of all mankind.

VI. NAHUM. (710.)

The orations of the prophet Nahum present, in one particular at least, a striking contrast to most of the other prophetic utterances. These generally describe the trials and the desolation about to fall upon the Holy Land, and they convey remonstrances mingled with solemn advice, or threats of punishment and disgrace. Not so the writings of Nahum. Called forth during one of those rare periods when brighter prospects seemed to dawn upon the fortunes of the Hebrews, they announce the doom of a powerful foe and the deliverance of Israel; indeed they almost bear the character of songs of praise and thanksgiving.

Of Nahum's life we know nothing except the fact that he was an "Elkoshite", that is, a native of the town of Elkosh, the situation of which is doubtful; he is never mentioned in the historical Books; and he is associated only with one great event, on which he commented with equal grace and power. Personally, therefore, he can not awaken the deep interest inspired by those whose labours lay in the sphere of public life. Nor can he, as far as we can judge, be called an instructor of the people, in the same sense as Isaiah, Jeremiah, or Micah; he did not attempt to guide the state, to cheer the failing courage of his countrymen, or to reprove the dangerous pertinacity and blindness of their leaders; and although he dwelt upon an event of the utmost political importance for his own people, he was more directly concerned with the errors and the fate of a foreign empire.

A few years only had elapsed since Micah had lamented and rebuked the sins of the Hebrews; but these few years formed no unimportant portion of king Hezekiah's long and eventful reign; for the lowering clouds that had menaced the horizon had burst and caused a terrible storm. The people of Judah had witnessed a catastrophe which, though long predicted and apparently inevitable, had been wilfully ignored. They had seen with dismay the invasion and conquest of the sister kingdom of Ephraim by the Assyrian monarch Shalmanassar. But they were soon to have themselves a direct cause of alarm. For in the fifteenth year of Hezekiah's rule, Sennacherib, the successor of the conqueror, whose glory he emulated, made an unopposed entry into the territory of Judah. The strong and fenced cities surrendered to his invincible forces; and fear and terror preceded him to the very gates of the capital. But when the danger assumed so threatening a form, when rescue seemed impossible, and the most fearful misfortune was imminent, the miraculous destruction of Sennacherib's army, filling all minds at once with amazement and exultation, created an instantaneous revulsion of feeling. The vague anticipations of a sanguinary and hopeless war, of ruin and captivity, gave suddenly way to the certainty of deliverance from an insatiable and apparently all-powerful enemy.

It was the happy task of the prophet Nahum to expatiate on this great theme, to portray in his own glowing colours the gratitude and the joy which must have filled the heart of every inhabitant of Judah, and to point out the Divine retribution which had crushed the daring Assyrians; for the Medes also, undaunted and aspiring, revolted against their rule, and declared their independence under their just and wise king Dejoces.

These striking events were highly suggestive to the poet, the patriot, and the prophet. In the rescue of his people, Nahum saw a guarantee of their peace and power; while the misfortunes of the invaders appeared to him the beginning of a chastisement which would fill the world with awe and consternation.

The Book commences with a grand hymn of thanksgiving admirably interpreting the feelings which must have thrilled through every breast: "A zealous God and an avenger is the Lord, an avenger is the Lord and full of wrath, an avenger is the Lord to His adversaries, and He keeps His anger against His enemies. The Lord is slow to anger and great in power, and never acquits the wicked; the Lord has His way in the whirlwind and in the storm, and the clouds are dust of His feet. He rebukes the sea and makes it dry, and parches up all the rivers. Bashan languishes, and Carmel, and the flower of Lebanon languishes. The mountains quake before Him, and the hills melt, and the earth is lifted up at His presence, yea, the world and all that dwell therein. Who can stand before His indignation, and who can abide the fierceness of His anger? His wrath is poured out like fire, and the rocks are hurled down by Him. The Lord is good, a refuge in the day of trouble, and He loves those that trust in Him. But with a rushing flood He brings destruction to their abode, and darkness pursues His enemies. — What do you (Assyrians) meditate against the Lord? He brings ruin; the affliction shall not rise up a second time. For entwined like thorns, and as if drunk by their drink, they are consumed fully as dry stubbles. There came out of thee (Nineveh) one that imagined evil against the Lord, a wicked counsellor. — Thus says the Lord, though they be in full numbers, and also many, yet thus they shall be cut down, and it is done with them; and though I afflicted thee (Judah), I will afflict thee no more. For now I will break his yoke from thee, and will tear thy bonds asunder; but concerning thee (the Assyrian), the Lord has commanded, that no more of thy name be sown; out of the house of thy god I will cut off the graven and the molten images; I will make thy grave, for thou art despised. Behold upon the mountains the feet of the messenger who brings good tidings, who declares peace! O Judah, keep thy solemn feasts, perform thy vows, for the wicked shall no more pass through thee — he is utterly cut off."

These last words introduce the main subject of the Book — the destruction of Nineveh, which the prophet predicts as the inevitable sequel of Sennacherib's fatal expedition against the chosen people. He feels that God's wrath was not exhausted in the terrible defeat caused by no human hands, aided by no human skill. His indignation rises; his words become more pointed and more ominous; and he thus describes the fall and plunder of Nineveh: "The destroyer marches on against thee (Nineveh): keep the fortress, watch the way, gird thy loins, strengthen thy power mightily . . . . . He recounts his heroes; they stumble in their walk; they hasten to the wall; but the defence is prepared. The gates of the rivers are opened, and the palace shall be dissolved. And it is decreed — she (Assyria) shall be led into captivity, and she shall be taken away, and her servants shall mourn like the voice of doves, beating their breasts. Yet Nineveh was (full of men) like a pond full of water from the time of her existence; but they flee: 'Stand, stand!' Yet no one turns back. Take the spoil of silver, take the spoil of gold: there is no end of the treasures, abundance of all precious vessels. She is empty, and void, and waste, and her heart melts, and her knees totter, and pain is in her whole loins, and the faces of all lose their brightness. Where is (now) the lair of the lions, and the pasture of the young lions, whither the lion, the lioness, and the lion's whelp went, while no one threatened them? The lion made prey for his whelps, and strangled for his lionesses, and filled his dens with prey, and his caves with booty. Behold, I come against thee, says the Lord of hosts, and I will consume thy chariots in smoke, and the sword shall devour thy young lions, and I will cut off thy prey from the earth, and the voice of thy messengers shall no more be heard ... The noise of the whip, and the noise of rattling wheels and prancing horses and bounding chariots! Horsemen approaching, and the flame of the sword and the lightning of the spear, and a multitude of slain, and a pile of carcasses! And there is no end of corpses; they stumble upon their corpses .... And whoever sees thee, shall flee from thee, and say, 'Nineveh is laid waste, who will bemoan her? whence shall I seek comforters for thee?'"

Nineveh's fall was indeed a mournful catastrophe; yet it was fully deserved by the crimes and the corruption which had preceded it. The impious invasion of the sacred soil by the Assyrians was one of the many proofs of their presumption and covetousness, and of their cruelty to less powerful nations. "Woe to the bloody city," exclaimed the prophet, "it is all full of lies and robbery; it desists not from plunder." The proud city of Thebes had already experienced the fate which Nahum anticipated for Nineveh. The waves that formed a rampart around her, could not protect her; the help of Egypt was futile and unavailing; for in spite of many alliances "she was carried away, she went into captivity, her young children were dashed in pieces at the corners of the streets, and they cast lots for her honoured men, and all her chiefs were bound in chains." Such was to be the destiny of Nineveh. "Thou also," the prophet declared, "shalt be inebriated, and shalt hide thyself, thou also shalt seek refuge before the enemy ... Draw for thyself water for the siege, fortify thy stronghold; step upon the clay, and tread the mortar, repair the brick-kiln. There shall the fire devour thee, the sword shall cut thee off, it shall consume thee like a cankerworm." — The wealth and influence of the Assyrians were indeed great, but their leaders would be powerless in the day of desolation: "Thou hast multiplied thy merchants above the stars of heaven; ... thy crowned are as the locusts, and thy captains as the swarms of grasshoppers, that camp in the hedges in the cold season, but when the sun arises, they flee away, and their place is not known where they are."

The Assyrians were not merely to suffer severe losses, but they were to be partially exterminated, and their former greatness and power forgotten. "Thy shepherds slumber, O king of Assyria, thy nobles are at rest, thy people is scattered upon the mountains, and no man gathers them ... There is no healing of thy bruise, thy wound is deadly. All that hear the report of thee, shall clap their hands over thee; for upon whom has not thy wickedness passed continually?"

This conclusion aptly conveys the prophet's object, and illustrates the Divine justice which never fails to vindicate the wrongs of the oppressed and to humble the pride of the arrogant. This idea pervades the whole work, which chronicles the glory of God and the triumph of His faithful servants, as well as the fall of a political foe; and although treating of an event of paramount worldly importance, Nahum, unlike his great contemporary Isaiah, never comes forward as a statesman, weighing political details or calculating human influences. Therefore, in a purely religious point of view, the orations of Nahum are of singular interest, setting forth God's power and justice with the utmost earnestness and dignity. They are distinguished by a unity of thought and expression, not easily attainable in works which embrace a variety of events, or refer to different epochs.

The language is always adapted to the subject, and it exhibits a rare intensity of feeling and great elevation of thought. Brilliant imagery adorns the hymn of thanksgiving; and Nineveh's doom is announced in accents of awe-stirring solemnity.

VII. ZEPHANIAH. (640.)

The reign of Hezekiah, memorable as it proved for the political history of Judah, was even more important in the annals of prophecy. It was distinguished by a bright constellation of those great men, who elevated their age and immortalised their nation; but it was followed by a long period of idolatry and moral degeneracy, during which no inspired voice seems to have been raised.

The first heralds of the return of a better time were the utterances of the prophet Zephaniah. Not that the influence of many years of wickedness had already yielded to a happier dawn and a purer light; for the baneful and protracted reign of Manasseh, standing out in sad contrast to that of the pious king Hezekiah, and the equally iniquitous, though short, rule of his son Amon, had inflicted upon the nation deadly wounds that could not so easily be healed. But the throne which Amon had desecrated, and which was vacated by his violent death, was left to his son Josiah, who was destined once more to raise and to restore it to its ancient honour. It was in the earlier part of Josiah's reign that Zephaniah prophesied; and his efforts may have contributed to stimulate the pious young king to those religious reforms which secured the stability of Mosaism for ever. His indignant invectives were hurled against a depraved people, long left to their own unchecked recklessness, as well as against those who should have been their guides and instructors. They reflect a time of anarchy and violence, when no Divine or human authority had the power of restraining licentiousness and idolatry. They dwell on that ever fruitful theme of prophetic eloquence — the punishment of the people for sins committed during generations with revolting pertinacity. He predicted to the rebellious community a complete and universal doom, which would embrace the king on his throne, the nobles in their palaces, and the merchants in their abodes of wealth and luxury — in fact, all those who with mocking incredulity had exclaimed, "The Lord will not do good, neither will He do evil." He announced this doom in decisive, though somewhat general terms: "I will utterly destroy all things from off the land, says the Lord. I will destroy man and beast, destroy the fowls of the heaven, and the fishes of the sea, and the ruined houses with the wicked; and I will cut off man from the face of the earth, says the Lord. And I will stretch out My hand upon Judah, and upon all the inhabitants of Jerusalem; and I will cut off the remnant of Baal from this place, and the name of the ministers of the idols with the priests, and those who worship the host of heaven on the roofs, and who worship and swear by the Lord, and swear also by their idol, and those who have turned back from the Lord, nor seek the Lord, nor search after Him. Silence in the presence of the Lord God! for the day of the Lord is at hand: for the Lord has prepared a sacrifice, He has sanctified His guests. And in the day of the Lord's sacrifice, I will punish the princes and the king's children, and all that are clothed with foreign apparel.... Their wealth shall become a booty, and their houses a desolation; they build houses, but do not inhabit them; and they plant vineyards, but do not drink the wine thereof." —

He then made an allusion to some dreaded event, though its interpretation remains a matter of conjecture. The source of alarm to which he referred was most probably the danger which was then threatening Judea either from the invasion of the Chaldeans or of the hordes of Scythians, whose thirst for adventure and rapine spread terror far and wide; for those ravaging tribes were looked upon as the instruments of God's vengeance, and the scourge appointed by Him to punish the Hebrews for their wickedness and disobedience: "The great day of the Lord is near, it is near, and hastens greatly; the day of the Lord calls aloud; then the hero cries bitterly. That day is a day of wrath, a day of trouble and distress, a day of destruction and desolation, a day of darkness and gloom, a day of clouds and black shadows, a day of the trumpet and alarm against the fenced cities, and against the high towers. And I will bring anguish upon men, that they shall walk like blind men, because they have sinned against the Lord; and their blood shall be poured out as dust, and their flesh as the dung. Neither their silver nor their gold shall be able to deliver them in the day of the Lord's wrath; and the whole land shall be devoured by the fire of His zeal: for He will annihilate, nay crush suddenly all the inhabitants of the land."

Predicting misfortune as the inevitable result of sins, Zephaniah hardly mitigated the dread announcement by an expression of hope or encouragement. Yet he could not refrain from a word of advice deeply felt but diffidently uttered, and he urged upon all that it still lay in their own power somewhat to shield themselves from the impending calamities: "Assemble, yea assemble, O shameless nation, before His decree matures — like chaff passes the time — before the fierce anger of the Lord comes upon you, before the day of the Lord's anger comes upon you. Seek the Lord, all ye meek of the earth, who exercise His judgment; seek righteousness, seek meekness: perhaps you may be protected in the day of the Lord's anger."

But he promised no happier fate to the heathen nations which had taken up arms against the people of the Lord, and which, ever restless and aggressive, had alternately triumphed over the Hebrews and succumbed to their valour. The Philistines, the Moabites, and the Ammonites trembled no less than the Jews before the invading hosts; nor should the two greatest countries, Egypt and Assyria, those strongholds of ancient idolatry, escape the general desolation. "For Gaza shall be forsaken and Ashkelon be a waste: Ashdod shall be driven out at the noon-day, and Ekron shall be uprooted.... I have heard the taunt of Moab, and the revilings of the children of Ammon, wherewith they taunted My people, and rose up against their boundaries. Therefore, as I live, says the Lord of hosts, the God of Israel, surely Moab shall be as Sodom, and the children of Ammon as Gomorrah, a breeding-place of nettles, and salt pits, and a perpetual desolation: the remnant of My people shall spoil them, and the residue of My nation shall possess them..... Ye Ethiopians also, you shall be slain by My sword. And He stretches out His hand against the north and destroys Assyria, and makes Nineveh a desolation, and parched up like a wilderness.... This is the exulting city that dwells carelessly, that says in her heart, I am, and there is none beside me: how is she become a desolation, a den for beasts! every one that passes by her hisses, and waves his hand."

Then the prophet returns to his chief subject — his own people. His language becomes more vivid and more forcible, as he dwells upon their fatal wickedness, and unfolds a picture full of gloom and despair: "Woe to her that is refractory and polluted, to the city of oppression. She obeys no voice; she accepts not correction; she trusts not in the Lord; she draws not near to her God. Her princes within her are roaring lions, her judges evening wolves that save nothing till the morrow; her prophets are boasters and traitors, her priests pollute the Sanctuary, and do violence to the Law."

But although he repeatedly described the awful trials that awaited the people, he also assured them of the efficacy of repentance, and promised that after years of varied fortunes, of ruin, and degradation, peace and happiness were certain to return. These good tidings were not intended for the listless multitude, but for the virtuous few, who by strenuous efforts would escape the general calamity — for the remnant of the nation, small indeed and poor, bereft of land and honours, yet richer than their proud ancestors by their trust in God and by their moral strength. "The residue of Israel shall not do iniquity nor speak lies, nor shall a deceitful tongue be found in their mouth; for they shall feed and lay down, and none shall make them afraid." In contemplating this happy prospect, the prophet forgets all the misery and shame of the past. "Sing, O daughter of Zion, shout, O Israel; be glad and rejoice with all thy heart, O daughter of Jerusalem. The Lord has removed thy judgments, He has cast out thy enemy, the Lord is the King of Israel in the midst of thee: thou shalt not see evil any more." The power of God had been felt by His wrath; but in the expected time of happiness it should be known by His boundless love. "The Lord thy God in the midst of thee is mighty; He will save, He will be jubilant over thee with joy, He will be silent in His mercy, He will rejoice over thee with gladness." To crown this felicity, even those members of God's people who had been scattered among foreign nations, would be restored to their native soil, and live in comfort and honour. Thus the last utterances of the prophet are messages of cheerfulness and hope.

Though these themes may have suggested sublimer flights of oratory, the style of Zephaniah is not deficient in impressiveness and dignity. His descriptions of terror and desolation do not reach the truth and pathos of Isaiah or Hosea, and his more peaceful pictures fall short of the poetical beauty of Amos; yet he succeeds in conveying the indignation, the fear, and the hope, that alternately pervaded his mind. Here and there a well-known burden of Isaiah or of Joel meets the ear; and though it would be too much to assert that Zephaniah's orations are essentially reproductions of earlier authors, they show few traces of a striking originality; they contain no new ideas on the attributes of God or the destinies of His people; but they are confined to the narrow circle of passing events.

VIII. HABAKKUK. (610.)

The name of the prophet Habakkuk is never mentioned in the historical records of Judah, and is only preserved to us through his own writings. But these reveal a soul so sublime, a character so pure, and a genius so lofty, that we would fain know more of his life and personal influence. Tradition has endeavoured to fill up the deficiency; but the legends relating to him are fanciful and unreliable.

It is easy to infer from the prophecies of Habakkuk the events by which they were called forth. Impregnated by an atmosphere of despondency and sorrow, they were evidently composed in dark and troubled times; and their sad forebodings are relieved by no anticipations of happiness. Even if we had no other and more direct evidence, this tone of Habakkuk's writings would suggest that he was the immediate predecessor of Jeremiah. Yet his grief is less bitter, and his lamentations are less mournful; for he watched only the approach of those events, the reality of which Jeremiah witnessed and bewailed. The picture which he draws both of the moral and political condition of his time points to the reign of Jehoiakim (611 — 599) — a period when the much-tried people saw their misfortunes rapidly thickening, and when, enfeebled by the severe taxation of an unscrupulous monarch, they heard of the successful inroads of the wild and rapacious Chaldeans. With the deepest grief Habakkuk alludes to the unopposed progress of the enemy; and roused by the imminent danger which threatened the people, he exclaims: "O Lord, how long have I cried, and Thou wilt not hear! I cry to Thee of violence and Thou wilt not save!" On all occasions he discloses the depth and energy of his great nature; predictions of evil and indignant remonstrance are wrung from him by a painful struggle; and they are generally coupled with expressions of grief both at the people's sins and their misfortunes.

He manifests, at the very outset, a disinclination to comment upon those failings which his mission made it his duty to rebuke. "Why," he cries, "dost Thou show iniquity, and cause me to behold misery? for oppression and violence are before me, and strife arises, and contention is kindled." From the signal triumphs of the wicked he apprehends an ascendency of vice and scepticism concerning the justice of God: "Therefore the law languishes, and judgment does not go out for truth; for the impious encompasses the righteous, therefore judgment goes forth perverted." Then he describes the invading Chaldeans with a pith and power rarely excelled: "Behold among the nations and regard, and marvel marvellously! For I will work a work in your days, which you will not believe if it be told you. For behold, I raise up the Chaldeans, that fierce and nimble nation, which marches to distant lands to take possession of abodes that are not theirs. They are awful and formidable, their judgment and their glory proceed of themselves. And their horses are swifter than leopards, and quicker than the evening wolves, and their horsemen dash along, and their horsemen come from afar, and fly as the eagle that hastens to his prey. They come all for violence; they rush onward to the east, and they gather captives as the sand. And they scoff at the kings, and the princes are a scorn to them; they scorn every stronghold, they heap up earth and conquer it. Then they pass along like a storm, and march on, and are guilty — they who make their power their god." — The prophet appears to recoil from the harrowing vividness of his own words; for a moment a glimmering of hope crosses his mind; he cannot believe that the destruction of his people by such foes has indeed been decreed. This hope is not inspired by patriotism alone; it is suggested by that moral problem which at all times engaged pious and enquiring minds: for he finds it difficult to associate reckless violence and bloodshed with agencies of Divine Providence. Full of faith and trust in the merciful attributes of God, he cannot persuade himself, that the triumphs of unscrupulous ravagers are final and lasting. He knows too well the measure of his people's sins, and he is certain that they cannot escape Divine punishment; but he knows also that their cruel enemies are infinitely more iniquitous; should they, he asks, not in a spirit of bitterness but of sorrow, be chosen as the scourges of retribution? "Art Thou not from primeval times, O Lord my God, my Holy One? We shall not die. O Lord, Thou hast ordained them for judgment; and O Rock, Thou hast decreed them for correction. Thy eyes are too pure to look upon evil, and Thou canst not behold iniquity: wherefore dost Thou behold the traitors, and art silent when the wicked devours the more righteous, and makes men as the fishes of the sea, as the creeping things that have no ruler over them? He lifts up everything with the angle, draws it out with his net, and gathers it in with his drag; and they rejoice and exult. Therefore he offers sacrifices to his net, and burns incense to his drag, because by them their prey is fat and their food abundant. Shall he therefore empty his net, and massacre nations continually without mercy?"

A long interval may have elapsed before the answer to this often-repeated question was suggested to the prophet; he may have read in the signs of the times the coming events which were to calm his doubts and his conflicting thoughts; certain it is that in some measure his gloomy despair gave way, and that from the high eminence of his wisdom and faith, he looked with new hope upon the vindication of the ways of God at an appointed and not far distant time, when the just would be rewarded and the wicked of all nations would meet with well-merited punishment. He patiently waited for the heavenly missive: it came at last, and it came in words of such sublimity, of such truth and grandeur, that all doubts were silenced: "I will stand upon my watch-tower, and place myself on the height, and I will look out to see, what He will say to me, and what answer I shall receive to my lament. And the Lord answered me, and said, Write down the vision, and engrave it upon the tablets, that it may be read fluently. For still the vision points to a distant time, yet it hastens on to the end, and deceives not; though it tarry, wait for it, for it will surely come, it will not fail to come. — Behold, his soul is inflated, it is not upright in him: but the just shall live by his faith. Yea the wine also makes treacherous, the man is made reckless and cannot rest, he enlarges his desires as the grave, and he is like death and cannot be satisfied, and gathers to himself all nations, and collects together all people. Will not all these pronounce a taunt and a mocking sneer against him, and say: Woe to him who piled up what was not his — how long? — and who loaded himself with a burden of guilt! Will not suddenly rise up those that pay tribute to thee? Will not those rise who shall expel thee? And thou shalt be a booty to them, because thou hast spoilt many nations, all the remnant of the people shall spoil thee on account of man's blood and of the violence done to the land, the town, and all its inhabitants. — Woe to him that covets the evil gain of the covetous for his house, that he may set his nest on high, that he may save himself from the hand of the wicked! Thou hast devised shame for thy house by cutting off many people, and hast brought guilt upon thy soul. For the stone cries out of the wall, and the beam out of the timber answers it. — Woe to him that builds towns with blood, and founds cities by iniquity! Behold, it is decreed by the Lord of hosts, that nations shall labour for the fire, and the people shall toil for nothing. For the earth shall be filled with the knowledge of the glory of the Lord, as the water covers the sea... The cup in the Lord's right hand will be turned against thee, and disgrace shall fall upon thy glory. For the violence of the Lebanon shall cover thee, and the destruction of the beasts which terrified them, on account of man's blood and of the violence done to the land, the town, and all its inhabitants."

In such language the prophet describes the judgment of God against cruel oppressors. To enhance the effect of the picture by contrast, he adds a few words deriding the impotence of the idols, on whose protection the invaders relied: "What does the graven image avail, that the maker thereof has graven it? the molten image and the teacher of lies, that the maker of his work trusts therein, making dumb idols? Woe to him that says to the wood, Awake; to the dumb stone, Arise. Shall it teach? Behold it is set with gold and silver, and there is no breath at all within it! But the Lord is in His holy Temple. Silence before Him, all the world!"

Once again the scene is changed; Habakkuk is no more the chronicler of political events; and his language, no longer vague and oracular, conveys his innermost feelings with fervent enthusiasm. He chose in this concluding portion the form of prayer unusual in prophetic works; for he evidently desired to give vent to his own feelings, rather than to compose a public address. Remembering the guilt of his countrymen and of their heathen enemies, and reflecting on the deserved punishment of both, he prays with trembling lips: "O Lord, I have heard Thy report, and am afraid: O Lord, achieve Thy work within years; within years make it known: in wrath remember mercy." Then leaving his immediate theme, he describes in a few words the miracles wrought by God on behalf of Israel at the time of their deliverance from Egypt — the consternation of their proud foes, the drying up of the sea, the revelation of God on Sinai, and the other marvellous events of that time. In this survey, which combines the glow of the poet and the elevation of the prophet with the patriot's earnestness, Habakkuk approaches the genius of Isaiah, while in fervour and in aptness of similes he is equal to the most gifted of the Psalmists. He dwells upon God's greatness and anger not with the unadorned plainness of Zephaniah, nor with the terror-inspiring sternness of Hosea; but he breathes into his words that deep regret and pathos which pervade the strains of Jeremiah, and infuses into them the power and the spirit of a war song:

"God came from Teman, and the Holy One from Mount

Paran. [Selah.] His glory covered the heavens and the earth was full of His praise. And His brightness was like the light of sun, rays beamed forth from His hand, and there was the veil of His majesty. Before Him went pestilence, and consuming plagues came before His feet; He stood and measured the earth, and made the nations tremble; and the everlasting mountains were scattered, the perpetual hills were bent low; He went His eternal ways. I saw the tents of Cushan in affliction, and the curtains of the land of Midian trembled. Was the Lord wroth against the streams? was Thy anger against streams, was Thy wrath against the sea, that Thou didst ride along upon Thy horses and Thy chariots of victory? Thy bow was bare and unsheathed, the arrows were satisfied. [Song of triumph. Selah.] Thou didst cleave the earth with rivers; the mountains saw Thee and trembled, a flood of water rushed by; the deep uttered its voice, and lifted up its hands on high. The sun and moon stood still in their habitation, like the light went Thy arrows, and like splendour Thy glittering spear."

Why did the prophet recall these wondrous scenes? The Chaldeans were no less dangerous to the Hebrews in his time, than the Egyptians of old had been to their ancestors: would God show the same mercy to His people, and punish their enemies with the same rigour, in order to glorify His own name and truth? The prophet is full of confidence, for he sees the signs of approaching deliverance.

"Thou marchest through the land in indignation, Thou crushest the nations in anger: Thou goest forth for the salvation of Thy people; for the salvation of Thy anointed Thou dashest to pieces the head of the race of the wicked, laying bare foundations high up to the neck. [Selah.] Thou piercest with his spears the head of his leaders, who storm along to scatter us, whose delight it is to devour the poor in an ambush. Thou treadest the sea with Thy horses, the mire of great waters."

Yet he knows that the Hebrews must first suffer misery, want, and oppression; and he is full of sorrow when he thinks of these bitter trials that await his people. "I heard it," he exclaims, "and my body trembled, my lips quivered at the voice, rottenness entered into my bones, and my knees trembled that I must look forward quietly to the day of trouble, to the approach of the people that presses upon us. For the fig-tree shall not blossom, nor the vines yield produce, the crop of the olive shall fail, and the fields bring forth no food; the flock will be cut off from the fold, and there shall be no ox in the stalls."

But he is sure that the day of redemption will come, and he is firm in his hope and confidence. He silences all doubts and dismisses all evil foreboding, and he preserves his calmness and resignation: "Yet I will rejoice in the Lord, I will exult in the God of my salvation. The Lord is my strength, and He will make my feet like the hind's, and He will cause me to walk upon my heights."

There can be little doubt as to the place which Habakkuk occupies among the Hebrew prophets. In depth of feeling and largeness of sympathies, he resembles Jeremiah; while in vigour of thought and pithy expression, he rivals the greatest masters of Hebrew song. He combines the past, the present, and the future into one grand historical picture, and indeed by his immortal work he has in no slight degree contributed to the glory of that people for which he alternately trembled and hoped.

IX. OBADIAH. (About 580.)

Between the two Books of Amos and Jonah, our Canon has placed the vision of Obadiah. We are left in complete ignorance with regard to the life of the author, from whose hand one solitary oration has been transmitted to us. But tradition has endeavoured to associate him with several familiar events of Jewish history. It was variously suggested that he was a disciple of Elijah, and a leader in the army of Ahab; or the husband of the poor woman, whose cruse of oil was miraculously replenished by Elisha. However, as in the case of Habakkuk, Zephaniah, and others, his writings alone can help to dispel the mystery which veils his life, and they lead us to conclude that he lived during the Babylonian captivity and in the distant land of exile. At this period of Jewish history, when the prophet could no more rouse the warrior or counsel the statesman, remembrance and hope were left as the only themes of his eloquence; and it is natural that his mind should have reverted to those nations, with which the Hebrews had so often been brought into hostile contact. Among these tribes the Edomites were the most conspicuous. They had from very early times displayed a hatred to the Hebrews, which gradually increased into fierce enmity, and at last, when Jerusalem fell, gave rise to ungenerous exultation. Obadiah, whose affections clung to the home of his fathers, looked on their conduct with indignation. He declared that in spite of their vaunted power they would not be able to escape destruction. He described their callous unconcern, which arose from their belief that they were secure within their rock-encompassed fastnesses, doubly shielded by their cunning and worldly wisdom, for which qualities they had become proverbial. But all their advantages would be unavailing against the wrath of God, which they had provoked by their cruelty. "The pride of thy heart", said the prophet, "has deceived thee, thou that dwellest in the clefts of the rocks, whose habitation is high, that says in his heart, 'Who shall bring me down to the ground?' Though thou exalt thyself as the eagle, and though thou set thy nest among the stars, thence will I bring thee down, says the Lord... Shall I not in that day, says the Lord, destroy the wise men out of Edom, and understanding out of the mount of Esau?" — Such was to be their punishment, because, after the capture of Jerusalem, they had shared the spoil with the invader, and had delivered up the fugitives to slaughter. "For thy violence against thy brother Jacob shame shall cover thee, and thou shalt be cut off for ever. In the day that thou stoodest by, in the day that the strangers carried away captive his army, and foreigners entered into his gates, and cast lots upon Jerusalem, thou also wast as one of them. Yet do not look with delight at the judgment-day of thy brother, at the day of his misery; rejoice not over the children of Judah in the time of their ruin; do not talk proudly in the time of their distress, nor enter in the gate of my people;... do not lay hands on their substance in the day of their calamity; do not stand in the cross-way to cut off his fugitives, nor deliver up their remnant in the day of distress."

But after having announced the fall of Edom, the prophet turns to his own people, and in prophetic strains promises them a happy future. Returning from their dispersion, they will reconquer their land, and live undisturbed under the protection and guidance of God. "And the house of Israel shall be a fire, and the house of Joseph a flame, and the house of Esau for stubble, and they shall kindle them, and devour them, and there shall not be any remainder of the house of Esau, for the Lord has spoken it. And those in the south shall take possession of the mount of Esau, and those in the plain shall occupy the land of the Philistines; and they shall take the fields of Ephraim and the fields of Samaria, and Benjamin shall possess Gilead... And deliverers shall come up on Mount

Zion to judge the mount of Esau; and the kingdom shall be the Lord's."

With these consoling words ends the short address of Obadiah.

The voice of the seer had indeed lost much of the vigour of former ages; yet the oration of Obadiah is no unworthy echo of the stirring eloquence of his predecessors, and it recalls the spirit of Jeremiah, though it reveals also the bonds which fettered the genius of prophecy as well as the strength of the Hebrew nation.

X. HAGGAI. (520.)

The Hebrews had suffered the misfortune which their prophets had long announced to them as inevitable. But happily they were to experience not only the bitterness of subjection and exile, but also the deliverance foreshadowed by their great leaders. After more than half a century, the gates of their captivity were opened, and they returned, a small and tributary band, to the land of their ancestors.

The period of adversity had united the conflicting members of the community; and this happy result was mainly owing to the care and jealousy with which they now guarded their faith. It is to this scrupulous adherence to the rites and ceremonies of their religion, that the Jews owed their preservation as a distinct people, since it placed a strong barrier between them and their conquerors. The immigrants, under the leadership of their appointed governor Zerubbabel, arrived in the spring-time in Judea, and were welcomed by the children of those poor co-religionists whom the invaders had deemed too insignificant for captivity.

The small colony immediately commenced to re-establish itself, and not long afterwards we hear of the erection of large and splendid dwellings. The zealous settlers then felt a strong desire to restore the Temple, the chief pride of Jerusalem of old. But the energy which in earlier days had enabled the Hebrews to acquire territory and power in spite of the greatest obstacles had waned away in consequence of their long inertness, and not even their genuine religious ardour could rouse them to sustained exertions. They had indeed many reasons to be dispirited. The first Temple had been erected, in the proudest period of Hebrew history, with all the wealth and skill of Phoenicia: how poor were now their means, how deficient their appliances! Where should they find the materials which, at the command of the great king, had been brought in profusion from far and near? And not unnaturally distrusting the fortunes of the future, they delayed their great work: "the time is not yet come," they said, "the time that the Lord's House should be built."

But the voice of the prophetic adviser, which had never been silent in Israel, did not tarry to make itself heard in the young colony. The prophet Haggai felt it to be his mission to rebuke the apathy of the people, and to strengthen their good intentions. Summoning them to a public assembly, he reproachfully asked them, how they could have the heart to dwell in richly-roofed mansions, while they allowed the House of God to lie in ruins? They pleaded the great difficulties under which they were labouring in an exhausted country; but the prophet insisted that earnest zeal would overcome all obstacles. "Consider your ways," he said; "go up to the mountain, and bring wood, and build the House; and I will take pleasure in it, and I will be glorified, says the Lord. You look for much and lo, it comes to little, and when you bring it home, I blow it away. Why? says the Lord of hosts; because of My House, that is waste, while you run every man to his own house. Therefore the heaven over you is stayed from dew, and the earth is stayed from its fruit. And I call for a draught upon the land, and upon the mountains, and upon the corn, and upon the new wine, and upon the oil, and upon the produce of the ground, and upon men, and upon cattle, and upon all the labour of the hands."

His words had at first an inspiriting effect. Zerubbabel the governor, and Joshua the High-priest, and "the remnant of the people", obeyed, and all cheerfully joined in the holy work. But their eagerness soon abated. Disheartened by the difficulties which seemed to increase as they proceeded in their labours, they relinquished a task that appeared to them hopeless. The prophet, far from undervaluing their difficulties, addressed them with pity rather than bitterness: "Who is left among you that saw this House in its first glory? and how do you see it now? is it not in your eyes in comparison as nothing? Yet now be strong, O Zerubbabel, says the Lord, and be strong, O Joshua, son of Josedeck the High-Priest, and be strong, all ye people of the land, says the Lord, and work, for I am with you, says the Lord of hosts."

He raised their drooping spirits by promising God's assistance in their great undertaking, and by assuring them that His favour would shine even more brightly on the second Temple than on the first. Peace and piety should render it more beautiful than it could be made by skill and splendour, which had been unable to save the former structure from the sacrilege of the destroyer.

Again three weary months had elapsed, and once more the workmen stopped dejected and dissatisfied. And now the prophet appeared before them with a message not of commiseration or encouragement but of indignant reproof.

The delay had not been caused by indifference to the ceremonials of their religion; for these had evidently been kept with the utmost strictness. In somewhat enigmatical language, Haggai declared that the people, unable to rouse themselves at God's bidding, presented offerings that were not acceptable to Him; and he urged that the mildew and the hail which had blasted their harvests, were the instruments of God's anger, but that the soil would again bring forth abundant crops if they resumed and accomplished the sacred work.

Now the people were prompted to assiduous exertions, in acknowledgment of which the prophet predicted to them happiness at home and triumph over their heathen enemies; and he invoked a fervent blessing upon Zerubbabel, under whose guidance the Temple had at last been completed.

The Book of Haggai affords an interesting insight into a remarkable period of Jewish history, and presents a vivid picture of the people, humbled and depressed indeed by suffering, yet retaining in some measure the high aspirations of former days. But it reveals no striking peculiarities of the prophet himself. His language is clear and appropriate, but it lacks the fervour and the eloquence of his predecessors who wrote under the impulse of more varied events and of a more stirring public life. Instead of the originality and freedom of an Isaiah or a Joel, we find in Haggai a remarkable advance in levitical ceremonialism, and frequent allusions to ritual questions. "Thus says the Lord of hosts, Ask now the priests concerning the Law, saying, If one bear holy flesh in the skirt of his garment, and with his skirt touch bread or pottage, or wine, or oil, or any meat, shall it be holy? And the priests answered and said, No. Then said Haggai, If one that is unclean by a dead body touch any of these, shall it be unclean? And the priests answered and said, It shall be unclean. Then answered Haggai, and said, So is this people, and so is this nation before Me, says the Lord; and so is every work of their hands: and that which they offer there is unclean." No more striking evidence is needed to show how much the character of Hebrew prophecy had changed.

XI. ZECHARIAH. (520.)

The same period that witnessed the active endeavours and practical advice of Haggai, called forth some of the most mystical orations bequeathed to us by prophecy. Zechariah is the author of an obscure and in some parts almost unfathomable work. He was the son of Barachiah, and grand-son of the prophet Iddo; he prophesied in the second year of the reign of the Persian king Darius; and his youth must consequently have been spent in the land of exile. There, surrounded by Chaldean superstition, he became familiar with that fantastic imagery and those strange conceptions which pervade also the writings of Ezekiel. He probably returned to his native land among the first immigrants, and at once aided the leaders in their efforts for promoting the organisation and spiritual welfare of the colonists. About four months after the energetic appeals of Haggai, the apathy of the people excited once more prophetic admonition. Among the obstacles which paralysed their exertions in building the new Temple, perhaps the most serious was the unconquerable enmity which raged between Samaria and Judah. Also the Persian dynasty had at first been unwilling to assist a tributary people in restoring a monument of their ancient glory. Therefore, although the foundation stone was laid in the year 534, apparently little progress was made within the next six years. But the new king Darius Hystaspes, unlike his predecessors Cambyses and the false Smerdes, entertained friendly feelings towards the Jews, and promised them his aid in their great undertaking. The inaction, however, which circumstances had partially forced upon the people, had become so habitual to them, that they lacked the courage to make use of their newly acquired rights and resources. The energetic appeals of Zechariah followed, after a very short interval, the repeated remonstrances of Haggai; but he had not to rebuke a defiant or refractory people. Softened by present as well as past misfortunes, the Jews were humble and obedient, though hesitating and apathetic. Their character had indeed greatly changed since the time of Isaiah and Jeremiah. They required now a powerful monitor to rouse them from their despondency, and a moral guide to rescue their religion from servile attachment to outward forms; and they found both in Zechariah, whose efforts make themselves apparent in spite of the mysticism of his orations.

The Book which bears his name is divided into two parts so dissimilar in many respects, that their common authorship has often been disputed. The earlier part, comprising the first eight chapters, bears almost entirely upon the erection of the Temple, and pronounces the displeasure or the favour of God according to the delay or the alacrity with which the work was carried on. The introductory verses are sufficiently clear in language and meaning. The prophet warns the people, by referring to the fate of their ancestors, to keep aloof from iniquity, and to listen to the Divine commands: "Be not as your fathers, to whom the former prophets have cried, saying: Thus says the Lord of hosts, Turn ye now from your evil ways and your evil doings, but they did not hear nor hearken to Me, says the Lord. Your fathers, where are they? and the prophets, do they live for ever?"

But soon this plain style changes, and we find a succession of visions, the exact aim and purpose of which are concealed by a veil of dark imagery. These visions, a form of composition that had become popular, bear a strong resemblance to those of Ezekiel. They abound in metaphors; they present ideas very different from those that meet us in the earlier writings; and they bear the impress of Babylonian influence both in the introduction of strange conceptions, and in the use of Chaldean forms which affect the purity of the language. But they differ from those of Ezekiel in as much as they are more practical, and are designed to convey an immediate lesson; they are less poetical, and their allegorical meaning is often still more difficult of interpretation. The decay of prophetic power which is visible in the plain and sober words of Haggai, is no less evident in the soaring strains of Zechariah.

The first vision represents in several images the renewed bestowal of God's favour upon Jerusalem, and the fall of those nations which had been instrumental in the ruin of Judah. These are portrayed first as horsemen who roam through the earth, and then as strong horns which a supernatural guide shows to the prophet. "And I said to the angel that talked with me, What are these? And he answered me, These are the horns which have scattered Judah, Israel, and Jerusalem, and the Lord showed me four smiths. Then said I, What come these to do? and He spoke saying, These are the horns which scattered Judah; so that no man lifted up his head, but these are come to frighten them, to cast down the horns of the nations, which lifted up their horns over the land of Judah to disperse it."

The same idea is carried on in the next vision, which represents with greater distinctness the ultimate power and triumph of Jerusalem. The prophet beholds a man with a measuring line, and when he asks for an explanation, he receives the reply, that Jerusalem is to be measured out in its length and its breadth; for, says the angel, "Jerusalem shall be inhabited as towns without walls, on account of the multitude of men and cattle therein; for I, saith the Lord, will be to her a wall of fire round about, and will be her glory in the midst of her." Therefore the prophet issues a powerful appeal to the scattered Jews, especially those of the northern or Babylonian regions, to return to the sacred soil, and to occupy again the homes of their ancestors. He adds words full of terror for the enemies, full of comfort and hope for the oppressed Jews: "Behold, I will shake My hand upon the nations that spoiled you, and they shall be a spoil to their servants, and you shall know that the Lord of hosts has sent me. Sing and rejoice, O daughter of Zion; for, behold, I come, and I will dwell in the midst of thee, says the Lord ... And the Lord shall inherit Judah, His portion, in the holy land, and shall choose Jerusalem again. Be silent, all flesh, before the Lord! for He rises up out of His holy habitation."

The following vision is more distinctly characterised by the eastern atmosphere in which the youth of the prophet had been spent. It prominently introduces the spirit of evil. Satan appears tempting the High-priest Joshua, in whom we recognize the embodiment of the Jewish people with their religious aspirations and their mission of holiness. But the spirit of evil is powerless; for God has not rejected Israel; and He says to Satan: "The Lord rebuke thee, O Satan, the Lord rebuke thee, that has chosen Jerusalem! Is Israel not a brand plucked out of the fire?" Joshua, as befitted one accused under judgment, had appeared in poor and sullied garments; but as a sign that he was acquitted and graciously accepted, he was now by the direction of the angel clad in new raiments, and a splendid mitre was placed on his head. However, the Divine promises can only be fulfilled on condition that both the priests and the people remain steadfastly in the path of virtue. "Thus says the Lord of hosts, If thou wilt walk in My ways, and if thou wilt keep My charge, then thou shalt judge My house, and shalt also keep My courts, and I will give thee associates among those that stand by." And then the prophet conveys in obscure, yet not quite unintelligible terms the gracious assurances of God: the foundation stone of the Temple would soon be laid; and on it would be engraven seven eyes, typifying God's watchful providence and love, and implying that His merciful forgiveness would diffuse both moral purity and outward prosperity.

Notwithstanding the peculiarity of style, and the apparently abrupt termination of the different visions, they are sufficiently linked together. In darkly allegorical language, the author describes the only means by which the Jews could attain their cherished objects. Human power had proved to be only human frailty; aid of a very different kind was necessary for success — inward grace or heavenly instruction and guidance. This is symbolised by the next vision of a golden candlestick with seven lamps, placed between two olive trees. The candlestick and the lamps were meant to typify, like the seven eyes on the foundation-stone of the Temple, enlightenment through God's grace, and His fatherly help; and the two olive trees were the Jewish people and their priesthood, or "the two anointed ones", that is, their spiritual and wordly chiefs, the High-priest and the Ruler, who were the recipients of that enlightenment and help. The prophet was astonished and perplexed. The angel asked him, "Dost thou not know what these are?" And when he replied, No, the angel gave him the explanation in these pithy and significant words: "Not by might and not by power, but by My spirit, says the Lord of hosts." The obstacles that impeded the great national work might be formidable, and might appear insurmountable; but by God's help they would vanish: "Who art thou, O great mountain? Before Zerubbabel thou shalt become a plain; and he shall produce the corner-stone with shoutings, Grace, grace him." And the Divine promise continued: "The hands of Zerubbabel have laid the foundation of this House; his hands shall also finish it; and thou shalt know that the Lord of hosts has sent me to you. For who will despise the day of small beginnings? for those seven, the eyes of the Lord, which pervade the whole world, see with rejoicing the plummet in the hand of Zerubbabel."

As the work advances, the visions become more and more fantastic in form, and events and ideas are strangely personified. The prophet urges that the people should be freed from moral stains and sin. This idea is first conveyed by the picture of a flying roll bringing a curse into the house of the unrighteous, and causing its destruction; and then by the allegory of wickedness, which, in the form of a woman, is placed into an ephah-measure closed by a heavy leaden lid, and thus carried away by two women with storks' wings to Babylon, where it thenceforth remains. Thus by the same act, the land of the Hebrews is cleansed from defilement, and that of their enemies infected with it.

Then follows the description of the judgment of the heathens, among whom are sent forth, as the instruments of God's anger, four chariots with horses of various colours, of inauspicious black and bloody red. Two of the chariots take their way northwards to Babylon, and the two others to all parts of the earth. The mission of the two former is especially important in the prophet's eye: "Behold those that go toward the north country satisfy My anger in the north country."

From these hostile anticipations, Zechariah turns

to more congenial scenes and prospects. Messengers had arrived in Jerusalem from the Jews of Babylon with rich presents of gold and silver. Zechariah recognised in this token of brotherly interest a hopeful sign for the future; and kindled into new enthusiasm, he was anxious to mark the gifts as pledges of coming success and greatness. He desired especially to see the worldly and the spiritual power acting together in harmony; and he therefore declared that a descendant or branch of the royal house of David would come to sit on his throne, and by his side the High-priest on his throne, both working in unison for the welfare of the nation. "Take silver and gold", he said in the name of God, "and make crowns, and set them upon the head of Joshua, the son of Josedek, the High-priest, and speak to him, saying, Thus speaks the Lord of hosts: Behold, a man whose name is The Branch shall grow up in his place, and he shall build the Temple of the Lord. He shall build the Temple of the Lord, he shall bear the royal splendour; and the Priest shall be on his throne, and the counsel of peace shall be between them both. And the crowns shall be for a memorial in the Temple of the Lord." — This would surely come to pass, he concluded, if the Jews faithfully obeyed the voice of God.

After having thus expressed his national hopes, the prophet leaves the mysterious sphere of vision, and casting aside the veil of allegory, he comes forward as the practical counsellor and guide of the people. About two years had elapsed since his urgent remonstrance had given a new stimulus to those engaged in the building of the Temple; but when the great work was completed, and all the Jews went joyfully to worship in Jerusalem, the question arose, whether it was appropriate still to observe those mournful fasts which had been ordained to commemorate the perils and the fall of the capital. Zechariah, appealed to by the people, gave them an answer worthy of Isaiah or Amos, strongly setting forth the superiority of active virtue over fasts and ceremonies: "The word of the Lord of Hosts came to me, saying, Speak to all the people of the land, and to the priests saying, When you fasted and mourned in the fifth and seventh month, those seventy years, did you really fast for Me, for Me? And when you ate and when you drank, did not you eat for yourselves and drink for yourselves?... Thus spoke the Lord of hosts, saying, Execute true judgment, and show mercy and compassion every man to his brother; and oppress not the widow, nor the fatherless, the stranger, nor the poor; and let none of you imagine evil against his brother in your heart." And then he assured them that a time of gladness would follow the time of distress; men would live to a good old age, and the streets of Jerusalem would ring with the songs of young men and maidens; the very recollection of past misfortunes would be effaced, and the days of fasting and mourning would be changed into days of joy and thanksgiving: "Thus saith the Lord of hosts, the fast of the fourth month and the fast of the fifth, and the fast of the seventh, and the fast of the tenth shall be to the house of Judah joy and gladness, and cheerful feasts." But these promises of happiness were mingled with the earnest warning, that their fulfilment mainly depended on the people themselves, who would be dealt with according to their merits.

This address, so solemnly appealing to the nobler side of human nature, concludes the first part of the Book. But now we are suddenly transported into a different and larger sphere; for the interest of the work is no longer confined to the one great object of the people's toil, the building of the Temple; and the usual form of prophetic oratory is substituted for vision, symbol, and allegory. Yet the composition is not clearer or more transparent.

First the prophet, in the name of God, pronounces judgment upon the heathens, who had for many centuries been hostile to the Hebrews — upon Persia which is introduced by the name of Hadrach; upon Syria and Damascus; Tyre and Sidon, those luxurious and opulent communities, upon Ashkelon and Gaza, and all the other towns of the Philistines, which had long been defiled by rapine and murder, but were soon to be inhabited by a new race, worshippers of the only true God. He next promises to the Jews the assistance of the Lord, who would fight for them against all their adversaries; and he encourages them by the prospect of a glorious future. "Rejoice greatly, O daughter of Zion, shout, O daughter of Jerusalem, behold, thy king comes to thee; he is just and victorious, lowly and riding upon an ass, upon a colt, the foal of an ass." Thus the prophet pictures perfect peace, of which the patient ass was the type; whereas he declares that the horse, which was looked upon as the war-like animal that "smells the battle from afar", will no longer exist in those happy times. "And I will cut off the chariot from Ephraim, and the horse from Jerusalem, and the battle bow shall be cut off; and he shall speak peace to the heathen; and his dominion shall be from sea to sea, and from the river to the ends of the earth." Moreover, all the captives will return from their dispersion, and the places of their exile will be like "pits in which there is no water" — "Return to the stronghold (of Zion), ye hopeful prisoners, even to day I announce it: I render double to you."

This joyful message, intended to revive the waning courage of the struggling colonists, was supplemented by promises of more immediate help: "I bend Judah for Me as a bow, fill the quiver for Ephraim, and raise up thy sons, O Zion, against thy sons, O Greece, and make thee as the sword of a hero. And the Lord shall appear to them, and his arrow shall go forth as the lightning: and the Lord God shall blow the trumpet, and pass along with whirlwinds of the south. The Lord of hosts shall protect them; and they shall devour their enemies, and tread upon them as sling stones; and they shall drink and be noisy as through wine; and they shall be filled like offering-bowls, and as the corners of the altar. And the Lord their God shall save them in that day as the flock of His people; for they are as the stones of a crown, lifted up as an ensign upon His land."

But did the Hebrews deserve so much mercy? Had they been purified in the furnace of misery? Even Zechariah was compelled to repeat the complaints which had so constantly been raised by his predecessors. Idolatry and superstition were still rife among the people — "The Teraphim speak vanity, and the diviners behold lies, and the dreamers speak falsehood, they comfort with shadows." The guides of the people were as reckless and treacherous as ever — "My anger is kindled against the shepherds, and I will punish the leaders." Yet God in His compassion, so the prophet declares, will overlook all their sins and failings — "He remembers His flock, the house of Judah, and makes it His splendid battle-horse", by means of which the proud heathens will be cast down into the dust. He will bring back to the Holy Land not only Judah, but Ephraim also, crowned with victory and invested with renewed glory — "And I will take away his blood out of his mouth, and his abominations from between his teeth: but he that remains, even he, shall be for our God, and he shall be as a governor in Judah, and Ekron as a Jebusite. And I will encamp about My house because of the army, because of him that passes by, and of him that returns, and no oppressor shall pass through them any more: for now have I seen with My eyes." And while the enemies will be defeated and scattered, escaping from their native towns over seas and deserts, and seeking refuge in distant lands, the Hebrews, restored to their own soil, freed from civil strife and foreign danger, will be fortified with that courage which is inspired by faith and virtue — "I will strengthen them through the Lord, and they shall proceed in His name, says the Lord."

About this time, some atrocious deed was perpetrated — probably the murder of some distinguished men, whom the prophet, in a bitter lamentation, introduces by the image of lofty cedars — "Open thy doors, O Lebanon, that the fires may devour thy cedars. Howl, fir-tree, for the cedar is fallen, because the mighty is spoiled; howl, O ye oaks of Bashan, for the forest of the vintage is come down. — There is a voice of the howlings of the shepherds, for their glory is spoiled; a voice of the roaring of young lions, for the pride of Jordan is spoiled."

Then he describes, in a remarkable parable, the efforts he had so often and so fruitlessly made to advise and to guide the community. A flock of sheep, neglected by its shepherd, is straying about, and is in danger of falling a prey to wild beasts. The prophet pities the flock, and by God's command undertakes to tend it. For this purpose he chooses two rods, one of which he calls Beauty and the other Unity. But the flock heeds him not, and refuses to obey his call. In his anger he exclaims, "I will not feed you: that which is to die, let it die; and that which is to perish, let it perish; and let the rest devour, every one the flesh of the other." Now disobedience and strife cause havoc among the sheep, and as a sign that they will be without shelter and safety, the prophet breaks the staff Beauty. He now demands his wages; and the people, to show their contempt for his services, offer him no more than thirty pieces of silver, which he put into the Temple treasury; and then he breaks the staff Unity also. In His wrath God menaces that He will give the people a faithless shepherd, who "shall not look after the sheep that perish, nor search for those that go astray, nor heal those that are wounded, nor feed those that are healthy, and who eats the fat ones, and allows their hoofs to be torn"; but who shall suffer no less than those he so shamefully betrays: "Woe to the worthless shepherd that deserts the flock! The sword shall be upon his arm and upon his right eye; his arm shall be altogether dried up, and his right eye shall be utterly darkened."

By allegories like these the prophet hoped to rouse the young settlement to a sense of their heedlessness and their dangers; and in order to encourage them in their efforts of improvement, he again pronounced promises of deliverance: Jerusalem would be a devouring sword for heathen nations, and all the enemies of Judah would be visited with destruction and ruin. "I will make the governors of Judah like a hearth of fire among the wood, and like a torch of fire in a sheaf, and they shall devour all the people round about, on the right hand and on the left, and Jerusalem shall be inhabited again in its own place. In that day shall the Lord defend the inhabitants of Jerusalem; and he that is feeble among them in that day shall be as David; and the house of David shall be as God, as the angel of the Lord before them." But infinitely more precious than these material blessings will be the spiritual gifts that are to be diffused among the nation: all minds will be freed from error, and all hearts cleansed from sin; and the bonds of affection will unite the people and their once persecuted prophets: "Then I will pour out upon the house of David and upon the inhabitants of Jerusalem, the spirit of grace and of supplication; and they shall look upon me whom they have pierced, and they shall mourn for him as one mourns for his only son, and shall weep for him bitterly, as one weeps for his first-born." Pious thoughts will result in virtuous deeds;

every idol will be dashed to pieces, and idolatry detested. Above all, the chief tempters to error, the false prophets, will be banished or annihilated; and even if they continue their deluding speeches, they will be unable to lead the people astray; so that the rough garment, symbolical of the prophetic office, will no more be desecrated, nor shield its deceitful wearer; nay those nearest and dearest to him will bear witness against him, and bring him to punishment — "And it shall come to pass that when any shall yet prophesy, then his father and mother that begat him shall say to him, Thou shalt not live, for thou speakest lies in the name of the Lord." Two thirds of the evildoers will perish, and the surviving third will "be refined as gold is refined", and will be true servants of the Lord — "They will call upon Him, and He will hear them; the Lord speaks, It is My people, and they speak, Jehovah is our Lord": they will be the holy seed destined to perpetuate God's glory and truth in all eternity.

Then the prophet resumes his chief theme once more, and he dwells upon it in glowing language. He speaks in metaphors and similes which indeed seem at first sight obscure, but become clear if read in the light of his previous addresses. He announces, in no lenient terms, misfortunes which the Jews will have to suffer — the enmity of all nations, the ruin of their cities, the plunder of their property; but though many will be carried off into captivity, "the residue of the people shall not be cut off from the city", but will behold God's mercy, and rejoice in their safety. Then, desirous to describe God's omnipotence, the prophet shows that the laws of nature which men regard as immutable, are subject to His command; and evidently taking his images from an earthquake, he says: "And His feet shall stand on that day upon the Mount of Olives, which is before Jerusalem in the east, and the Mount of Olives shall be cleft in the midst, towards the east and towards the west, and there shall be a very great valley, and half of the mountain shall remove towards the north, and half of it towards the south ... And the Lord, my God, appears — all the holy ones with Thee." Then comes the great act of salvation. The time itself—which will be neither day nor night, but the evening twilight — will mysteriously forebode the impending event, the spiritual grandeur of Israel, of which all the nations of the earth will be eager to partake. "And it shall be on that day, that living waters shall go out from Jerusalem, half of them towards the eastern sea, and half of them towards the western sea, in summer and in draught shall they remain. And the Lord shall be King over all the earth; in that day shall there be one Lord and His name One." This was the great object of all prophetic teachings, the ideal of all prophetic aspirations. The Divine light shall not be limited to the chosen people, but shall reach all nations, to dispel the mists of vice and ignorance. Then Jerusalem will be the centre of the earth, and the enemies of Israel will feel God's retribution. The world being purified from idolators and sinners, all men will join in the same worship, as the type of which the prophet takes one of the most joyous of the Jewish festivals: "And it shall come to pass that every one that is left of all the nations which came against Jerusalem, shall go up from year to year to worship the King, the Lord of hosts, and to keep the Feast of Tabernacles. And it shall be, that whosoever will not come up of all the families of the earth to Jerusalem to worship the King, the Lord of hosts, upon them shall be no rain. And if the family of Egypt do not go up and come not, it will have no rain; there shall be the plague wherewith the Lord will smite the heathen that do not come up to keep the Feast of Tabernacles." This feeling of universal brotherhood will produce a state of active virtue and of unalloyed piety, which will not only be witnessed within the walls of the Temple, but will be exercised in the gates and the market-place, in the open streets and at the domestic hearth: "In that day shall there be written upon the bells of the horses, 'Holiness unto the Lord', and the pots in the House of the Lord shall be like the bowls before the altar. Yea every pot in Jerusalem and in Judah shall be holy to the Lord of hosts, and all those that sacrifice shall come and take of them, and seethe therein; and in that day there shall be no more Canaaite in the House of the Lord of hosts."

Thus concludes one of the most remarkable Books of the Biblical Canon. If it is inferior to some other prophetic productions in clearness, simplicity, and beauty, it yields to none in force and sublimity. It breathes the loftiest patriotism, and the most ardent zeal for the spiritual progress of mankind. The author never fails to engage the imagination or to rouse the reflection of the reader; and many of his expressions have become current among all nations.

XII. MALACHI. (About 430.)

The Book of Malachi embodies some of the latest utterances of prophecy. Although we have no details of the prophet's life, it may be safely concluded from his orations that he was a contemporary of Nehemiah, and wrote about a hundred years after the return of the first colonies from Babylon. For the same offences and follies which excited the indignation and prompted the exertions of the great statesman, are rebuked by Malachi. At that period of Jewish history, which is contemporary with the latter part of the reign of the Persian king Artaxerxes Longimanus (464—424), extraneous causes were again at work to endanger the morality, and the ever vacillating faith of the people. Freedom from care and immediate perils proved, as usual, a severe temptation. Religious ardour, which past misfortunes had for a time fanned into enthusiasm, was waning away, and was replaced by a fatal indifference to those laws and ordinances which experience had proved to be necessary for the political as well as the religious stability of the commonwealth. The energy and zeal with which the Temple had been erected, vanished when it was completed; and the sacred rites began to be tainted by the same abuses which had prevailed in the first Sanctuary. Moreover the strict isolation which the Jews had attempted after their return from Babylon, was relaxed, and numerous intermarriages with heathen tribes threatened a renewal of all the old dangers of idolatry.

The style of Malachi's orations is peculiar. As a rule, the prophets conveyed their ideas either in the form of a Divine oracle, a vision, and an allegory, or in a simple address or narrative. But the Book of Malachi teaches by questions and answers, and is almost one continuous dialogue. The questions generally disclose the people's faithlessness and disbelief, and their self-sufficient reliance upon their own excellence. The prophet sometimes retorts with an emphatic counter-question, but usually rebuts the insolence of the queries by pithy rebuke or severe menace. He thus succeeds in imparting to his speeches a certain dramatic animation and impressiveness, and in placing the ingratitude and constant rebellion of the people in striking contrast to the unbounded mercy and forgiveness of their God.

The character of the Book and the temper of the people are well illustrated in the very opening words: "I have loved you, says the Lord; yet you say, Wherein hast

Thou loved us? — Was not Esau Jacob's brother? says the Lord; yet I loved Jacob, and hated Esau, and laid waste his mountains, and made his heritage abodes of the wilderness." Israel had been favoured beyond his merits, but refused to own it. God's reply involves indeed censure, but it is tempered by indulgence: He is sure that the people will, in due time, recognise His untiring compassion — "Your eyes shall see it, and you shall say, Great is the Lord beyond the boundaries of Israel."

Like many of his predecessors, Malachi attributes the deplorable state of the commonwealth to the recklessness and indifference of its leaders, or the priests, who after the Babylonian period had acquired unusual power. To them, therefore, he first addresses his reproaches. "A son honours his father, and a servant his master: if then I be a father, where is My honour? and if I be a master, where is My fear? says the Lord of hosts to you, O priests that despise My name! And you say, Wherein have we despised Thy name? You offer polluted bread upon My altar; and you say, Wherein have we polluted Thee? In that you say, The Table of the Lord is contemptible. And if you offer the blind for sacrifice, is it not evil? and if you offer the lame and sick, is it not evil? Offer it to thy governor; will he be pleased with thee, or accept thy person? says the Lord of hosts. And now, I pray you, beseech God that He will be gracious to us: this has been by your means — will He regard your persons? says the Lord of hosts." Then he chastises the negligence with which the priestly functions were performed, the cupidity of withholding the firstlings from their sacred destination, and the irreverence of presenting on the altar of God maimed and worthless beasts. In reviewing these offences, he is unable to restrain his wrath: "Cursed be the deceiver that has in his flock a male, and vows and sacrifices to the Lord a faulty female: for I am a great King, says the Lord of hosts, and My name is dreaded among the nations." He then contrasts the noble mission of the priests with their contemptible conduct, and the happy influence they ought to exercise with the baneful effects of their heedlessness. "My covenant was with him for life and peace; and I gave them to him for the fear wherewith he feared Me, and revered My name. The law of truth was in his mouth, and iniquity was not found in his lips; he walked with Me in peace and equity, and turned away from iniquity. For the priest's lips should keep knowledge, and they should seek the law at his mouth: for he is the messenger of the Lord of hosts." The true priest, as Malachi pictured him in his mind, leads a life of peace and usefulness, tries to improve and encourage the people, and finds other duties to perform besides those connected with sacrifice and religious ceremonies. But the whole order had deserted its high avocation, and proved unworthy of the sacred offices entrusted to its care: "You have swerved from the way; you have caused many to stumble at the Law; you have corrupted the covenant of Levi, says the Lord of hosts." But punishment and humiliation are announced as inevitable: "Therefore will I also make you contemptible and base before all the people, since you have not kept My ways, but have been partial in the law . . . If you will not hear, and if you will not lay it to heart, to give glory to My name, says the Lord of hosts, I will surely send a curse upon you, and I will curse your blessings; yea, I have cursed them already, because you do not lay it to heart."

Then the prophet inveighed against the people themselves, and especially against their intermarriages with heathen nations. He started indeed with the principle, "Have we not all one Father? has not one God created us?" Yet he intimated, that an indiscriminate intercourse between those who believe in Him and those who do not, is "a profanation of the holiness of the Lord", fraught with serious evils, since the young and still unsettled colony was sure to be endangered by the infusion of heathen elements. But with even greater earnestness the prophet denounced the levity with which husbands seem to have divorced their wives; and he declared that because the House of God was filled with the cries and weeping of discarded women, the Lord rejected the people's sacrifices and prayers. To palliate their frivolity, they quoted the example of Abraham, who sent away Hagar; but the prophet replied that Abraham was in an exceptional condition which obliged him to act as he did — "that he might seek a godly seed"; and he added, "Therefore take heed of your souls, and let none deal treacherously against the wife of his youth: for the Lord, the God of Israel, says that He hates divorcing."

The habitual disregard of God's commands resulted in moral callousness, which recognised no duties and dreaded no punishments: "You have wearied the Lord with your words; yet you say, Wherein have we wearied Him? When you say, Everyone that does evil pleases the Lord, and He delights in them; or, Where is the Lord of justice?"

But the day of judgment approaches, God appears to pronounce sentence upon the righteous and the wicked, and He sends His messenger to execute it. This messenger will be like the fire of the refiner, which burns out all dross, and removes all alloy. He will bring terror and destruction upon the evil-doers, but relief and salvation to the innocent. "And I come to you for judgment, and I am a swift witness against the sorcerers and against false swearers, and against those that oppress the hireling in his wages, the widow and the fatherless, and that turn aside the stranger from his right, and fear not Me, says the Lord of hosts." But when the time of retribution is completed, peace and happiness will prevail for ever: "Then shall the offering of Judah and Jerusalem be pleasant to the Lord, as in the days of old, and as in former years."

After reproving the people for their "spoliation of the Lord" in not paying the tithes and other imposts, the prophet turns once more to the impending chastisement, which calls forth his fervent eloquence. He is unable to understand the hardihood and folly which presume to question the justice of God, expect prosperity from a life of sin, and declare virtue unavailing for happiness. But the day is near when the scoffers will tremble, and their eyes will be opened. It will be a terrible time: "Behold, the day comes, burning as an oven; then all the proud and all the evildoers shall be stubble, and the day that comes shall burn them up, says the Lord of hosts, and shall leave them neither root nor branch." — "But", he continues, "to you that fear My name shall the sun of righteousness arise with healing in his wings; and you shall go forth and bound as calves of the stall." However, some preparation was to precede the awful judgment, for the weakness of man claims compassion and indulgence. Therefore Malachi declares, that God will send another messenger to precede the dreaded requiter of good and evil; and a great prophet like Elijah will re-appear to restore peace and good-will among men, and appease God's anger: he will "turn the heart of the fathers to the children, and the heart of the children to the fathers."

With these allusions to a bright future, Malachi closes his orations. Throughout the Book, he avoids doctrinal questions, and advocates with much earnestness a simple and elevated code of morality; his plain and appropriate language, if not enriched with striking similes, nor displaying sublime flights of oratory, is free from obscurity and fantastic imagery.

D. THE BOOK OF DANIEL.
(About 160.)

The Book of Daniel, though invested, like all prophetic works, with universal interest, and replete with examples and lessons to which every age may turn for guidance and instruction, is most closely identified with the remarkable time to which it owes its origin. Warning and encouragement, menace and entreaty — the ordinary themes of Hebrew patriots — appear in this work in a peculiar and novel form; for the illustrations are not, as usual, suggested by the genius of the poet or the orator, but they are based upon historical facts; and these are held up as a mirror to the author's own contemporaries for the double purpose of showing the evildoers their inevitable downfall, and of inspiring the oppressed with fortitude. Therefore, the picture of presumption and pride on the part of Israel's enemy is skilfully contrasted with that of a wise and pious Israelite, unwavering in courage and in faith.

Daniel, who was descended from a distinguished family, was taken to Chaldea after the capture of Jerusalem by Nebuchadnezzar. There, in conjunction with three other young men, he was for several years prepared for the royal service, his Hebrew name being altered into the Babylonian one of Belshazzar. In consequence of his happy interpretation of a dream, he was entrusted with an important office at the court, and was appointed chief of the caste of magicians.

When the Medes conquered Babylon, and a change of dynasty ensued, he rose to the place of first minister, which post he seems to have occupied for some time also under Cyrus. Thus the history of Daniel has, to a certain extent, its prototype in that of Joseph; and we are again introduced to Oriental despotism with its capricious modes of bestowing approval and censure, and to a court addicted to magic lore and oracular interpretation. In the recollection of the Hebrews, Daniel was associated with all that is wise and good; and he is not only known to us through the pages of the Book which bears his name, but by the allusions made to him in other parts of Scripture. The prophet Ezekiel, in describing the incredible presumption of the prince of Tyre, declares that he thought himself wiser than Daniel; later writers attributed to him every kind of miraculous power; and tradition made him the hero of many wonderful tales. Indeed his memory became, in the lapse of generations, so deeply rooted in the reverence of the people, that, in the momentous time of the Syrian conqueror Antiochus Epiphanes, it suggested itself to a Hebrew writer, to place his life before his desponding contemporaries as a great example of endurance and piety, and to raise their hopes by prophetic predictions ascribed to Daniel's pen.

Not even the long periods of hardship which the Jews endured after the first loss of their independence, had prepared them for the wrongs inflicted upon them by the cruelty of Antiochus. For some time after their return from the Babylonian captivity, they enjoyed comparative freedom and quiet. Engrossed by the development of their religious literature and their civil organisation, they found few opportunities for military enterprise, and when the Macedonian invasion swept over the East, the small commonwealth, paying homage to the conqueror, escaped unhurt. The Jews were less fortunate during the reign of Alexander's successors, and they repeatedly became the victims of that jealousy which divided the kingdoms of Syria and Egypt. Yet neither their resources nor their liberties were materially curtailed. But the wars of Antiochus inaugurated a new era of suffering. Then for the first time raged that fierce and fanatic persecution which has since so often stained humanity in the name of religion. Massacres perhaps as cruel as those perpetrated by the Syrian king, had indeed before been caused by the animosity of hostile races, or had been prompted by ambition or revenge; but now a far wilder hatred was kindled between antagonistic creeds, and a whole nation was tortured into compliance with the commands of an idolatrous conqueror. An attempted rising of the Jews increased his wrath and matured his plans. He shrank from no form of oppression or cruelty, and recoiled from no sacrilege. But the very excess of his fanaticism tended to defeat its object. His wanton barbarity roused the Hebrews into action, and called forth prodigious feats of valour which revived the ancient fame and glory of the people. This patriotic enthusiasm was, in no small degree, fostered by their national literature; and it appears that it was particularly nourished by the records of Daniel's constancy, and of his encouraging prophecies. Those records were now written down in that form in which they have been preserved to us, and with that practical purpose which they were so well calculated to serve. The Book of Daniel appears indeed at first glance to be a mere biography, interwoven with historical allusions; but not even the language of allegory can conceal its ulterior object of stimulating and advising the oppressed Hebrews, of pointing out God's terrible judgment, and of announcing the annihilation of the apparently invincible Syrian empire.

 The beginning of the narrative carries us back to the siege and destruction of Jerusalem by Nebuchadnezzar. The sacred vessels were taken from the House of God to be profaned in Babylonian temples or banqueting halls. The bulk of the people was led away to enrich the territories of the conqueror by their labour and their skill. But the captives were treated with leniency, and not a few of them rose to honour and distinction. Thus the king commanded that some Hebrew youths, conspicuous for comeliness and intelligence, should be brought to his palace, where for three years they should partake of his own food and wine, and be instructed in the language of the Chaldeans. Among those youths were Daniel and his three friends Hananiah, Mishael, and Azariah, who received the Chaldean names Shadrach, Meshach, and Abednego. But though they all acted and suffered alike, the character of Daniel alone stands out with a distinct individuality. He is from the first described as possessed of a rare combination of great qualities. His remarkable firmness was blended with a modesty which soon gained him the affection of the high official to whom the king's command had been entrusted.

When installed at the palace, he declined to eat the proffered food, because it was such as was forbidden by his faith. The officer feared the displeasure of his master, if he permitted a departure from his orders; but Daniel persisted in his refusal, and pleaded both for himself and his friends: "Prove thy servants, I beseech thee, ten days; and let them give us pulse to eat and water to drink; then let our countenances be looked upon before thee, and the countenances of the young men that eat of the portion of the king's meat, and as thou seest, deal with thy servants." The proposal was accepted, and when it was found that the frugal meals had in no way changed the healthy appearance of the four Hebrews, the steward furnished them permanently with their lawful food. At the expiration of the period of trial, they were brought before Nebuchadnezzar, who admired their knowledge and intelligence.

Not long afterwards an event occurred which was to test their abilities. The king had a remarkable dream, which Daniel alone was able to interpret. That dream was employed by the author of our Book for unfolding the great historical picture which he was anxious to submit to his readers, and from this time he made the personal history of Daniel subservient to prophetic delineations: for, with the exactness of the historian and the keensightedness of the politician, he represented, in the form of dreams and visions, the events of many generations and the fate of succeeding dynasties, the violence of conquerors and the vicissitudes of the conquered. The dream of Nebuchadnezzar (ch. II) serves as the first introduction to these changeful scenes, which are at first vaguely hinted at, but are afterwards clearly and minutely worked out.

The character of Nebuchadnezzar combined all the peculiarities of the Oriental despot. He was superstitious and easily alarmed, unable to bear contradiction, and resenting the slightest censure, capriciously lavish in bestowing favours, and cruel in inflicting punishment. The dream which had troubled his sleep, had left no distinct recollection, nothing but a fevered sensation. He summoned all the wise men of his court, the soothsayers and magicians, and bade them tell him the forgotten dream and its interpretation; if they were unable to do so, he menaced them with instant death and the destruction of their houses and families. In vain they remonstrated against this unreasonable demand, and the king ordered that they should all be massacred. Among the doomed counsellors were Daniel and his friends; the former entreated a short respite, which was granted; and soon afterwards he was favoured by a Divine vision revealing to him the dream and its meaning. He then sought the king's presence, and anxious only to exalt the glory of God, the Bestower of all wisdom, he said that it was not in the power of soothsayers and magicians to disclose the secret; nor was he himself specially gifted for such a task; but God desired to reveal to the king the events of later days, and had chosen him as His humble instrument. He then continued: "Thou, O king, sawest and behold a great image. This great image whose brightness was marvellous, stood before thee; and the form thereof was terrible. The head of this image was of fine gold, its breast and its arms of silver, its belly and its thighs of brass, its legs of iron, its feet partly of iron and partly of clay. Thou sawest till a stone was cut out without hands which struck the image upon its feet that were of iron and clay, and broke them to pieces. Then was the iron, the clay, the brass, the silver, and the gold broken to pieces together, and became like the chaff of the summer threshing-floors; and the wind carried them away, that no place was found for them: and the stone that struck the image became a great mountain, and filled the whole earth." The dream did not refer to occurrences affecting the life or reign of Nebuchadnezzar, but to revolutions and changes to be wrought in the course of centuries after him; for this was its interpretation. The parts of the strange image represent the empires which successively ruled over Asia during four hundred years from the time of Nebuchadnezzar, and which are briefly but most appropriately described. The head of gold means the powerful and far-famed kingdom of Babylon, or of Nebuchadnezzar and his immediate successors (to B. C. 560). The kingdom of the Medes and the Persians, flourishing from the time of Cyrus to that of Alexander the Great (560—330), and described by Daniel as inferior to the preceding one, is indicated by the arms and breast of silver. The body and the loins of brass are the vast and formidable empire of the Macedonian conqueror, which "bore rule over all the earth". Alexander's successors, the kings of Macedon, of Syria, and of Egypt, unequal in power, and often at war with each other, are alluded to by the feet partly of iron and partly of clay; and their rule was protracted, amidst feuds and disturbances, to the time of Antiochus Epiphanes, the king of Syria (B. C. 170). But over the ruins of great and proud empires, a kingdom more glorious and more lasting than all will arise — the dominion of the Messiah, which was expected to commence after the unhappy times of Antiochus. "And in the days of these kings", said Daniel, "shall the God of heaven set up a kingdom which shall never be destroyed, and the kingdom shall not be left to other people, but it shall break in pieces and consume all these kingdoms, and it shall stand for ever." Thus the suffering Hebrews were cheered not only by the hope of political deliverance but of spiritual comfort, and by the near prospect of a future of unexampled happiness and splendour.

The author next desired to strengthen the religious fortitude of his contemporaries by a striking example of heroic resistance on the part of Daniel and his companions. The haughty king, he relates (ch. III), resolved to try the loyalty of his subjects by an expedient which tyrants of later days have imitated. Not content with being worshipped wherever he appeared, he caused a colossal golden image of himself to be erected before a vast assembly of the chiefs, the scholars, and high officials of the land; and a proclamation was then issued that, at a given time to be announced by the sound of music, all persons of whatever tribe or language, should fall down before the figure and worship it, and that whosoever disobeyed the decree, should be cast into a fiery furnace. The first offenders reported to the king were the three Jews, the friends of Daniel, who had been promoted to offices of great distinction, and who declared that they bowed down only before God. Their courage did not waver when they were brought before the monarch; and in reply to his angry threats, they said: "If it be so, our God, whom we serve, is able to deliver us from the burning furnace, and He will deliver us out of thy hand, O king; but if not, be it known to thee, O king, that we will not serve thy gods, nor worship the golden image which thou hast set up." Enraged at this defiant reply, the king ordered that the three men should at once be thrown into the furnace, which by his command was heated seven times more than usually. This injunction was so faithfully carried out, that the men who executed it were burnt by the blazing flames. But God did not forsake the three valiant Israelites. Entirely unhurt, their garments even remaining intact, they were seen by the awe-struck monarch himself walking fearlessly in the midst of the fire, and protected by a figure that appeared to him like a "Son of God". Nebuchadnezzar, humbled and terrified, called to them from the furnace, and exclaimed, "Blessed be the God of Shadrach, Meshach, and Abednego, who sent His angels and saved His servants that trusted in Him, and have trespassed the king's word, and yielded up their bodies, that they might not serve nor worship any god except their own God."

The preceding account is calculated to prove God's care for the Jews in their distress, and to show the insignificance of even the mightiest despot directing his power against Divine omnipotence. This last point is now once more illustrated by the sudden insanity of the king.

The account of this calamity (ch. IV) is put in the mouth of Nebuchadnezzar himself, who, in the form of a confession addressed to his subjects, humbly declares his own weakness and the superior wisdom of Daniel, and acknowledges the greatness of the God of Israel. He relates that he had been troubled by a dream which the Chaldean soothsayers were unable to interpret, and about which he at last consulted Daniel, who, when hearing it, was much embarrassed, because in his opinion it foreboded evil. The dream was as follows: "I saw, and behold a tree in the midst of the earth, and its height was great. The tree grew and became strong, and its height reached up to heaven, and its sight to the end of all the earth; the leaves were fair, and the fruit plentiful, and on it was food for all; the beasts of the field had shadow under it, and the fowls of the heaven dwelt in its boughs, and all flesh was fed of it. I saw in the visions of my head upon my bed, and behold, a watchman and a holy one came down from heaven; he cried aloud and said thus, Hew down the tree, and cut off its branches, shake off its leaves, and scatter its fruits; let the beasts flee away from under it, and the fowls from its branches: nevertheless leave the stump of its roots in the earth with a band of iron and brass, in the tender grass of the field; and let it be wet with the dew of heaven, and let its portion be with the beasts in the grass of the earth. Let his heart be changed from man's, and let a beast's heart be given to him; and let seven times pass over him." When the king finished, Daniel earnestly exclaimed: "My lord, the dream be to those that hate thee, and the interpretation to thy enemies." For, he explained, the tree meant the king himself, whose "greatness reached to the heavens, and whose dominion was extended to the end of the earth." But, he continued, "they shall drive thee from men, and thy dwelling shall be with the beasts of the fields, and they shall make thee eat grass as oxen, and they shall wet thee with the dew of heaven, and seven times shall pass over thee, till thou knowest that the Most High rules in the kingdom of men, and gives it to whomsoever He pleases . . . Yet thy kingdom shall be sure to thee, when thou shalt have learnt that the heavens rule." And he concluded with this admonition: "Wherefore, O king, let my counsel be acceptable to thee, and break off thy sins by righteousness, and thy iniquities by showing mercy to the poor; it may perhaps prolong thy happiness."

At the very moment when Nebuchadnezzar was glorying in his magnificence, when he said, "Is not this the great Babylon that I have built for the house of the kingdom by the might of my power, and for the honour of my majesty?" the fatal prediction came suddenly to pass: "he was driven from men, and ate grass as oxen, and his body was wet with the dew of heaven, till his hairs were grown like eagles' feathers, and his nails like birds' claws." But the hand of affliction was removed at last; and when his reason returned, he was humble and contrite. He rejoiced at his recovery not for his own sake, but on account of his kingdom; and he revered the Lord in whose eyes "all the inhabitants of the earth are reputed as nothing, who does according to His will in the army of heaven and among the inhabitants of the earth; and none can stay His hands or say to Him, What doest Thou?... and all His works are truths and His ways judgment, and those that walk in pride He is able to abase."

And in this account of Nebuchadnezzar a warning was given to Antiochus Epiphanes that the same fate would surely befall him, if he did not abandon his arrogance and cruelty.

Now, in order to terrify the tyrant still more, the author sets forth another instance of the vanity of earthly greatness, and of well established power suddenly destroyed (ch. V).

The repentance of Nebuchadnezzar failed to inspire his successor Belshazzar with moderation and piety, and a fearful punishment was reserved for him. This time Belshazzar serves as the type of Antiochus, who resembled him in his iniquity, and who was certain to share his downfall. For Antiochus had dared to pollute the Temple of Jerusalem with his impious orgies, and had robbed it of its costly vessels to profane them at his licentious feasts; but he was to be punished by the ruin of the Syrian dynasty. All this is foreshadowed in the history of Belshazzar. This monarch, so relates our Book, once gave to his nobles and their wives a sumptuous banquet. On this occasion, he ordered the golden vessels which his father Nebuchadnezzar had taken from the Temple of Jerusalem, to be used as drinking cups. During the feast, hymns of praise were sung in honour of the Babylonian gods—"their gods of gold and silver, of brass, iron, wood, and stone". But suddenly the festive scene was thrown into confusion: the fingers of a hand came forth upon the wall, and the king saw them trace mysterious characters which he was unable to read. Terror-struck, he called loudly upon his sooth-sayers and astrologers, promising honours and riches to the successful interpreter. But this time their science was at fault, and they remained silent. Now the queen remembered that, in the time of Nebuchadnezzar, a Hebrew captive, famous for his wisdom, had been the chief of the sages of Babylon. At her suggestion, Daniel was once more summoned into the royal presence, and he acquitted himself of his ungrateful task with his usual frankness. Disdaining all rewards, he answered: "Let thy gifts be to thyself, and give thy recompense to another; yet I will read the writing to the king, and make known to him the interpretation." He commenced by pointing out, not the writing and its meaning, but the cause of the doom which the mysterious words announced. On account of his presumptuous pride, Nebuchadnezzar had been bereft of his glory, his kingdom, and his reason. "And thou, his son, O Belshazzar", the prophet continued, "hast not humbled thy heart, though thou knowest all this." The writing consisted of four Chaldee words — "*Mene, Mene, Tekel, Upharsin,*" which signify literally, "Numbered, numbered, weighed, and dividing"; and Daniel explained that they meant, that God had numbered the kingdom of Belshazzar, and was about to make an end of it; that the king had been weighed in the balance, and had been found wanting; and that his empire would be divided, and given to the Medes and Persians.

In that very night the terrible message was fulfilled: Belshazzar was slain, and Babylon was taken by Darius the Mede (that is, Cyaxares II), the predecessor of Cyrus.

The Book, now continuing the history of Daniel, relates (ch. VI) how Darius, anxious to reward the Hebrew prophet for his devotion and his services, raised him to the most important position in the kingdom. This signal preferment of a foreigner gave great offence to the Persian nobles who conspired to effect his downfall. They searched in vain for some neglect of his public duties, or for some offence in his private life; but not even slander could assail his zeal and his honesty. They determined, therefore, to use his faith as a snare, and they devised a plan which, by flattering the king's pride, offered well-founded prospects of success. Appearing before Darius in great numbers, they suggested, that a decree should be issued to the effect that, whoever should, during the next thirty days, ask a petition of anyone except the king himself, should be cast into a den of lions. The decree was written, signed, and published with all the formalities which made it unalterable according to the Median laws. But Daniel did not heed the proclamation. During all the years of his captivity, it had been his custom to kneel down and to pray three times a day in his chamber before the opened windows, which were in the direction of Jerusalem. He remained faithful to tha custom, and he prayed to his God as before. His enemies watched him, and they soon felt sure that he had disobeyed the royal command. They hastened to Darius to report his offence and to demand his punishment. The king was grieved, and would fain have saved the most gifted and most faithful of his ministers. But the accusers impetuously urged the authority of the law, and he was compelled to yield. When Daniel was thrown into the lions' den, the king accompanied him to the spot, saying, "Thy God, whom thou servest continually, He will deliver thee"; and in order to prevent treachery, he sealed the den with his own ring. He passed the night in fasting and sleepless anxiety. At early dawn, he repaired to the place, and cried out, "O Daniel, servant of the living God, has thy God whom thou servest continually, been able to deliver thee from the lions?" And the voice of Daniel responded from the den declaring, that the angel of God had saved him and closed the lions' mouths so that they did not hurt him. Thereupon Daniel's accusers were thrown into the pit, in which they instantly perished; and a royal decree was published commanding the worship of the God of the Hebrews, "of the God who delivers and rescues, and works signs and wonders in heaven and on earth, who has delivered Daniel from the power of the lions."

Thus the Jews of the Maccabean age were again admonished to keep steadfastly to the faith of their ancestors, and fearlessly to practise its observances; and they were once more assured, that, however cruelly the Syrian tyrant might act against them, they would be saved by that God who was able to curb the instincts of savage beasts, and to change the powers of nature according to His will.

After this narrative of miraculous release, the personal history of Daniel passes into the background; his destinies are no more interwoven with the historical portions of the Book; and he only appears as the favoured prophet to whom the fate of nations is revealed. For the remainder of the work is devoted to a survey, almost minutely exact, of the dynasties which followed one another in rapid succession, and prepared the way for the disastrous reign of Antiochus. The prophetic form is retained; and important historical facts are conveyed in dreams or visions, the interpretations of which are usually given in the Book itself.

In the first dream (ch. VII), Daniel saw four strange beasts which typify four kingdoms. The one, a lion, represents the Babylonian empire. The second, a bear "with three ribs in the mouth between the teeth", is the rapacious dynasty of the Medes and the Persians. The third, resembling a leopard with four wings and four heads, denotes the kingdom of Alexander the Great, the number four expressing completeness, and consequently pointing to the perfect dominion which the great conqueror obtained over the nations of the East. But the most remarkable was the fourth beast, "terrible and dreadful and strong exceedingly; it had great iron teeth... and it had ten horns." From these horns sprang up a smaller one, which, however, grew by degrees, tore out three of the larger horns with their roots, and, being endowed with human eyes and a human mouth, spoke with proud arrogance. The interpretation of these details appears obvious. The fourth beast is evidently the Macedonian kingdom; its ten horns are the ten kings of the dynasty of the Seleucidae, who ruled over Syria from the death of Alexander the Great to the time of Antiochus Epiphanes.*) This ruthless monarch himself is meant by the small horn

---

*) Viz. 1. Seleucus I Nicator (312—280); 2. Antiochus I Soter (279—261); 3. Antiochus II Theos (260—246); 4. Seleucus II Callinicus (245—226); 5. Seleucus III Ceraunus (225—223); 6. Antiochus III the Great (222—187); 7. Seleucus IV Philopator (186—176); 8. Heliodorus; 9. Demetrius; and 10. Ptolemaeus IV Philometor.

which, springing up from the other ten horns, uprooted three of them: for Heliodorus, Demetrius, and Ptolemy IV, repeatedly attempted to establish themselves on the Syrian throne, but were violently expelled by Antiochus. He is the mouth "which spoke great things against the Most High, and thought to change times and laws"; it is he whose look was more haughty than that of his fellows, who carried on an implacable warfare against the people of God, and mocked their sacred observances. But the period of this reign of terror is limited: "The Jews shall be given into his hand until one time, and two times, and half a time."

The facts of history explain these somewhat enigmatical words. In the beginning of the year 168, Antiochus sent his general Apollonius against Jerusalem; he himself followed in the month of June of the same year, laid siege to the town, and captured it. Then commenced the cruelties which have before been described, and the Temple was desecrated by idolatrous rites and forbidden sacrifices. At last the energies of the Jews were roused; the heroic struggle of the Maccabees began, and was brought to a successful issue; and on the 25th day of the 9th month (Kislev) in the year 165, the Temple was purified and re-consecrated, and the lawful worship restored. Shortly afterwards, in the eleventh month of the same year, Antiochus died; and then, three years and a half after his attack upon Jerusalem, that is, "after one time, and two times, and half a time", the Jews expected the arrival of the Messiah, the Divine judgment of the heathen kingdoms, and the establishment of a glorious Jewish empire that was to last for all eternity.

These events and anticipations are thus described in Daniel's vision: "I beheld till the thrones were cast down; and the Ancient of Days [God] was sitting, whose garment was white as snow, and the hair of His head like pure wool; His throne was like the fiery flame, and His wheels as burning fire. A fiery stream issued and came forth from before Him; thousand times thousands ministered to Him, and myriads times myriads stood before Him: the judgment was set, and the books were opened. I beheld then on account of the presumptuous words which the horn spoke, I beheld, till the beast was slain, and its body destroyed, and thrown into the burning flame. As concerning the rest of the beasts, they had their dominion taken away; for the length of their lives was fixed for season and time. I saw in the night visions, and behold, one like the Son of Man [the Messiah] came with the clouds of heaven, and came to the Ancient of Days, and they brought him near before Him. And there was given him dominion, and glory, and kingdom, that all people, nations, and languages should serve him: his dominion is an everlasting dominion, which shall not pass away, and his kingdom shall never be destroyed." Daniel's interpretation alludes to the fulfilment of these hopes in the following terms: "And the kingdom, and dominion, and the greatness of the kingdom under the whole heaven, shall be given to the people of the Saints of the Most High whose kingdom is an everlasting kingdom, and all dominions shall serve and obey Him." Thus a gloomy present and a bright future, earthly greatness and spiritual distinction, are blended in the same picture.

The next vision (ch. VIII) presents again the rapid succession of the Eastern dynasties; it is shorter, but even more striking and graphic than the preceding one; and an intelligible explanation follows the allegory. The united kingdom of the Medes and the Persians is figured by a ram with two horns, one larger than the other, to indicate the superior strength of the Persians, who rapidly extended their empire, "so that there was no one that could deliver out of their hands". Their power, however, was not of long duration. It was supplanted by the Macedonian rule, which is introduced as a he-goat coming from the west, and furnished with "a conspicuous horn between his eyes", which points to Alexander, the conqueror of Asia. For some time the "great horn" had unlimited sway; the ram with two horns lay crushed before it; and "the he-goat grew very great and very strong". But the days of its might were numbered; it broke to pieces, and instead of it appeared four horns turned towards the four sides of the heavens. These were the four kingdoms which arose out of Alexander's empire after his death — in the east, the Syrian kingdom under the rule of Seleucus Nicator; in the north, the Thracian monarchy under Lysimachus; in the west, the Macedonian under Cassander; and in the south, the Egyptian under Ptolemaeus Lagi. From one of these horns—the Syrian—there came forth a small one, "which grew exceedingly great, even to the host of heaven, and it cast down some of the hosts and stars [the Jews] to the ground, and stamped upon them: yea he magnified himself even to the Prince of the host, and by him the daily sacrifice was taken away, and the place of His Sanctuary was cast down." This is of course the hated Antiochus, "the king of the fierce countenance, understanding dark sentences, who destroys wonderfully, and prospers, and practises, and annihilates the mighty people." But after two thousand and three hundred days, or about six years and four months, they should be avenged; and then the Sanctuary should be cleansed from heathen pollutions. All this corresponds exactly with historical events; for just so much time elapsed from the first attacks of Antiochus upon the Jews, in the middle of the year 171, to the ninth month of the year 165, when he was defeated and expelled, and the ancient worship of the Temple restored.

The next section (ch. IX) brings before us Daniel eagerly searching the writings of Jeremiah, and vainly endeavouring to harmonise their bright promises of happiness and release with the mournful reality. Unreconciled to the bitterness of captivity even by his high honours and distinctions, he sorrowfully counted the seasons, as they passed without bringing the hoped-for deliverance. Jeremiah had announced seventy years as the appointed duration of the exile; now the sixty-ninth year was already at hand, and yet no sign of redemption could be discovered. The beloved city and the Temple, towards which the captives constantly directed their supplications, were still in ruins. Daniel, deeply distressed, sought for light and consolation in a fervent prayer. The Jews, he declared, suffered indeed grievously, but they suffered only in proportion to their sins; and their miseries could not be removed except by true and sincere repentance. Neither anger nor menace mingled with his expressions of sorrow; he took upon himself the burden of the people's misdeeds; and identifying himself with their affliction also he exclaimed: "We have sinned, and have committed iniquity, and have done wickedly, and rebelled, by departing from Thy precepts and from Thy judgments;... neither have we obeyed the voice of the Lord our God, to walk in His laws which He set before us by His servants the prophets. Yea all Israel have transgressed Thy Law by revolting, that they might not obey Thy voice; therefore, the curse is poured upon us, and the oath that is written in the Law of Moses, the servant of God, because we have sinned against Him." This confession is followed by an earnest appeal for Divine help and pardon: "Now, therefore, O Lord our God, hear the prayer of Thy servant and his supplications, and cause Thy face to shine upon Thy Sanctuary that is desolate for the Lord's sake ... O my God, incline Thy ear and hear; open Thy eyes and behold our desolations, and the city which is called by Thy name, for we do not present our supplications before Thee for our righteousness, but for Thy great mercies."

Daniel's prayer did not remain unanswered; for the angel Gabriel appeared to him, and gave him the following explanation: "Seventy weeks are determined upon the people, and upon thy holy city, to finish the transgression, and to make an end of sins, and to make reconciliation for iniquity, and to bring in everlasting righteousness, and to seal up the vision and prophecy, and to anoint the Most Holy. Know, therefore, and understand, that from the going forth of the command to restore and build Jerusalem unto an anointed prince shall be seven weeks, and within sixty-two weeks the street shall be built again, and the wall, yet in troublous times. And after sixty-two weeks shall an anointed be cut off, and there is none who belongs to him: and the people of a prince shall come and shall destroy the city and the Sanctuary; and his end shall be as in a flood, and unto the end of the war desolations are determined. And he shall confirm the covenant with many for one week; and in the midst of the week he shall cause the sacrifice and the oblation to cease, and over the pinnacle of abominations the destroyer will be, even until destruction and decree are poured out upon the destroyer."

All these words become clear if read by the light of history and Biblical allegory. The seventy years, said the angel, were not to be regarded as seventy ordinary years, but as seventy "year-weeks", or as seventy times seven years, at the end of which period the prophecy of Jeremiah would be fulfilled not merely in its literal, but in a much higher sense; for not only would the holy city and the Temple be restored to their former splendour, but the people would receive forgiveness of their sins, and would begin a new career of happiness and virtue. In this explanation we must keep in mind, that in Scriptural phraseology the number seventy often represents a period of long and indefinite duration, so that the term "seventy times seven years" denotes not precisely four hundred and ninety, but *many* years, whether more or less than that number. Now, from the destruction of Jerusalem "unto an anointed prince", that is, to Cyrus, who permitted the Jews to return to Palestine, elapsed "seven weeks", that is, seven "year-weeks" or 49 years (from 588 to 539), and then the town and the Temple were indeed rebuilt, but "in troublous times", and poorly and imperfectly. Then followed a very long period, set down at sixty-two year-weeks, comprising the time from the conquest of Babylon by Cyrus to the first acts of violence committed by Antiochus Epiphanes against the author's contemporaries (539 — 171). The warfare of the Jews with this tyrant was continued up to his death, during one year-week, or seven years (from 171—164). Thus the 70 year-weeks were accounted for (viz. $7 + 62 + 1$); but it must again be observed, that the number of 62 year-weeks is not to be taken literally, but was necessarily introduced by the writer to make up the 70 year-weeks, if added to the two numbers which were historically fixed, namely, the 7 year-weeks between Jeremiah and Cyrus, and 1 year-week of Syrian hostilities. The "anointed one" who was "cut off", is Seleucus IV Philopator, who was in reality the predecessor of Antiochus Epiphanes, since the three men who intervened between them (viz. Heliodorus, Demetrius, and Ptolemaeus IV), could hardly be said to have occupied the throne (see p. 208). Yet although Antiochus Epiphanes harassed the Jews for about seven years, the regular worship in the Temple of Jerusalem was interrupted for no more than half that period, or during three years and a half (see p. 208). At the end of this time the oppressor died, and then it was expected that a reign of glory and happiness would dawn upon the faithful worshippers of God.

The next vision (ch. X—XII) is remarkable for its detail and precision, and it reads almost like an ordinary historical narrative, but little concealed by its allegorical form. It comprises the time between Cyrus and Antiochus; and as the events touched upon were of vital importance for the welfare of the Jews, their record in the attractive form of the Book of Daniel must have proved of the highest interest.

A long introduction prepares the reader for the momentous subject. It was in the third year of the reign of Cyrus, that Daniel beheld a man "clothed in linen, and whose loins were girt with fine gold; and his body was like chrysolith, and his face as the appearance of lightning, and his eyes as torches of fire, and his arms and his feet like the appearance of polished brass, and the voice of his words like the voice of a multitude." Daniel, awe-struck at the sight of that figure, fell to the ground; but a hand raised him up, and he heard the following words of encouragement: "O Daniel, a man greatly beloved, understand the words that I speak to thee, and stand upright ... Fear not, Daniel; for from the first day that thou didst set thy heart to understand and to chasten thyself before thy God, thy words were heard." But when the prophet was informed that the destinies of his people were about to be revealed to him, he was again unable to master his fears; once more the strange voice cheered and comforted him; and at last he was prepared to listen, and he said, "Let my Lord speak, for Thou hast strengthened me."

"Behold", the angel began, "there shall stand up yet three kings in Persia; and the fourth shall be far richer than they all; and when he is strong by his wealth, he shall stir up all against the realm of Greece" (XI. 2). The three first kings are Cyrus, Cambyses, and Darius Hystaspes, and the fourth Xerxes, who undertook the famous expedition against Greece.—"But a mighty king shall stand up, that shall rule with great dominion, and do according to his pleasure. And when he has risen, his kingdom shall be broken, and shall be divided towards the four winds of heaven, yet not to his posterity, nor like his dominion with which he ruled: for his kingdom shall be plucked up, and be divided among others beside those" (XI. 3, 4). This refers of course to the destruction of the Persian monarchy by Alexander the Great, whose empire, however, as he left no heir, fell to pieces after his death, and was divided among his generals. — "And the king of the south shall be strong; but one of his captains shall be stronger than he and have dominion; his dominion shall be a great dominion" (XI. 5). The most powerful of Alexander's successors was Ptolemaeus Lagi, king of Egypt, who was, however, dethroned by his valiant general Ptolemaeus Philadelphus. — "And in the end of years they shall be reconciled; for the daughter of the king of the south shall come to the king of the north to establish peace; but she shall not retain the power of the arm; nor shall he stand, nor his arm; but she shall be given up, and they that brought her, and he that begat her, and he that seized her in these times" (XI. 6). Ptolemaeus Philadelphus gave his daughter Berenice in marriage to the Syrian king Antiochus Theos, and thus established friendly relations with the northern kingdom; yet Berenice was murdered soon afterwards. — "But out of the branch of her root shall one stand up in his place, and he shall come to the army, and shall enter into the fortresses of the king of the north, and shall act against them and shall prevail; and he shall carry as booty into Egypt their gods with their images and their precious vessels of silver and gold; and he will desist for some years from the king of the north, who, however, marches against the land of the king of the south, yet he shall return into his own country" (XI. 7—9). Ptolemaeus Euergetes, the successor of Philadelphus, avenged the murder of Berenice by plundering Syria, whose king then attempted an unsuccessful invasion of Egypt. — "But his sons shall bestir themselves, and shall assemble a multitude of great armies; and the one shall march and deluge, and pass through and return; and they will carry on the war up to his fortress. Then the king of the south shall be wroth, and shall come forth and fight with the king of the north, and he will gather a great multitude, and the multitude shall be given into his hand. And the multitude shall rise, and his courage shall grow, and he shall cast down many myriads, but he will not obtain the victory. For the king of the north shall return and shall gather a multitude greater than the former, and shall come after a few years with a large army and great riches" (XI. 10—13). Antiochus the Great and Seleucus Ceraunus, the sons of Antiochus Theos, advanced with a large army against Egypt, were at first defeated, but finally achieved brilliant victories.

In this manner the history of Egypt and of Syria continues to be sketched, but it will be sufficient here to mention the chief events alluded to in the next sections.

In the reign of Ptolemaeus Epiphanes, Egypt, considerably weakened, was convulsed by rebellions and invasions, but ultimately regained peace (XI. 14). Yet the king of the north, Antiochus the Great, appeared once more in Egypt, captured Alexandria and several other fortified towns, and occupied a large part of the country. But on his return into Syria, he was attacked by the Roman general Lucius Scipio, was defeated at Magnesia (190), and compelled to give up many of his east-Asiatic provinces (XI. 15—19).— After his death, Heliodorus attempted to secure the vacant throne, but he was speedily expelled, "not in anger nor in battle", but by the deceitful machinations of Antiochus Epiphanes, "who came in peaceably and obtained the kingdom by flatteries." Antiochus made a successful raid upon Egypt, and broke the power of the king Ptolemaeus Philometor. By perfidy he obtained possession of the finest portions of the land, which he then devastated and plundered (XI. 20—24). Deserted by his friends and surrounded by traitors, the Egyptian king, unable to hold out any longer, made peace with the king of Syria; and the two sovereigns determined to undertake a joint expedition against Judea; "for both these kings' hearts were set upon evil" (XI. 25—27). But the execution of the scheme was delayed; and Antiochus, returning to Syria with great spoil, meditated a single-handed invasion of Palestine (XI. 28). Shortly afterwards, in the year 168, the old enmity between Syria and Egypt was re-kindled; Antiochus marched southwards, but his plans were frustrated by the Roman fleet, "the ships of Kittim", and he was compelled to return (XI. 29, 30). Now his thoughts were busily engaged upon the conquest of Judea; he undertook the long-projected campaign, which was entirely successful; he occupied the province, and forced Jerusalem to surrender; he then entered the Temple and polluted it by the introduction of heathen rites, and by the erection of a statue of Jupiter Capitolinus (XI. 31, 32). Then followed the heroic struggle of the Jewish patriots under the leadership of the Maccabees, the sanguinary encounters, and the arrogance of the tyrant, who blasphemed the God of Israel, and mocked his own deities, paying homage to Jupiter alone, "the god of forces whom he honoured with gold and silver, and with precious stones and pleasant gifts." Flattering the Jewish renegades, and merciless to those who adhered to their faith, unbending in his fanaticism, and deaf to all appeals of compassion, he pursued his object with remorseless audacity; and, relying on his power and constant success, "he exalted himself and magnified himself above every god, and spoke marvellous things against the God of gods" (XI. 33—39*).

---

*) In vers. 40—45, the preceding events are once more briefly reviewed.

But suddenly all this power was overthrown. Antiochus "came to an end and none helped him" (XI. 45). The Jews were saved, and restored to liberty. Then they expected a time of Messianic happiness — of prosperity and virtue, of universal love and justice; and they were prepared for the Divine judgment and the resurrection of the dead: "Many of them that sleep in the dust shall awake, some to everlasting life, some to shame and everlasting contempt; and they that are wise shall shine as the brightness of the firmament, and they that turn many to righteousness, as the stars for ever and ever."

The precise time when all these events would occur, was revealed to Daniel in a last vision. He was told, that 1290 days, or about $3\frac{1}{2}$ years, would elapse from the first invasion of Judea by Apollonius, the general of Antiochus, to the re-consecration of the Temple under the Maccabees; and 1335 days, or about 3 years and 8 months, from the same event to the death of Antiochus, which was to usher in the glorious age of the Messiah.

With this promise the Book of Daniel concludes. But in the course of time, it was enriched with many additions. The great wisdom of Daniel, his firmness and justice, and above all the Divine protection which delivered him from every danger, were more fully developed in the apocryphal writings of "Bel and the Dragon" and the "History of Susanna"; and a beautiful Psalm was attributed to his three friends, when they prayed for safety in the fiery furnace.

In the Book of Daniel, the historical events are at first briefly sketched, and then step by step defined with greater distinctness, till at last the veil of allegory is almost entirely removed, and the well-known names of empires and rulers replace the typical images by which they were at first represented. The composition is strongly characteristic of a later age, and the effects of foreign influence are visible in the mixture of the Chaldee and Hebrew languages, in the frequent introduction and the strange attributes of angels, and in the conception of the nature and mission of the Messiah.

II. THE POETICAL WORKS.

A. GENERAL SURVEY.

The prophets clothed their writings in poetical language which often attains the highest beauty; and in enforcing their sublime teaching, they did not disdain the arts of rhythm and euphony. But these were naturally subordinate to the ends they had in view: poetry found a more genial sphere away from the turmoil of political life, and became essentially the province of the philosopher and the moralist. Lyrical poetry was particularly congenial to the character of the Hebrews, who were easily carried away both to pathetic lament and to soaring exultation; and their productions, true in feeling and admirable in form, have gained a powerful hold upon all civilised nations.

Words alone appeared insufficient to convey an idea of the greatness of God, to describe the wonders of nature, and to give due utterance to joy or anguish; the voice was therefore uplifted to the sound of the harp and the timbrel; and the sister arts of poetry and music flourished together. An event of national importance would stir up the genius of the people, and give rise to some lyrical effusion which remained as a lasting monument: thus the Song of Moses resounded when the waves had closed over the enemy, as well as over an age of bondage and disgrace, and it was re-echoed in the thanksgivings of Miriam; and during the disturbed period of the Judges, the fall of the Canaanite foes was celebrated in a powerful song by the prophetess Deborah. Also personal feelings of joy or sorrow would find expression in verse like the beautiful prayer, in which Hannah poured forth her gratitude to God. And when at last anarchy and confusion ceased among the Hebrews, the arts of peace were zealously cultivated, and the schools of prophets diffused religious knowledge, and fostered taste and refinement.

Lyric poetry received a new stimulus by the genius of David, who was not only skilled in the use of the sling and the bow, but was also a master of the harp, a poet and a minstrel, whose melodies had the power to chase gloom and sadness away. In the eventful moments of a chequered life, he gave vent to his emotions in thrilling song; and in the intervals of repose, he glorified God in ardent hymns. His love of art was inherited by his son Solomon, who summoned all the talent of his time to adorn the public worship. In the splendid Temple he had erected hundreds of voices rose to the sound of many instruments; and music and song thenceforth remained powerful aids to religious devotion. Thus a new and important branch of literature was created; and lyric poetry retained its freshness and vigour almost to the latest periods of Hebrew history; for like the efforts of the prophets, it survived the fall of the two kingdoms, flourished in the land of exile, found successful votaries among the small community that returned to the Holy Land, and re-echoed within the walls of the second Temple.

Besides the lyrical productions scattered in the historical Books, the Hebrew Canon contains the Book of *the Psalms*, the *Lamentations of Jeremiah*, and *the Song of Solomon*.

Although the moralist was often blended with the poet, the didactic style was cultivated by the Hebrews independently of the lyrical form, and gave birth to several noble productions. Practical experience and advice were imparted in short and pithy sentences, which, easily impressed upon the memory, were welcomed as guides in the various relations and difficulties of life. Solomon was considered to have been the greatest master in this mode of teaching, and to him were attributed an almost endless number of *Proverbs*. But the advance of thought and experience soon demanded a higher form of expression. Earnest minds investigated the laws which rule the world, and attempted to fathom the mysteries which encompass the life of man. The great questions of Divine justice, as suggested by the perplexing inequality of human destinies, form the theme of the *Book of Job*. The meditations, the doubts, and the conclusions of a great observer of life are contained in the confessions of *Ecclesiastes*. In much later times, the progress of didactic literature is apparent in the beautiful ethics of *Jesus Sirach* and the *Wisdom of Solomon*, which have been embodied in the Apocrypha.

Yet though all these works prove that the Hebrews were no strangers to speculative thought, their genius inclined more strongly towards lyrical poetry, in which they have remained unsurpassed.

B. THE PSALMS.

The Psalms, as their name indicates, are a collection of poems intended to be sung with the accompaniment of the lute or psaltery. The later Jews designated them by the Hebrew word *Tehillim* (תְּהִלִּים) or "songs of praise", an appellation suitable only to a portion of them, and especially to those employed in the Temple. That they were designed to blend music and poetry, is not only proved by their striking rhythm, but by the distinct directions given in many of their headings; and we can well imagine the powerful effects of fine hymns of praise sung with the accompaniment of the harp and the timbrel, the clear notes of the cornet, or the blast of the trumpet.

The collection contains poems of an almost endless variety, dwelling upon every possible phase of human life, and interpreting all the emotions of the human heart — faithfully reflecting sorrow and joy, hope and fear, love and hatred, fervent gratitude and pious resignation.

Although the whole Book is generally described as "the Psalms of David", only a few of them are from his pen; both before and after his time, lyrical poems were written; and extensive as is the Book of Psalms, our gratitude for its preservation is mingled with deep regret for the loss of many other poetical productions. For such poems only were chosen for embodiment in the Book, which, apart from their literary merit, are distinguished by a religious tone and tendency; while those of a worldly nature, which no doubt existed among the Hebrews, were carefully excluded; though even a few of the latter class found their way into the sacred Volume. Those principles of selection will not appear surprising if it be remembered, that the Canon was fixed during the time of the second Temple, when the zealous and pious chiefs aimed principally at the religious education of the community. The Book of Psalms may, therefore, be considered as a kind of liturgy of the Jewish Church; the poems were made to serve this purpose, however different their original object might have been.

The 150 Psalms, of which the work consists, are neither arranged chronologically nor according to their contents; and they are divided into five groups or "books", all of which contain productions of various dates. Yet many poems are kindred in subject, and seem to have been suggested by the same or by similar occasions.

Perhaps the chief portions are those devoted to *the praise of God* and the glorification of His attributes. They point out His ruling Providence and His omnipotence, they expatiate on His wisdom, and they declare, above all, His boundless mercy. They are subdivided into various classes. Some of them describe the power of God as Lord of all nature: "He spoke and it was done; He commanded and it stood fast." He makes the waters rise or flee at His rebuke, or lets them flow gently in the valleys to give drink to every beast of the field. He has brought forth those marvels which shine in the firmament, and He is the Creator of man, the noblest of all works: "Thou hast made him only a little lower than the angels, and hast crowned him with glory and honour; Thou hast given him to have dominion over the works of Thy hands; Thou hast put all things under his feet." He has not only produced all beings, but He constantly provides for their sustenance, and He extends His forethought to the weakest as well as to the most powerful creatures: "The hills are a refuge for the wild goats, the rocks for the conies; the darkness ushers forth the stealthy beasts of prey, and the beasts of the forest creep forth to seek their food from God"; the lofty cedars offer shelter "where the birds build their nest, while the stork finds its home in the fir-trees".

Some other songs of praise dwell upon the relation of God towards kings and empires. They declare the eternity of His power, and contrast it with the shortlived greatness of earthly rulers; they describe how He raises up kingdoms and nations, and casts them into the dust, according to their deserts; and they set forth how He watches over His chosen people and delivers them from all dangers: "Shout joyfully to God, all ye lands; sing forth the honour of His name, make

His praise glorious... O bless our God, ye people, and make the voice of His praise to be heard... For Thou, O God, hast proved us, Thou hast tried us as silver is tried. Thou hast brought us into the net, Thou hast laid affliction upon our loins. Thou hast caused men to ride over our heads, we went through fire and through water; but Thou hast brought us to abundance" (Ps. LXVI). He is peculiarly "the God of Jacob"; His praise "is proclaimed in the city of their God, in the mountain of His holiness"; He is "known in Judah, His name is great in Israel; in Salem also is His Tabernacle, and His dwelling-place in Zion."

In another category of the songs of praise, God is exalted as the source of all honour and distinction, in strains like these: "Unto Thee, O God, do we give thanks, unto Thee do we give thanks: for Thy name is near, all declare Thy wondrous works ... The earth and all its inhabitants tremble; I establish its pillars. Selah. — Therefore I said to the proud, Do not be proud, and to the wicked, Do not lift up your head; do not lift up high your head; do not speak with an insolent neck. For honour does not come from the east, nor from the west, nor from the south; but God is the Judge: He makes low one and sets up high another. For in the hand of the Lord there is a cup, in which the wine ferments, and it is full of mixture; and He pours out of it: all the wicked of the earth wring out its dregs and drink them. But I will declare it for ever; I will sing praises to the God of Jacob. All the heads of the wicked I will cut off; but the heads of the righteous shall be exalted" (Ps. LXXV).

The most touching, if not the most fervent, songs of praise are those composed in grateful acknowledgment of some special proof of God's mercy and love; for in them the poets expressed their own experiences, and described how they had themselves been uplifted from misery to happiness.

They depict not so much the awful Judge of mankind, as the Protector of the weak, the Guide of the erring, and the Deliverer of the oppressed. Perhaps the most beautiful example of this class of composition is the Psalm written by David when he had triumphed over his enemies, and when, after a long career of adventure and danger, he believed he might hope for years of peace and tranquillity:

"I love Thee, O Lord, my strength. The Lord is my rock and my fortress, and my deliverer. The God of my rock, in Him will I trust, He is my shield, and the horn of my salvation, and my high tower. I called upon the Lord who is worthy of praise, and I was saved from my enemies.

"The bands of death encompassed me, and the floods of destruction terrified me. The bands of hell encompassed me, the snares of death seized me. In my distress I called upon the Lord, and I cried to my God, He heard my voice out of His Temple, and my cry came before Him into His ears.

"Then the earth shook and trembled; the foundations of the mountains moved and were shaken, because of His wrath. There went up a smoke out of His nostrils, and fire out of His mouth devoured, coals burnt out of Him. And He bent the heavens and came down, and darkness was under His feet. And He rode upon a cherub, and did fly, and He hovered upon the wings of the wind. He made darkness His cover, and His tent round about Him, darkness of waters and thick clouds. Out of the brightness before Him His thick clouds passed, hail-stones and coals of fire. And the Lord thundered in the heavens, and the Most High gave His voice, hail-stones and coals of fire. And He sent out His arrows and scattered them; and He shot out lightnings and discomfited them. Then the beds of the seas were seen, and the foundations of the world were uncovered at Thy rebuke, O Lord, at the blast of the breath of Thy nostrils.

"He sent from above, He took me, He drew me out of many waters. He delivered me from my strong enemy, and from them that hated me; for they were too strong for me. They surrounded me in the day of my calamity; but the Lord was my support. He brought me forth into safety; He delivered me, because He delighted in me. The Lord rewarded me according to my righteousness; according to the cleanness of my hands has He recompensed me. For I have kept the ways of the Lord, and have not wickedly departed from my God. For all His judgments were before me, and I did not put away His statutes from me. And I was also upright before Him, and I kept myself aloof from my iniquity. Therefore has the Lord recompensed me according to my righteousness, according to the cleanness of my hands in His eyes. With the merciful Thou showest Thyself merciful; with the upright man Thou showest Thyself upright; with the pure Thou showest Thyself pure; and with the froward Thou showest Thyself froward. For Thou savest the lowly people, but bringest down high looks.

"For Thou art my lamp, O Lord, and the Lord will lighten my darkness. For by Thee I have run through troops; by my God have I leaped over walls. As for God, His way is perfect; the word of the Lord is tried: He is a buckler to all those that trust in Him. For who is God save the Lord, and who is a rock save our God? God is my strength and power, and He makes my way perfect. He makes my feet like hinds' feet, and sets me upon my high places. He teaches my hands to war, so that my arm draws the bow of steel. And Thou hast given me the shield of Thy salvation, and Thy compassion has made me great. Thou hast enlarged my steps under me, so that my feet did not slip.

"I have pursued my enemies and destroyed them, and turned not again until I had consumed them. I have smitten them that they were not able to rise; they are fallen under my feet. For Thou hast girt me with strength for the battle, Thou hast subdued under me those that rose up against me, Thou hast also given me the necks of my enemies, and I have destroyed those that hated me. They cried, but there was none to save them; even to the Lord, but He answered them not. And I crushed them as the dust before the wind; I cast them out as the dirt in the streets. Thou hast delivered me from the struggles of my people, Thou hast guarded me to be the head of nations: many a people I knew not serve me; strangers submit to me; hearing the report of my fame, they are obedient to me; strangers tremble in awe, and come forth in fear from their fastnesses.

"The Lord lives, and blessed be my rock, and exalted be the God of the rock of my salvation. It is God who avenged me, and who brought down the nations under me, who rescued me from my enemies; Thou also hast lifted me up high above my adversaries, Thou hast delivered me from the men of violence. Therefore, I will give thanks to Thee, O Lord, among the nations, and sing praises to Thy name. He makes glorious the salvation for His king, and shows mercy to His anointed, to David, and to his seed for evermore" (Psalm XVIII).

Hebrew poets were naturally fervent in their praise of the holy city, and of the Temple, the centre of national worship: "For the Lord has chosen Zion; He has desired it for ever and ever." — "This is My rest for ever; here will I dwell, for I have desired it." But they urged again and again, that the pure-minded and the virtuous only could hope to be accepted by God when they came to bow down in His courts. This idea is, for instance, forcibly set forth in the following Psalm:

15*

"The earth is the Lord's, and the fulness thereof, the world and they that dwell therein. For He has founded it upon the seas, and established it upon the floods. Who shall ascend the hill of the Lord? or who shall stand in His holy place? He that has clean hands and a pure heart, who does not lift up his soul to vanity, nor swears deceitfully. He shall receive the blessing from the Lord, and righteousness from the God of his salvation. This is the generation of those that worship Him, that seek Thy face, O Jacob. Selah.

"Lift up your heads, O ye gates, and lift yourselves up, ye everlasting doors, that the King of Glory may come in. Who is the King of Glory? The Lord strong and mighty, the Lord mighty in battle. Lift up your heads, O ye gates; yea, lift them up, ye everlasting doors, that the King of Glory may come in. Who is the King of Glory? The Lord of Hosts, He is the King of Glory. Selah" (Psalm XXIV).

Nor was praise denied to the kings, the anointed of the Lord, and many Psalms dwell upon their wisdom, their power, or their glory. But the pious poets never failed to point to God as the source of all greatness and success: "For the king trusts in the Lord, and through the mercy of the Most High he shall not be moved." "The Lord said to my lord, Sit thou at My right hand until I make thy enemies thy footstool; the Lord at thy right hand shall strike through kings in the day of His wrath."

There is a group of Psalms which record the changeful history of the Israelites, and which, at the same time, remind them of their sins and their ingratitude, of benefits conferred and forgotten, of commands disobeyed, and of forgiveness constantly granted by a longsuffering God. They were intended to exhort later readers to "set their hope in God, and not to forget the works of God, but to keep His commandments, that they might not be as their fathers, a stubborn and rebellious generation; a generation that set not their heart aright, and whose spirit was not steadfast with God." One of these Psalms (the 78th) gives a rapid sketch of the destinies of the Hebrews from the time of Moses to the reign of David; and another (the 105th) relates the wonders and blessings which enabled them to take possession of the Promised Land, "that they might observe God's statutes and keep His laws."

A numerous class of Psalms consists of those which may be called *Psalms of lamentation*. These have perhaps exercised the most wide-spread and the most lasting influence; and to them sufferers have ever turned, finding therein not only the apt expression of their own sorrows, but the best comfort and solace. They are eminently religious and solemn, and are pervaded by a spirit of humble submission. Some of them dwell indeed with doubt and perplexity upon the trials and the misery of the righteous; but they finally acknowledge God's justice and wisdom, and teach resignation to His inscrutable decrees. Though they tell of physical suffering and mental anguish, they are free from the gloom of despair; for they invariably point to God as the merciful Deliverer and the unfailing Healer of all wounds. Most touching are the descriptions of individual affliction and distress. Thus a sufferer exclaims: "Oh, that I had wings like a dove, for then would I fly away and be at rest." For a cruel blow has wounded him, and his affection and friendship have been betrayed: "It was not an enemy that reproached me, then I could have borne it; neither was it he that hated me, that magnified himself against me, then I would have hidden myself from him. But, it was thou, a man, my equal, my guide, and my acquaintance — the words of his mouth were smoother than butter, but war was in his heart; his words were softer than oil, yet they were drawn swords." Deceived and outraged, yet not despairing, the poet turns to God, and not only finds help and consolation, but points out to others the means of rescue and comfort: "Cast thy burden upon the Lord, and He shall sustain thee; He shall never suffer the righteous to be moved."

Other Psalms of lamentation are the outpourings of patriots mourning over national misfortunes. They usually describe God's mercy to the Israelites, express sorrow for the ingratitude and the chastisements of the latter, and finally implore God's forgiveness in troubled times; they speak of faded glory and waning strength, and generally reflect the sad condition of the monarchy in later periods, when the people vainly struggled to recover their power and independence. The following is an example:

"O God, how long shall the adversary insult, shall the enemy insult Thy name for ever? Why withdrawest Thou Thy hand, even Thy right hand? take it out of Thy bosom and destroy them. For God is my King of old, working salvation, in the midst of the land. Thou didst divide the sea by Thy strength, Thou brokest the heads of the monsters in the waters. Thou hast crushed the heads of crocodiles, and gavest them for food to the people inhabiting the wilderness; Thou didst cleave the fountain and the flood; Thou didst dry up mighty rivers. The day is Thine, the night also is Thine; Thou hast prepared the light and the sun. Thou hast set all the borders of the earth; Thou hast made summer and winter. Remember this, the enemy insults the Lord, and wicked people blaspheme Thy name. Oh deliver not the soul of Thy turtle dove [Israel] to the wild beast: forget not the life of Thy poor for ever. Have regard of the covenant; for the dark places of the earth are full of the habitations of cruelty. Oh let not the oppressed return ashamed; let the poor and needy praise Thy name. Arise, O God, plead Thy own cause; remember how the impious insult

Thee daily. Forget not the voice of Thy enemies; the tumult of those that rise up against Thee increases continually" (LXXIV. 10-23).

Such effusions illustrate perhaps better than any record of history the terrible events which preceded and followed the overthrow of the commonwealth, the calamities of the war, the horrors of the siege, and the dreariness of exile. It will suffice to quote the following Psalm:

"By the rivers of Babylon there we sat down and wept, yea we wept when we remembered Zion. We hanged our harps upon the willows in the midst thereof. For they that carried us away captive required of us a song, and they that oppressed us required mirth, saying, Sing us one of the songs of Zion. How shall we sing the Lord's song in a strange land? If I forget thee, Jerusalem, let my right hand forget its cunning. If I do not remember thee, let my tongue cleave to the roof of my mouth; if I prefer not Jerusalem above my chief joy. Remember, O Lord, the children of Edom in the day of Jerusalem; who said, Destroy it, destroy it, even to the foundation thereof. O daughter of Babylon who art to be overthrown; happy shall he be that requites thee as thou hast served us. Happy shall he be that takes and dashes thy little ones against the stones" (Psalm CXXXVII).

Thus national reverses were felt as personal misfortunes, but consolation was derived from the confident hope that God would protect Jerusalem, rebuild the cities of Judah, and allow His people to inhabit them again and for ever. One of the sufferers declares that his heart is smitten and withers like grass; that his days are like a shadow that declines; yet he is sure that God will have mercy on the Israelites; and that "the time to favour them, yea the set time is come, when the Lord shall build up Zion, and shall appear in His glory... For He looks down from the height of His Sanctuary; from heaven the Lord beholds the earth to hear the groaning of the prisoner, to loosen the fetters of those that are appointed to death."

But some Psalms of lamentation describe the people's corruption and iniquity, their sinfulness and ingratitude; and in the manner of the prophets they combine rebuke with terrible predictions. "Help, O Lord, for the righteous man ceases, and the faithful fail from among the children of man." "The sinner in his pride persecutes the poor; but he will be taken in the schemes he has devised."

On the other hand, the collection of Psalms includes many *Songs of Thanksgiving*, composed when danger had been overcome, and sorrow and suffering were seen through the softening veil of the past. They have a great affinity to the hymns of praise, but they are less joyous and exuberant, because subdued by the influence of recent affliction; and they are sighs of relief, rather than shouts of exultation: "I will bless the Lord at all times, His praise shall be constantly in my mouth; for I sought the Lord, and He heard me, and delivered me from all my fears."

However, many of these Psalms cannot be classified with precision. The religious spirit of the Hebrews was averse to unrestrained effusions of gladness or of sorrow. Therefore, a feeling of solemnity and dependence generally toned down the brilliant colouring of the hymns of gratitude; and the piercing cries of distress were usually softened into accents of resignation, if not changed into strains of hopefulness.

Other poems are the productions of contemplative or philosophical minds, and may, in some measure, be regarded as expositions of the creed of the Hebrews. They include several odes not indeed composed with the enthusiasm of the hymns of praise, nor betraying the strong emotions of the songs of thanksgiving, but describing with great fervour the power of God which makes itself felt throughout the universe. As a specimen may be taken the "Prayer of Moses":

"O Lord, Thou hast been our dwelling-place in all generations. Before the mountains were brought forth, or before Thou hadst formed the earth or the world, even from eternity to eternity, Thou art God. — Thou turnest man to dust, and sayest, Return, ye children of men. For a thousand years in Thy sight are but as yesterday when it is past, and as a watch in the night. Thou carriest them away, they are as a sleep: in the morning they are like grass which grows up. In the morning it flourishes and grows up; in the evening it is cut down and withers. For we are consumed by Thy anger, and by Thy wrath are we terrified. Thou settest our iniquities before Thee, our secret sins in the light of Thy countenance. For all our days pass away in Thy wrath; we spend our years like a thought. The days of our years are threescore years and ten, and if in strength fourscore years, and their pride is labour and sorrow; for it is soon cut off, and we fly away. Who knows the power of Thy anger? even according to Thy fear so is Thy wrath. So teach us to number our days, that we may acquire a wise heart. Turn, O Lord! How long? and have compassion with Thy servants. O satisfy us soon with Thy mercy; that we may rejoice and be glad all our days. Make us glad according to the days wherein Thou hast afflicted us, and the years wherein we have seen evil. Let Thy work appear to Thy servants, and Thy glory to their children. And let the beauty of the Lord our God be upon us; and establish Thou the work of our hands upon us; yea, the work of our hands establish it" (Psalm XC).

Other Psalms of this class are intended to express faith and trust in God alone, those mainsprings of the Hebrew creed; as for instance the following beautiful hymn:

"The Lord is my shepherd; I shall not want. He makes

me lie down in green pastures, He leads me beside still waters, He refreshes my soul, He guides me in the path of righteousness for His name's sake. Even though I walk through the valley of the shadow of death, I fear no evil; for Thou art with me; Thy rod and Thy staff they comfort me. Thou preparest a table before me in the presence of my enemies; Thou anointest my head with oil; my cup runs over. Surely, goodness and mercy follow me all the days of my life; and I dwell in the House of the Lord for ever" (Psalm XXIII).

To this Psalm may be joined another of a similar import: "I lift up my eyes to the hills: whence shall my help come? My help comes from the Lord who made heaven and earth. — He will not suffer thy foot to be moved. He that keeps thee will not slumber. Behold, He that keeps Israel neither slumbers nor sleeps. The Lord is thy keeper, the Lord is thy shade upon thy right hand. The sun shall not smite thee by day, nor the moon by night. The Lord shall preserve thee from all evil, He shall preserve thy soul. The Lord shall preserve thy going out and thy coming in, from this time forth, and even for evermore" (Psalm CXXI).

The Psalmists constantly depict the futility of human efforts unaided by God's blessing: "Except the Lord build the house, they labour in vain that build it; except the Lord keep the city, the watchman watches, but in vain"; and they never omit to acknowledge that to His power Israel owed deliverance from so many dangers: "If it had not been the Lord who had been on our side, when men rose up against us — then they had swallowed us up quickly, when their wrath was kindled against us; then the water had overwhelmed us, the stream had gone over our soul" (Psalm CXXIV).

Other Psalms are confessions of sinfulness, or self-exhortations to virtue and repentance:

"Lord, my heart is not haughty, nor my eyes proud; neither do I exercise myself in great matters, or in things too high for me. Surely I have silenced and quieted my soul, as a child that is weaned of his mother, my soul is as a weaned child. Hope, O Israel, in the Lord from henceforth and ever" (Psalm CXXXI).

"I will sing of mercy and judgment: Thee, O Lord, will I praise. I will attend diligently to a righteous way. — Oh when wilt Thou come unto me? — I will walk within My House with a perfect heart; I will set no wicked things before My eyes; I hate transgressing, it shall not cling to Me. A froward heart shall be far from Me; I will not know a wicked person. Whoso secretly slanders his neighbour, him will I cut off; him that has a haughty look and a proud heart will I not suffer. My eyes shall be upon the faithful of the land, that they may dwell with Me: he that walks in a perfect way, he shall serve Me. He that works deceit shall not dwell within My House; he that tells lies shall not abide in My sight. Every day I will destroy all the wicked of the land; I will cut off all the evildoers from the city of the Lord" (Psalm CI).

Dogmas are rarely introduced in the writings of Hebrew poets and prophets; yet many didactic Psalms enforce the doctrine of retribution, and declare that punishment follows sin surely, though often tardily. "Be not revolted on account of evildoers, nor be thou envious against the workers of iniquity; for they are soon cut down like the grass, and wither as the green herb; trust in the Lord and do good, dwell in the land and foster righteousness" (Psalm XXXVII). Sometimes the Psalmists were indeed perplexed by the apparent success of the wicked: "For I was envious at the mockers when I saw the prosperity of the wicked. For they have no troubles until their death, and their body is well-fed; they are not in misery as other men, nor are they plagued like other people... Behold these ungodly! and still in perpetual rest, they increase in riches." Yet finally they never failed to acknowledge God's wisdom and justice, and to foretell the downfall of the unrighteous, and the deliverance of the humble-minded and the virtuous: "Surely Thou didst set them in slippery places, Thou didst cast them down into destruction. How are they brought into desolation as in a moment! they are utterly consumed with terrors" (Psalm LXXIII).

"Hear this, all ye people; give ear, all ye inhabitants of the world : both low and high, rich and poor together. My mouth shall speak of wisdom, and the meditation of my heart is understanding. I will incline my ear to a parable; I will open my deep saying upon the harp. Wherefore should I fear in the days of evil, when the iniquity of my trespassers compass me about? of those that trust in their wealth, and boast themselves in the greatness of their riches? Man cannot redeem his brother, nor can he give God a ransom for himself (for the redemption of their souls is too precious, and He desists for ever): that he should still live for ever and not see corruption. For he sees that wise men die, likewise the fool and the silly person perish, and leave their wealth to others. In their own thoughts, their houses continue for ever, and their dwelling-places to all generations; their names are praised on earth. Yet man in honour abides not; he is like the beasts that perish.

"This their way is their hope, and they that follow them approve their sayings. Selah. — Like sheep they are laid in the grave; death shall feed on them; and the upright shall have dominion over them soon; and their beauty shall perish in the grave, in their dwelling. But God will redeem my soul from the power of the grave: for He shall protect me. Selah.

"Be not thou afraid when a man becomes rich, when the

wealth of his house is increased; for when he dies, he shall carry nothing away, his wealth shall not descend after him. Though while he lived he deemed himself happy, and men will praise thee, when thou doest well to thyself; yet shalt thou come to the abode of thy fathers, who shall never see the light. Man that is in honour and has no understanding, is like the beasts that perish" (Psalm XLIX).

Many of the Psalms are devoted to the praise of active virtue, and in denouncing unmeaning ceremonialism, they rival the works of the prophets in force and earnestness: "I will not reprove thee, says the Lord, for thy sacrifice; since thy burnt-offerings are continually before Me; I will take no bullock out of thy house, nor he-goats out of thy folds. For every beast of the forest is Mine, and the cattle upon a thousand hills. I know all the fowls of the mountains, and the wild beasts of the field are Mine. If I were hungry I would not tell thee, for the world is Mine and the fulness thereof. Will I eat the flesh of bulls or drink the blood of goats? Offer to God thanksgiving, and pay thy vows to the Most High; and call upon Me in the day of trouble: I will deliver thee and thou shalt glorify Me . . . Whoso offers praise glorifies Me; and to him that directs his way aright will I show the salvation of God. But to the wicked God says, What hast thou to do to declare My statute, or that thou shouldst take My covenant in thy mouth? seeing Thou hatest instruction, and castest My words behind thee. When thou seest a thief, then thou agreest with him, and hast friendship with adulterers. Thou openest thy mouth to evil, and thy tongue frames deceit. Thou sittest and speakest against thy brother; thou slanderest thy own mother's son. These things thou hast done, and I kept silence; thou didst think that I was like thyself: but I will reprove thee, and set it before thy eyes. Now consider this, ye that forget God, lest I tear you in pieces, and there be none to deliver" (Psalm L. 8—22).

What God really requires of His servants is set forth simply and comprehensively in Psalms like the following: "O Lord, who shall abide in Thy Tabernacle? who shall dwell in Thy holy hill? He that walks uprightly, and works righteousness, and speaks the truth in his heart; he that backbites not with his tongue, nor does evil to his neighbour, nor takes up a reproach against his fellow-man; in whose eyes a vile person is contemned; but who honours them that fear the Lord; he that swears to his own hurt, and changes not; he that puts not out his money to usury, nor takes a bribe against the innocent: he that does these things shall never be moved" (Psalm XV).

A picture of brotherly love is presented in the following Psalm: "Behold, how good and how pleasant it is for brethren to dwell together in unity! It is like the precious ointment upon the head, that runs down upon the beard, even Aaron's beard, that runs to the skirts of his garments; as the dew of Hermon, and as the dew that descends upon the mountains of Zion: for there the Lord commands His blessing, even life for evermore" (Psalm CXXXIII).

Words of wisdom and lessons of experience are scattered throughout the work; and one Psalm (the 119th) is exclusively devoted to such didactic teaching, being composed of many proverbial sayings, and conveying partly moral maxims and partly praise and glorification of God.

It will be seen from the preceding remarks, that any classification of the Psalms beyond the broadest divisions is impossible; for, being the effusions of many minds, they present an almost endless variety of shades in character, spirit, and theme; meditation is mingled with sentiment which, rapidly changing, appears in every form and in every degree of intensity.

Enquiry naturally turns to the authors whose genius has bequeathed to us these precious treasures. The opinion, for some time entertained, that all the Psalms were written by king David, has long been abandoned. The compilers of the collection attributed 74 of the Psalms to the pen of David; but it is impossible to ascribe to him even this limited number; for many of them mention events of a subsequent, and even of a very late epoch of Jewish history, and allude not only to the building of the Temple by Solomon, but to its destruction by the Chaldeans, and to the Babylonian exile; and others are both in style and matter entirely different from the genuine compositions of David. In these power and tenderness, elevation and simplicity are wonderfully blended. They are not speculative, didactic, or historical; for as David was the minstrel as well as the poet, his productions are essentially lyrical, and describe in tones which were probably mellowed by the accents of the lyre or the harp, the varied impulses and feelings which moved his heart in the stirring moments of his eventful life. In lofty, yet simple songs of praise he has hardly a rival; let one instance suffice:

"O Lord, the king rejoices in Thy strength; and by Thy salvation how gladdened is he! Thou hast given him his heart's desire, and hast not withheld the request of his lips. Selah. For Thou hast presented him with blessings of happiness; Thou hast set a crown of pure gold on his head. He asked life of Thee, and Thou hast given it him, even length of days for ever and ever. His glory is great by Thy salvation; honour and majesty hast Thou laid upon him. For Thou hast made him most blessed for ever; Thou hast made him exceedingly glad with Thy countenance. For the king trusts in the Lord, and through the mercy of the Most High he shall not be moved. — Thy hand shall find out all Thy enemies; Thy right hand shall find out those that hate Thee. Thou shalt make them as a fiery oven in the time of Thy anger; the Lord shall swallow them up in His wrath, and fire shall devour them. Their fruit shalt Thou destroy from the earth, and their seed from among the children of men. For they spread out the nets of evil against Thee; they imagined mischief, but did not prevail. For Thou puttest them to flight, and directest the arrow from Thy strings against their face. — Rise Thou, O Lord, in Thy own strength, we will sing and praise Thy power" (Psalm XXI).

History has preserved many instances of David's impulsiveness, of his struggles against sin and passion, of his moral failings and victories, and of his readiness to forgive the trespasses of others, as well as to acknowledge his own. The confessions of such a man are naturally invested with singular interest, especially if they are so touchingly expressed as in the following Psalm:

"Blessed is he whose transgression is forgiven, whose sin is covered. Blessed is the man to whom the Lord imputes not iniquity, and in whose spirit there is no guile. When I kept silence, my bones waxed old through my crying all the day long. For day and night Thy hand was heavy upon me: my moisture is turned into the draught of summer. Selah. — I acknowledged my sin to Thee, and my iniquity have I not hid. I said, I will confess my transgressions to the Lord; and Thou forgavest the iniquity of my sin. Selah. For this shall every one that is godly pray to Thee in a time when Thou mayest be found: surely in the floods of great waters they shall not come nigh to him. Thou art my hiding place; Thou shalt preserve me from trouble: thou shalt compass Me about with songs of deliverance. Selah. I will instruct thee and teach thee in the way which thou shalt go: I will guide thee with My eye. Be you not as the horse or as the mule, which have no understanding, whose mouth must be held in with bit and bridle, lest they come near to thee. Many sorrows shall be to the wicked, but he that trusts in the Lord, mercy shall compass him about. Be glad in the Lord, and rejoice, ye righteous; and shout for joy, all ye that are upright in heart" (Psalm XXXII).

And then, David lays down the whole sum of his inward experience in a few striking sentences:

"Come, ye children, hearken to me; I will teach you the fear of the Lord. What man is there that desires life and loves many days, that he may see good? Keep thy tongue from evil, and thy lips from speaking guile. Depart from evil and do good; seek peace and pursue it. The eyes of the Lord are upon the righteous, and His ears are open to their cry . . . The Lord is nigh to them that are of a broken heart, and saves those that are of a contrite spirit. Many are the afflictions of the righteous; but the Lord delivers him out of them all" (Psalm XXIV. 12—20).

Nor must we forget to mention David's beautiful elegy on the death of Saul and Jonathan (see Part I. p. 375).

Next to David, the most important of the Psalmists was his contemporary Asaph. This gifted man, at once musician, poet, and prophet, was probably the son of Berachiah, of the tribe of Levi. Twelve Psalms are ascribed to him, which secure his place among the first of Hebrew poets. They are quite distinct from those of David; for they convey thoughts rather than feelings, and have in general a moral or didactic tendency. In the elevated tone of his speculations and in the largeness of his sympathies, Asaph recalls, more than any other of the Psalmists, the noble ethics of the prophets. He has the same lofty ideal of human excellence, and recommends the same means of attaining it: "Defend the poor and fatherless, do justice to the humble and needy; deliver the poor and the destitute, and release them out of the hand of the wicked." The Psalm to which we have above alluded as one of the most beautiful of the didactic class (the 50th), is at the same time one of the best specimens of Asaph's productions; but on the whole, his poems are less remarkable for variety or power than for precision and clearness.

The sons of Korah, likewise Levites, are mentioned as the authors of eleven Psalms distinguished by depth of feeling and fervent eloquence. Never has man's yearning for the love, the mercy, and the knowledge of God been so ardently expressed; never has the voice of praise rung with a more cheering sound; and seldom have the descriptions of nature and the glorification of the Divine power been inspired by greater enthusiasm and awe. As an instance we may take a Psalm, in which the feelings of joy are turned into a religious channel:

"O clap your hands, all ye people; shout to God with the voice of triumph. For the Lord, the Most High, is terrible; He is a great King over all the earth. He subdues the people under us, and the nations under our feet. He chose our inheritance for us, the pride of Jacob whom He loved. Selah. — God rises with a shout, the Lord with a sound of the trumpet. Sing praises to God, sing praises; sing praises to our King, sing praises. For God is the King of all the earth; give Him praises and song. God reigns over the nations, God sits upon the throne of His holiness. The princes of the people assemble, of the people of the God of Abraham: for the chiefs of the earth belong to God — He is greatly exalted" (Psalm XLVII).

The more serious side of the author's mind is disclosed in another masterly Psalm, in which is expressed not so much a longing for deliverance from the troubles and cares of the world, as an ardent desire for the return of the fatherly favour and protection of God.

"As the hart pants after the water-brooks, so pants my soul after Thee, O God. My soul thirsts for God, for having no guide, overseer, or ruler, provides her meat in the summer, and gathers her food in the harvest." "He that gathers in summer is a wise man; but he that sleeps in harvest-time is a son that causes shame." "The slothful man roasts not that which he took in hunting; but the substance of a diligent man is precious." And then the happy results of labour and the baneful effects of idleness are pointed out: "In all labour there is profit, but the talk of the lips tends only to penury." "Slothfulness casts into a deep sleep, and an idle soul shall suffer hunger." "He that loves pleasure shall be a poor man, he that loves wine and oil shall not be rich." "Be thou diligent to know the state of the flocks, and look well to thy herds; for riches are not for ever." "He that tills his land, shall have plenty of bread; but he that follows after vanity shall have poverty enough." "I went by the field of the slothful, and went by the vineyard of the man void of understanding; and, lo! it was all grown over with thorns, and nettles had covered the face thereof, and the stone-wall thereof was broken down."— The habits of the idle man himself are graphically described: "Yet a little sleep, yet a little slumber, a little folding of the hands to sleep"; to which the stern moralist adds, "So shall thy poverty come as one that travels, and thy want as an armed man".

Yet the Proverbs aim at promoting the love of work and not the love of gain, and they denounce greed and covetousness no less severely than the apathy and sloth which lead to poverty: "Riches profit not in the day of wrath, but righteousness delivers from death." "He that trusts in his riches shall fall, but the righteous shall flourish as a branch." Nor do they fail to describe the wretchedness of the avaricious man himself, and the uncertainty of earthly possessions; and they are implacable against those who endeavour to acquire wealth by unscrupulous and fraudulent means. "He that is greedy of gain tumbles in his own house, but he that hates gifts shall live." "Wilt thou set thy eyes upon that which is not? for riches certainly make themselves wings; they fly away as an eagle towards heaven." "The getting of treasures by a lying tongue is a vanity tossed to and fro of them that seek death."

A modest competence earned by honest labour, and enjoyed with contentment and humility, is praised as the most desirable lot, and as best calculated to secure happiness. "Better is little with righteousness, than great revenues without right." "Better is a dinner of herbs where love is, than a stalled ox and hatred therewith." "Better is it to be of a humble spirit with the lowly, than to divide the spoil with the proud." "When pride comes, then comes shame, but with the lowly is wisdom." The only possessions in which men should glory are "meekness and the fear of the Lord: they are riches, honour, and life". All other distinctions are insignificant; for "the rich and the poor meet together; the Lord is the Maker of them all".

The Hebrew sages commend not only a contented but a gentle and a patient mind; they describe with great force the misery so often inflicted by anger and passion, both upon the wrathful persons themselves and upon their fellow-men; while they dwell with persuasive eloquence upon the merits of forbearance, pardon, and meekness. "Hatred stirs up strife, but love covers all sins." "As coals are to burning coals, and wood to the fire, so is a contentious man to kindle strife." "A soft answer turns away wrath, but grievous words stir up anger." "A wrathful man stirs up strife, but he that is slow to anger appeases strife." "He that is slow to anger is better than the mighty, and he that rules his spirit than he that takes a city." "The discretion of a man defers his anger; and it is his glory to pass over a transgression."

However, the Proverbs enjoin not merely the repression of evil passions, of rancour and revenge, but they endeavour to promote a true fellow-feeling between man and man; they abound with exhortations to pity the unfortunate, to uphold the friend, to forgive the enemy, and to show sympathy even to the dumb animals. These feelings of charity are again and again inculcated with every variety of illustration. "He that oppresses the poor, reproaches his Maker; but he that honours Him, has mercy on the poor." "Withhold not good from those to whom it is due, when it is in the power of thy hand to do it." "Say not to thy neighbour, Go and come again, and to-morrow I will give; when thou hast it by thee." "He that has a bountiful eye shall be blessed; for he gives of his bread to the poor." "He that gives to the poor shall not lack; but he that hides his eyes shall share many a curse." "A man that has a friend must show himself friendly, and there is a friend that clings closer than a brother." "A friend loves at all times, and a brother is born for adversity." "Ointment and perfume rejoice the heart; so does the sweetness of a man's friend by hearty counsel." "Rejoice not when thy enemy falls, and let not thy heart be glad when he stumbles." "If thy enemy be hungry, give him bread to eat, and if he be thirsty, give him water to drink." "Say not, I will do so to him as he has done to me; I will render to the man according to his work." "The righteous man regards the life of his beast."

No less earnestly are all domestic virtues and obligations enjoined in the Proverbs — filial obedience and brotherly affection, conjugal fidelity and the duties of parents with regard to the education of their children. "My son, hear the instruction of thy father, and forsake not the law of thy mother; for they shall be an ornament of grace to thy head, and chains about thy neck." "A wise son makes a glad father, but a foolish man despises his mother." "A brother offended is harder than a strong city, and their contentions are like bars of iron." "Chasten thy son while there is yet hope, and let not thy soul spare for his crying." "Correct thy son, and he shall give thee rest, yea, he will give delight to thy soul." "Train up a child in the way he should go; and when he is old he will not depart from it."

And as the foundation and safeguard of all other virtues, the duty of truthfulness is enforced together with its sister-qualities of justice, rectitude, and fearless courage. "He that walks uprightly, walks surely, but he that perverts his ways shall be known." "He that hides hatred with lying lips, and he that utters slander, is a fool." "A false balance is an abomination to the Lord; but a just weight is His delight." "A false witness shall not be unpunished, and he that speaks lies shall perish." "The just man walks in his integrity, his children are blessed after him." "Bread of deceit is sweet to a man, but afterwards his mouth shall be filled with gravel." "He that says to the wicked, Thou art righteous, him shall the people curse, nations shall abhor him."

In addition to injunctions which concern the relations between man and man, the Proverbs give advice for the self-improvement and well-being of individuals. They denounce especially arrogance and conceit, and show the great advantages of readily listening to counsel and reproof, by whomsoever these may be offered. "The way of a fool is right in his own eyes, but he that hears counsel is wise." "The wise in heart will receive commandments; but a prating fool shall fall." "Poverty and shame shall be to him that refuses instruction, but he that regards reproof shall be honoured." "All the ways of a man are clean in his own eyes, but the Lord weighs the spirits." "Let another man praise thee and not thy own mouth; a stranger, and not thy own lips."

Other maxims point out the value of wise discretion shown in judicious silence and timely speech. "In the multitude of words there wants not sin; but he that refrains his lips is wise." "As a ring of gold in a swine's snout, so is a fair woman without discretion." "In all labour there is profit, but the talk of the lips that is penury." "A man has joy by the answer of his mouth, and a word spoken in season how good it is!"

But practical as the tendency of the Book undoubtedly is, it insists upon a life of rectitude and self-denial not merely on account of the worldly advantages it may secure, but for its own sake and from religious motives. To the mind of the pious Hebrew God was ever present, watching over his actions, and awarding blessing or punishment in accordance with his deserts. Therefore, the Proverbs instil above all the love of God, which is frequently represented as synonymous with the love of good and the hatred of evil. For they look upon religion and virtue as identical; they teach a theology simple indeed, but all-sufficient for attaining moral strength and single-minded purity; and they denounce unkindness, deceit, and pride with double force, because they regard every vice as "an abomination to the Lord." Like so many Psalms, they describe trust in God and His decrees as the fountain of all safety and success, of all knowledge and wisdom; they never cease to impress the fact that man is powerless without His guidance and assistance. "Trust in the Lord with all thy heart, and lean not to thy own understanding." "Commit thy works to the Lord, and thy thoughts shall be established." "He that handles a matter wisely, shall find good, and whoso trusts in the Lord happy is he." "The lot is cast upon the lap, but the disposing thereof is of the Lord." "Say not thou, I will recompense evil, but wait on the Lord, and He shall save thee." "The fear of man brings a snare, but whoso puts his trust in the Lord shall be safe." "The designs of the heart are in man, but the answer of the tongue is of the Lord." "A man's heart desires his way; but the Lord directs his steps." "The hearing ear and the seeing eye, the Lord has made both of them." "There is no wisdom nor understanding nor counsel against the Lord." "The horse is prepared against the day of battle; but safety is of the Lord."

Thus we meet with the same thoughts and sentiments which so often occur in the Psalms, and though in the Proverbs they are not expressed in the lyrical language of the poet, they breathe the same earnestness of feeling and conviction. They furnish another proof that the best and most pious among the Hebrews understood religion not as consisting in outward observances, but in the fear of God and in the practice of all human duties. They do not indeed reject the willing sacrifice, as they enjoin, "Honour the Lord with thy substance, and with the firstfruit of all thy increase"; but they give more frequent utterance to maxims like these: "To do justice and judgment is more acceptable to the Lord than sacrifice." "The sacrifice of the wicked is an abomination, how much more when he brings it with a wicked mind."

And the Proverbs also uphold throughout the doctrine of retribution, promising God's favour for deeds of righteousness, and menacing evil-doers with His displeasure: "As the whirlwind passes, so is the wicked no more; but the righteous are an everlasting foundation." "The fear of the Lord prolongs days; but the years of the wicked will be shortened."

It was reserved for later stages of religious training to pass beyond this conception, and to search for other explanations of the destinies of man.

D. THE BOOK OF JOB.

Though remarkable for poetic beauty and tragical pathos, the Book of Job is chiefly interesting on account of the philosophic problem which it discusses. Leaving the beaten track, and boldly opening new paths of enquiry, it brings some of the most important questions nearer a satisfactory conclusion, and prepares the way to their final solution.

The doctrine of retribution pervades all the earlier productions of the Hebrews: the Law and the Prophets, the Historical Books, the Psalms, and the Proverbs, they all uniformly describe the short-lived happiness of the wicked, and the certain, though often long-deferred prosperity of the virtuous. That doctrine was deemed sufficient to check the misdeeds of the one, and to sustain the fortitude of the other; yet it could not fail to be rendered doubtful by daily experience, which showed that bad men often enjoyed every earthly blessing, while the pious frequently died in suffering and misery. Such doubts found utterance in some of the finest Psalms; but they led to no new result, and the writers finally acquiesced in the traditional belief of speedy retribution, as may be seen from the following verses: "Fret not thyself because of evildoers, neither be thou envious of the workers of iniquity. For they shall soon be cut down like the grass, and wither as the green herb.... Rest in the Lord, and wait patiently for Him: fret not thyself because of him who prospers in his way, because of the man who practises fraud. Cease from anger and forsake wrath; fret not thyself only to do evil; for the wicked shall be cut off; but those that wait upon the Lord, they shall inherit the earth" (Psalm XXXVII). Another Psalmist forcibly describes the great difficulties which he felt in reconciling his experience with the popular doctrine; yet his inward struggles made him cling all the more firmly to the old belief, as the only source of peace and comfort. "Truly God is good to Israel, even to such as are of a clean heart. But as for me, my feet had almost fallen, my steps had wellnigh slipped. For I was envious of the foolish, when I saw the prosperity of the wicked. For they have no torments until their death, but their strength is firm. They are not in trouble as other men; nor are they smitten like other men.... Behold, these are the ungodly who prosper in the world; they increase in riches. Verily I have cleansed my heart in vain, and washed my hands in innocence. For all the day long have I been plagued, and chastened every morning .... Then I considered to comprehend this: it was too hard for me; until I went into the Sanctuary of God, and looked upon their end. Surely, Thou settest them in slippery places; Thou castest them down into destruction. How are they brought into desolation, as in a moment! they are utterly consumed with terrors. As a dream when one awakes, so, O Lord, Thou awakenest them, and destroyest their delusion" (Psalm LXXIII).

But the same problem was forced again and again upon thinking minds; and the first real advance towards its solution was made in the Book of Job. The author succeeded in proving the fallacy of the old theory, and especially in showing that suffering is by no means in all cases a punishment for wickedness. He combated that theory not timidly and cautiously, but with searching boldness, and in a series of argumentative speeches which remove all doubt. He skilfully chose a form of discussion which allowed a combination of exact enquiry and dramatic vivacity, of logical argument and poetic composition; and as a framework for his enquiries he employed the following narrative:

"There was a man in the land of Uz, whose name was

Job; and that man was perfect and upright, and one that feared God, and avoided evil. And there were born to him seven sons and three daughters; and his cattle was seven thousand sheep, and three thousand camels, and five hundred yoke of oxen, and five hundred she-asses; and besides, he had a very great household; so that this man was the richest of all the men of the East. And his sons went and feasted in their houses, every one his day; and they sent and called for their three sisters to eat and to drink with them. And when the days of their feasting had gone round, Job sent and sanctified them, and rose up early in the morning, and offered up burnt-offerings according to the number of them all; for Job said, It may be that my sons have sinned, and cursed God in their hearts. Thus did Job continually.

"Now one day the sons of God came to present themselves before the Lord, and Satan came also among them. And the Lord said to Satan, Whence comest thou? Then Satan answered the Lord, and said, From going to and fro in the earth, and from walking up and down in it. And the Lord said to Satan, Hast thou considered My servant Job, that there is none like him on the earth, a perfect and an upright man, one that fears God and avoids evil? Then Satan answered and said, Does Job fear God for nought? Hast not Thou made a fence about him and about his house, and about all that he has, on every side? Thou hast blessed the work of his hands, and his cattle has increased in the land. But put forth Thy hand now, and touch all that he has, and he will curse Thee to Thy face. And the Lord said to Satan, Behold, all that he has is in thy power; only upon himself put not forth thy hand. So Satan went away from the presence of the Lord.

"And one day when his sons and his daughters were eating and drinking wine in their eldest brother's house, there came a messenger to Job and said, The oxen were ploughing and the asses feeding beside them; and the Sabeans fell upon them, and took them away; yea, they have slain the servants with the edge of the sword; and I only am escaped alone to tell thee. While he was yet speaking, there came another, and said, The fire of God is fallen from heaven, and has burnt up the sheep and the servants, and consumed them; and I only am escaped alone to tell thee. While he was yet speaking, there came another, and said, The Chaldeans formed three bands, and fell upon the camels, and carried them away, yea, and have slain the servants with the edge of the sword; and I only am escaped alone to tell thee. While he was yet speaking, there came another, and said, Thy sons and thy daughters were eating and drinking wine in their eldest brother's house; and behold, there came a great wind from the wilderness, and smote the four corners of the house, and it fell upon the young men, and they are dead; and I only am escaped alone to tell thee. Then Job arose, and rent his coat, and shaved his head, and fell down upon the ground, and worshipped, and said, Naked came I out of my mother's womb, and naked shall I return thither; the Lord gave, and the Lord has taken away; blessed be the name of the Lord. In all this Job sinned not, nor uttered a foolish word against God.

"Again there was a day when the sons of God came to present themselves before the Lord, and Satan came also among them to present himself before the Lord. And the Lord said to Satan, From whence comest thou? And Satan answered the Lord and said, From going to and fro on the earth, and from walking up and down in it. And the Lord said to Satan, Hast thou considered My servant Job, that there is none like him on the earth, a perfect and an upright man, one that fears God and avoids evil? and still he holds fast his integrity, although thou hast incited Me against him, to destroy him without cause. And Satan answered the Lord, and said, Skin for skin, yea, all that a man has will he give for his life. But put forth Thy hand now, and touch his bone and his flesh, and he will curse Thee to Thy face. And the Lord said to Satan, Behold he is in thy hand; only spare his life.

"So went Satan forth from the presence of the Lord, and smote Job with sore boils from the sole of his foot to his crown; and he took a potsherd to scrape himself therewith, and he sat down among the ashes.

"Then said his wife to him, Dost thou still retain thy integrity? curse God, and die. But he said to her, Thou speakest as one of the foolish women speaks. What? shall we receive good at the hand of God, and shall we not receive evil? In all this Job did not sin with his lips.

"Now when Job's three friends heard of all this evil that had befallen him, they came every one from his own place—Eliphaz the Temanite, and Bildad the Shuhite, and Zophar the Naamathite: for they had made an appointment together to come to mourn with him and to comfort him. And when they lifted up their eyes afar off, they did not recognise him; and they lifted up their voice, and wept; and they rent every one his coat and sprinkled dust upon their heads towards heaven. So they sat down with him upon the ground seven days and seven nights, and none spoke a word to him: for they saw that his grief was very great."

It is impossible to decide how far this narrative is founded on fact; whether a pious sufferer like Job, who from the greatest prosperity sank into the deepest misery, ever lived, or whether — as Jewish tradition contends — he is a purely fictitious person. The story itself certainly shows traces of the poet's free creation both in Job's ideal piety and ideal happiness; the number of his children—*seven* sons and *three* daughters, or *ten* in all—has symbolical significance; and the introduction of a council of God, at which the angels and Satan appear, brings us into the circle of Persian conceptions. But it must be admitted, that the character of patriarchal life and simplicity is admirably preserved in the nature of Job's possessions, in the dangers to which he is exposed, and in his position as chief of his family.

Now the author approaches his subject; and in order to prepare the way for its discussion, he puts into the mouth of Job a strong outburst of anguish and despair: "Let the day perish wherein I was born, and the night in which it was said, There is a man-child conceived. Let that day be darkness; let not God regard it from above; neither let light shine upon it ... Why did I not die from the womb? why did I not expire, when I was brought into life? ... For I should now lie still and be quiet; I should sleep and be at rest, with kings and counsellors of the earth, who built splendid tombs for themselves; or with princes that were rich in gold, who filled their houses with silver ... There the wicked cease from oppression; and there the weary are at rest. There the prisoners repose together; they hear not the voice of the tyrant. The small and great are there; and the servant is free from his master. Wherefore is light given to him that is in misery, and life to the bitter in soul, who long for death, but it comes not, and dig for it more than for hidden treasures? ... For my sighs come before I eat, and my cries are poured out like water. For the thing which I greatly feared is come upon me, and that which I was afraid of has fallen upon me. I have no rest and no peace and no repose; for trouble has come."

On hearing these vehement complaints, the friends of Job can no longer remain silent, and they endeavour to soothe his grief and to quiet his doubts; but Job answers them one by one; and this dialogue, which goes round three times, skilfully unfolds the arguments which were usually brought forward in support of the old doctrine, and those by which the author attempted to refute it.

FIRST SPEECH OF ELIPHAZ (ch. IV. V).

The most experienced of the friends, Eliphaz, begins by cautiously expressing his surprise that Job who had often been the comforter of sufferers, should be so desponding now that he was himself in distress: "If we try to commune with thee, wilt thou be vexed? but who can restrain himself from speaking? Behold, thou hast instructed many, and thou hast strengthened weak hands. Thy words have upheld him that was falling, and thou hast strengthened feeble knees. But now it is come upon thee, and thou faintest; it touches thee, and thou art perplexed." — Job should trust in his well-known piety, since a good man had never yet perished, nor had a wicked man ever triumphed: "Is not thy fear of God thy confidence, is not thy hope the uprightness of thy ways? Remember, I pray thee, who ever was destroyed, being innocent? or when were the righteous cut off? Even as I have seen, those that plough iniquity, and sow wickedness, reap the same. By the blast of God they perish, and by the breath of His nostrils are they consumed."

Job had spoken as if he were sinless; therefore Eliphaz related what a vision had taught him — namely, that not even the angels are pure before God, much less earthborn men: "A lesson was secretly conveyed to me, and my ear received a whispering thereof... When profound sleep had fallen on men, fear came upon me and trembling, which caused all my bones to shake. Then a spirit passed before my face; the hair of my flesh stood up... there was silence, and I heard a voice, saying, Shall mortal man be just before God? shall a man be pure before his Maker? Behold, He puts no trust in His servants, and His angels He charges with folly:

how much more those that dwell in houses of clay, whose foundation is in the dust, which are crushed before the moth?" Therefore, the friend continues, the lamentations of Job were unavailing, and instead of rising against the decrees of God, it would be wiser to invoke His help, which is never withheld from the virtuous sufferer: "I would seek God, and to God would I commit my cause, who does great and unsearchable things, marvellous things without number: ... He overthrows the devices of the crafty, so that their hands cannot perform their enterprise,... but He saves the needy from the sword, from their mouth, and from the hand of the mighty. So the poor has hope, and iniquity stops its mouth."

Indeed, Divine chastisements should be received as warnings and lead to improvement, and if Job would view his trials in this light, he might be sure of a better future: "Behold, happy is the man whom God corrects; therefore despise not thou the chastening of the Almighty: for He makes sore and binds up; He wounds and His hands make whole... And thou shalt know, that thy tent shall be in peace; and thou shalt examine thy habitation and shalt not be disappointed. And thou shalt know, that thy seed is great, and thy offspring as the grass of the earth. Thou shalt come to thy grave in a full age, like as a shock of corn rises in its season. Lo this, we have searched it, so it is; hear it, and know thou it for thyself."

JOB'S REPLY (ch. VI. VII).

Job first justifies the violence of his complaints by pointing to the unwonted severity of his calamities: "Oh that my grief were thoroughly weighed, and my misery laid in the balances together! For indeed it is heavier than the sand of the sea; therefore my words wander. For the arrows of the Almighty are within me, and my spirit drinks their poison:

the terrors of God are set in array against me." He then insists that even his longing for death can not be blamed, as his agonies are intolerable, and his waning strength forbids all hope of recovery: "Oh that I might have my request, and that God would grant me my desire! That it would please God to destroy me, that He would stretch out His hand, and cut me off! Then should I have yet a comfort, and I should exult in my pitiless sorrow, that I have not belied the words of the Holy One. What is my strength, that I should hope? and what is my end, that I should be longsuffering? Is my strength the strength of stones? or is my flesh of brass?"

With bitter grief he inveighs against his friends, to whom he says he had looked for solace, but who vexed him with their empty words: "My brethren have dealt deceitfully as a brook, and as a stream of brooks that passes by ... For now you are nothing; you see my terror, and are afraid. Did I say, Bring presents to me? or, Give a reward for me of your substance? or, Deliver me from the enemy's hand? or, Redeem me from the hand of the oppressor?" — He is ready to answer their imputations; they condemn him for words which despair had wrung from him; and he bids them retract their undeserved reproaches: "Teach me, and I will be silent, and make me understand wherein I have erred . . . Do you desire to reprove words? Yet the speeches of the desperate are as the wind. Yea, you cast lots over the fatherless, and dig pits for your friend ... Return, I pray you, let not iniquity be done; yea, return again, my righteousness is still within me."

Having thus disposed of the remarks of Eliphaz, Job indulges in reflections on human misery, and dilates particularly on his own unparalleled trials, which he describes with thrilling power: "Is there not warfare to man upon earth?

and are not his days like the days of a hireling? As a servant yearns for the shadow, and as the hireling looks for reward of his work: so have I inherited months of vanity, and wearisome nights are appointed to me. When I lay down, I say, When shall I arise, and when shall the night be gone? and I am tired of tossings to and fro to the dawning of the day. My flesh is clothed with worms and clods of dust; my skin hardens and breaks again. My days are swifter than a weaver's shuttle, and are spent without hope." He, therefore, entreats God to deliver him ere it will be too late, since he will soon sink into the grave, from which no mortal returns: "O remember that my life is wind, that my eye shall no more see good. The eye of him that has seen me shall see me no more; Thy eyes are upon me and I am no more. As the cloud disappears and vanishes away, so he that goes down to the grave shall come up no more. He shall return no more to his house, nor shall his place know him any more."

This thought rouses his grief to increased vehemence; he complains that God treats him like some mighty sea-monster, whereas he is a frail man whose strength is nearly exhausted, and he implores His help and His pardon: "I have sinned, what shall I do to Thee, O Thou who searchest men? why hast Thou set me as a mark against Thee, so that I am a burden to myself? And why dost Thou not pardon my transgression, and take away my iniquity? for soon shall I sleep in the dust, and Thou shalt seek me, but I shall be no more."

FIRST SPEECH OF BILDAD (ch. VIII).

The second friend, displeased with Job's angry refutations, addresses him less leniently than Eliphaz, though his disapproval also is expressed in veiled and tempered language; he is indeed convinced of Job's righteousness, but he upholds with equal firmness his belief in God's justice; Job's children, who died, no doubt merited their fate; and his future happiness is in his own hand: "Does God pervert judgment? or does the Almighty pervert justice? If thy children have sinned against Him, He has cast them away for their transgression. If thou wouldst seek God, and make thy supplication to the Almighty; if thou art pure and upright: surely, then He would watch over thee, and make thy righteous habitation prosperous. And thy beginning will be held small, but thy latter end will be great indeed."

To prove the truth of his words, Bildad quotes the views and the experience of their forefathers, who always maintained that the wicked man cannot escape a speedy doom: "For enquire, I pray thee, of the former generation, and listen to the search of their fathers ... So are the paths of all that forget God, and the hypocrite's hopes shall perish ... He is green before the sun, and his branch shoots forth in his garden ... Yet if they tear him from his place, then it shall deny him, saying, I have not seen thee. Behold, this is the joy of his way, and from the ground shall others grow." And then he concludes that, as Job is no evil-doer, he may hope for a return of brighter days: "Behold, God will not cast away the righteous man, nor will He help the wicked: till He fills thy mouth with laughing and thy lips with rejoicing. They that hate thee shall be clothed with shame; and the dwelling-place of the wicked shall come to nought."

JOB'S REPLY (ch. IX. X).

Job strongly condemns Bildad's repetition of the old and, as he thinks, fallacious theory. He is fully aware, he says, of the vast gulf which separates God's omnipotence from man's littleness, and which renders it impossible for man to assert his innocence before God; and he describes that omnipotence in many of its grand and terrible manifestations: "I know it is so: how should man be just before God?... He is wise in heart, and mighty in strength: who has revolted against Him and has prospered? He removes mountains, unawares; and overturns them in His anger. He shakes the earth out of its place, and the pillars thereof tremble. He commands the sun, and it rises not; and seals up the stars. He alone spreads out the heavens, and treads upon the waves of the sea ... Behold, He takes away, who can hinder Him? who will say to Him, What doest Thou? God does not withdraw His anger, and the proud helpers stoop under Him. How much less shall I answer Him, and choose my words, to reason with Him?"

Therefore, he is far from the presumption of arguing with God, in whose power he stands; for he knows, that even his defence would be turned into an accusation against himself. Nevertheless, he does not shrink from proclaiming his innocence, unconcerned at the consequences: "I am righteous, I do not care for my life; I despise my days"; nay he fearlessly declares: "It is all one; therefore I say, He destroys alike the righteous and the wicked. If the scourge slays suddenly, He laughs at the trial of the innocent. The earth is given into the hand of the wicked; He covers the faces of its judges; if not, who does it?"

He points to his own wretched condition as the strongest proof of his views; he can see no hope of returning happiness; and though his conscience is clear, he must even renounce the desire of justifying himself, because God's sovereign will has decreed him to be guilty, and His majesty would awe him into fear or silence, were he to undertake his defence: "I am to be an offender; why then do I labour in vain? If I wash myself with snow-water, and make my hands ever so clean; yet Thou plungest me into the ditch, and my own garments shall abhor me. For He is not a man, as I am, that I should answer Him, and that we should come together in judgment."

Yet Job cannot resist the temptation of showing, how he would address God, if he were permitted to speak in His presence without restraint. Beginning his appeal with the assurance that his life is a burden to him, and that, therefore, he has no desire to save it by suppressing or veiling the truth, he asks God, why He, the all-seeing Ruler, so cruelly persecutes him, His creature, though He is aware of his innocence; and what pleasure He can have in searching out and mercilessly punishing the failings of a weak mortal: "I should say to God, Do not condemn me; show me wherefore Thou contendest with me. Is it good for Thee that Thou shouldst oppress, that Thou shouldst despise the work of Thy hands, and let Thy light shine upon the counsel of the wicked? Hast Thou eyes of flesh? or seest Thou as man sees?... Thou knowest that I am not guilty; and there is none that can deliver out of Thy hand... Remember, I beseech Thee, that Thou hast made me as the clay, and that Thou wilt bring me to dust again." And he concludes with a fervent supplication to be favoured with some short moments of happiness before he sinks to his eternal rest: "Are not my days few? let Him cease then, and turn from me, that I may take comfort a little, before I go, never to return, to the land of darkness and the shadow of death, a land of gloom like utter darkness, and of the shadow of death, without order, and where the light is as darkness."

FIRST SPEECH OF ZOPHAR (ch. XI).

The third friend, no longer indulgent as the two former speakers had been, expresses his indignation at what he considers Job's unpardonable arrogance and blasphemy; he says that, if God were to appear and to reveal the whole truth, Job would be terrified, and would feel that, so far from suffering innocently, he has not been adequately punished for all his transgressions: "Should not the multitude of words be answered? and should a man full of talk be justified? Should thy foolish speech make men be silent, and when thou mockest, shall no man make thee ashamed? For thou sayest, My faith is pure, and I am clean in Thy eyes. But oh that God would speak, and open His lips against thee!... Then thou wouldst know that God imposes upon thee less than thy iniquity demands."

How could Job presume to rival God's wisdom, or hope to escape His judgment? For God only is all-knowing, and to Him the secrets of the human heart are revealed. Therefore Zophar exhorts Job to abandon his evil ways, and to walk before God in piety; if he did this, then his future days would be full of happiness and rich in every blessing; but if he persevered in his sinful life, he must expect fearful and hopeless destruction: "If thou prepare thy heart, and stretch out thy hands towards Him; if thou put away the iniquity which is in thy hand, and do not let wickedness dwell in thy tents: then thou wilt lift up thy face free from fault; yea, thou wilt stand firm, and wilt not fear. Then thou wilt forget thy misery, and remember it as waters that pass away; and thy life shall be clearer than the noon-day; thou shalt shine forth, thou shalt be as the morning. And thou shalt be secure, because there is hope; yea, thou shalt make a fence about thee, and thou shalt rest in safety. And thou shalt lie down, and none shall make thee afraid; yea, many shall do homage to thee. But the eyes of the wicked fail, and their refuge perishes, and their hope is — giving up the ghost."

JOB'S REPLY (ch. XII—XIV).

Job can no longer govern his impatience at being obliged to hear again and again the same ideas and consolations, and he exclaims in bitter irony: "Indeed, you are the people, and wisdom will die out with you!" He considers it an intentional insult on the part of his friends to repeat observations with which they know he is familiar, and which even the animals of the field, the air, and the water proclaim; he is indeed not surprised at their conduct, for the unfortunate must expect contempt, while the flourishing sinners are esteemed and in peace.

Yet Job, in order to give another proof that he is fully imbued with the greatness of God's attributes, elaborately describes His unlimited rule over the elements of nature, and over the destinies of even the most powerful men: "Behold, He breaks down, and it cannot be built again; He shuts up a man, and he cannot be released. Behold, He withholds the waters, and they dry up; He sends them forth, and they overturn the earth. With Him is strength and wisdom; the deceived and the deceiver are His. He leads counsellors away as captives, and makes the judges fools. He unties the bond of kings, and strengthens their loins with a girdle. He leads princes away as captives, and overthrows the mighty. He removes the speech of the trusty, and takes away the understanding of the aged. He pours contempt upon princes, and loosens the girdle of the strong. He discloses the depths of darkness, and brings forth to light the shadow of death. He increases the nations, and destroys them; He enlarges the nations, and restrains them again. He takes away the intelligence of the chiefs of the people of the earth, and makes them wander in a wilderness where there is no path. They grope in the dark without light, and He makes them stagger like a drunken man."

Then reverting again to his own fate, Job repeats that he is indeed anxious to lay his case before God, and before Him alone; for his friends have proved both faithless and ignorant: "You are forgers of lies, you are all valueless physicians"; he requests them to speak no more, and thus to hide their folly; and he censures them severely for having uttered what they must have known to be untrue, and for having imputed to him grievous sins, in the vain hope to win God's favour by falsehood: "Hear now my reasonings, and hearken to the pleadings of my lips. Will you speak wickedly for God, and talk deceitfully for Him? Will you flatter His person? will you contend for God? Is it good that He should search you out? and as one man mocks another, do you not mock Him? He will surely reprove you, if you secretly accept persons. Does not His grandeur terrify you? and does not His dread fall upon you? Your speeches are like ashes; your strongholds are like strongholds of clay."

He goes so far as to entreat God's presence, that he may submit to Him his defence, were he even to suffer death for his daring; for his innocence arms him with courage. But his prayer is not granted, and God does not appear to him; and this he takes as a proof that God intends to oppress and to persecute him still more, and to hasten his doom: "Wherefore hidest Thou Thy face, and holdest me for Thy enemy? Wilt Thou frighten a chased leaf? and wilt Thou pursue the dry stubble? For Thou writest bitter things against me, and makest me feel the iniquities of my youth. And Thou puttest my feet in the stocks, and guardest all my paths, and hedgest round the heels of my feet; although I am consumed like a rotten thing, like a garment that is moth-eaten."

This train of thought naturally leads Job again to a description of the frailty of man and of his own sad struggles. Man is weak, shortlived, and born for suffering; yet God searches out and punishes his most trifling fault, and hardly grants him respite in his old age: "Man that is born of a woman is of few days, and full of trouble. He comes forth like a flower and is cut down; he flees as a shadow and continues not. And Thou settest Thy eyes upon such one, and bringest me into judgment with Thee? How can a clean one come out of an unclean? not one. If his days are fixed, if the number of his months are with Thee, and if Thou hast appointed his bounds which he cannot pass, then turn from him that he may rest, that he may enjoy his day like a hireling." — The lot of the tree is more enviable; for if it is cut down, the roots often shoot forth again, and a new tree arises: "But man dies and wastes away; yea, man expires and where is he? ... and man lies down and rises not: till the heavens be no more, they shall not awake, nor be raised out of their sleep." Job declares, that he would not murmur, if man were kept in the grave for a certain period, to suffer his deserved retribution, but were then allowed to return to a new life: "If a man die, shall he live again? all the days of my struggle should I wait, till my relief come." But such was not God's decree; for He is unsparing in His wrath; it may be that when pious persons die, their children live in prosperity; but they themselves are unconscious of it, and they end their days in grief and sorrow, unrelieved by a single ray of hope.

SECOND SPEECH OF ELIPHAZ (ch. XV).

The first circle of the dialogue is completed, and the only result of the discussion has been an increased irritation both on the part of Job and his friends. Neither of them has been convinced: Job cannot admit that he has merited such awful chastisements, whereas the friends take these very chastisements as a proof that he must have been guilty of great offences; thus Job finds in his own experience a conclusive refutation of the doctrine of retribution, while the friends disregard experience in order to uphold it. The next dialogue proceeds still more emphatically.

Eliphaz, speaking for the second time, expresses his astonishment, how a man who aspires to be called wise, can indulge in such vapid talk, which not only betrays his folly but his wickedness: "Yea, thou destroyest the fear of the Lord, and forgettest the awe of God. For thy mouth utters thy iniquity, and thou choosest the tongue of the crafty. Thy own mouth condemns thee, and not I; yea, thy own lips testify against thee."

Job has spoken so contemptuously of his friends that Eliphaz feels justified in reproaching him with the assumption of a fancied superiority. But more reprehensible still than Job's conceit is his blasphemous revolt against the ordinances of God: "Why does thy heart carry thee away? and what do thy eyes wink at, that thou turnest thy wrath against God, and lettest such words go out of thy mouth? What is man that he should be clean? and he that is born of a woman, that he should be righteous? Behold, He puts no trust in His holy ones, and the heavens are not clean in His sight; how much less so is wretched and depraved man, who drinks iniquity like water!" Therefore, Eliphaz, far from holding out to him hopes of happiness, as he had done before, now places before him an awful picture of the misfortunes which are sure to befall the unrepenting and defiant sinner; and in order to increase the force of his observations, he assures him that they are made on no contemptible authority: "I will show thee, hear me, and that which I have seen I will declare; what wise men have told, and have not hid from the times of their fathers, to whom alone the earth was given, and no stranger had passed among them."

JOB'S REPLY (ch. XVI. XVII).

Job had hoped that his friends, in pity of his fearful calamities, would speak more compassionately; but he had been cruelly disappointed; and he now assures them, that if their positions were reversed, he would not pour forth empty and heartless words; he says that he is indeed in utter perplexity; for he sees no advantage in speaking, and yet can he derive no relief from silence; he cannot refrain from surveying once more the terrible course of his life, from the peaceful and happy days of the past up to his present misery: "I was at ease, but He has shaken me; He has taken me by my neck, and dashed me to pieces, and set me up for His mark. His archers encompassed me, He cleft my reins asunder without pity; He poured out my gall upon the ground. He broke me with breach upon breach, He run upon me like a giant. I sowed sackcloth upon my skin, and defiled my head with dust. My face is reddened with weeping, and on my eyelids is the shadow of death."

He protests that he has not deserved such a fate; for no violence was in his hands, and his "prayer was pure"; he is convinced that the future has nothing in store for him but death; yet it would be a consolation for him to know that when he has passed away, his innocence will be acknowledged; he expects no justice from his mocking friends, but he looks up to God and entreats Him to decide his cause before his short span of life is concluded: "O earth, cover not thou my blood, and let my cry have no place! And even now, behold, my Witness is in heaven, and my Champion is on high. My friends scorn me, but my eye pours out tears to God, that He may procure justice for a man against God, and for the son of man against his friends. For my few years come to an end, and I go the way whence I shall not return. My spirit is troubled, my days are extinguished, graves are ready for me."

For a moment he is cheered by brighter prospects, but soon relapses into his former gloom, and describes with renewed force his misery, his disgrace, and the horror of all pious men at his unmerited distress; and he concludes by bitterly attacking the folly of his friends, who presume to console him with earthly hopes, whereas he hardly belongs any more to the living, and is already standing on the very edge of the grave: "But as for you all, return, and go now: for I cannot find one wise man among you ... They change the night into day; the light touches close upon darkness. If I wait for the grave as for my home, and make my bed in darkness; if I say to the tomb, My father art thou, and to the worm, Thou art my mother and my sister: where is then my hope? and my hope who sees it? It sinks down to the bars of the pit, since in the dust is rest altogether."

BILDAD'S SECOND SPEECH (ch. XVIII).

Bildad, mortified at Job's contemptuous rejection of all friendly advice, turns the reproach upon Job himself, who appears to believe, that for his own sake God ought to reverse the eternal order of things, according to which sinners like himself are invariably punished: "Wherefore are we counted as beasts, and are despised in your sight? Thou who tearest thyself in thy anger, shall the earth be forsaken on thy account? and shall the rock be removed out of its place? Yea, the light of the wicked is extinguished, and the spark of his fire does not shine. The light is dark in his tent, and his lamp is extinguished with him. His mighty steps are straitened, and his own counsels cast him down; ... his strength is wasted by hunger, and destruction is ready at his side."

Then, in order to offer a terrible warning to Job, to whom he makes pointed allusions, Bildad pictures with rising indignation the fearful lot of the wicked: "Misfortunes consume the limbs of his body; the firstborn of death consumes his limbs. He is torn away from his tent, his refuge, and he is pressed on to the king of terrors. Evil dwells in his tent, which no more belongs to him; brimstone is scattered upon his habitation. His roots are dried up beneath, and above are his branches cut off. His remembrance perishes from the earth, and he has no name in the land ... They that come after him are amazed at his day of misfortune, and they that went before, are affrighted. Surely such are the dwellings of the wicked, and this is the place of him that knows not God."

JOB'S REPLY (ch. XIX).

Job feels every new speech of his friends like another wound inflicted upon him by their stinging insults and their hollow accusations; he therefore entreats them to speak no more, since both the wickedness with which they reproach him and the fate he suffers concern him alone. Yet he cannot believe that they seriously consider him guilty of crimes of such enormity as to deserve so awful a retribution; they must in sincerity acknowledge that he is overwhelmed by the wrath of God; and therefore, as he has been forsaken by all others, they should grant him their compassion, instead of joining God in His cruel persecution: "How long will you vex me, and crush me with words?... And be it indeed that I have erred, my error remains with myself... Know, I beseech you, that God has oppressed me, and has compassed me with His net. Behold, I cry out of wrong, but I am not heard; I cry aloud, but there is no justice... His wrath is kindled against me, and He counts me as His enemy... He has separated me from my brethren, and my friends are indeed estranged from me... I call my servant, and he gives me no answer; I must entreat him with my mouth. My breath is loathsome to my wife, and my supplication to my progeny. Even young children despise me; I arise, and they speak against me. All my dearest friends abhor me, and those I loved turn against me... Have pity upon me, have pity upon me, O my friends; for the hand of God has struck me. Why do you persecute me like God, and are not satisfied with my flesh?"

But Job has little hope to obtain justice from his friends or his contemporaries; and he, therefore, wishes that his defence may be written in a book to be handed down to future generations, or still better that it may be engraven in imperishable rocks. But no, he need not wait for the verdict of posterity; he is sure that God Himself will soon appear to vindicate his righteousness, and to release him from anguish and bodily suffering; then his faithless friends will be terrified to think that they have ill-treated an innocent man, and will tremble before the Divine jugdment. These hopes and convictions he expresses in the following words: "I know that my Redeemer lives, and that He will at last appear on this ground; and when this my skin is destroyed, and I am deprived of my flesh, I shall see God: I shall see Him for myself, and my eyes shall see Him, and not another: my heart within me is consumed with longing for that day. Then indeed you will say, Why did we persecute him? for the root of the matter will be discovered in me. Be ye afraid of the sword; for your wrath deserves the punishment of the sword, that you may know that there is a judgment."

However, the anxious prayer of Job for a Divine vision is not at once granted; the author desires still further to prove that no ingenuity or eloquence is able to uphold the popular doctrine, and he, therefore, continues the dialogue.

ZOPHAR'S SECOND SPEECH (ch. XX).

Entirely passing over the principal ideas of Job's address, Zophar merely dwells on some of his incidental remarks. He is revolted at the reproaches levelled by Job against himself and his companions; his anger does not permit him to remain silent, and yet he can only repeat what has so often been said before: "Dost thou not know this of old, since man was placed upon earth, that the triumph of the wicked is short, and the joy of the evildoer but for a moment?" He can only describe, with great power it is true, but without offering a single new idea, the sudden and fearful ruin of the wicked, the certain loss of his ill-gotten wealth, the fear and torture that poison his joys, and the punishments that never fail to overwhelm him: "Though his greatness mount up to the heavens, and his head reach to the clouds: yet he shall perish for ever like his own dung; they who have seen him ask, Where is he? He flies away as a dream, and is not found, and he is chased away as a vision of the night... Though wickedness be sweet in his mouth, though he hide it under his tongue,... his food is turned in his bowels, it becomes gall of asps within him... He does not rejoice in the brooks, in the streaming rivers of honey und butter... In the fulness of his abundance he is in distress; all the strokes of the wretched come upon him... If he flees from the iron armour, the steel pierces him through... The heaven reveals his iniquity, and the earth rises up against him. The increase of his house departs, and is consumed in the day of his wrath. This is the portion of the wicked man from God, and the heritage appointed to him by God."

Bus the very force of language and the great variety of illustration place the poverty of Zophar's argument in a more striking light, and help to refute the teaching which he is so anxious to support.

JOB'S REPLY (ch. XXI).

It is not difficult to see that the friends, in portraying the life and fate of the evildoer, intend to hold up the mirror to Job himself, and that they believe him to have provoked God's vengeance by his unparalleled wickedness. This rouses Job's uncontrollable indignation; and he now, without reserve, opposes his own experience to the empty declamation of his would-be comforters. In weighing the subject, he feels the utmost sorrow; for the result at which he has arrived renders a life of peace and faith impossible; it appears to his agonised mind that the only road to happiness is through iniquity; he has ever found that the worst sinners are the most prosperous; their household is blessed, they have flocks and herds in abundance, they live securely in a perpetual round of pleasures, they enjoy a long life, and have an easy death; yet all the while they say to God, "Depart from us; for we do not desire the knowledge of Thy ways! What is the Almighty that we should serve Him? and what profit should we have if we pray to Him?"

Job protests indeed, that not even the brightest happiness can tempt him to secure it by unrighteousness; but he is sure that sinners in misfortune are very rare exceptions: "How often is the lamp of the wicked extinguished? and how often does destruction come upon them? or when does God in His anger allot to them sorrow? When are they as stubble before the wind, and as chaff that the storm carries away?" It is frequently said, that the children of the evildoer are wretched; but Job cannot acknowledge the justice of absolving the sinner himself from his merited punishment. In fact, his friends, he declares, ignore the world as it is, and assume a fancied order of things, as if they desired to "teach God wisdom"; for the fact remains unshaken: "One dies in his full strength, quite at ease and tranquil,... and another dies in the bitterness of his soul, and has never tasted pleasure". This is confirmed by all who have studied life and gathered experience; nay the wicked are even spared in times of public calamity; no one dares to oppose or to punish them; not only do they rest peacefully in their graves, but their memory is honoured, because thousands after them follow their example.

These being Job's convictions, he concludes with a taunting rebuke to his friends — "How then do you comfort me in vain? your answers remain mischief!"

THIRD SPEECH OF ELIPHAZ (ch. XXII).

The discussion has again been concluded; Job has in the most unguarded terms dilated upon the injustice which everywhere prevails in the lives of men; and now Eliphaz, speaking for the last time, declares in equally undisguised language, that Job must be an inveterate sinner who has committed the most heinous offences against all moral laws: "For thou hast taken a pledge from thy brother for nought, and stripped the naked of their clothing. Thou hast not given water to the weary to drink, and thou hast withheld bread from the hungry... Thou hast sent widows away empty, and the support of the fatherless has been broken by thee. Therefore snares surround thee, and fear troubles thee suddenly; or dost thou not see the darkness and the floods of water that encompass thee?"

Then Eliphaz points out, that Job's impiety in questioning God's power and government equals that of the worst blasphemers in former times, and that, therefore, his chastisement will be as fearful as theirs has been. And yet Eliphaz, unable quite to forget his former friendship, tells him, that he may yet be happy if he renounces all unrighteous gain, and in future remains faithful to God and His laws: "Take thy refuge to Him, and it will be well with thee, thou wilt be at peace; thus happiness will come to thee. Receive, I pray thee, instruction from His mouth, and take His words to heart! If thou return to the Almighty, thou shalt be built up. Put away iniquity from thy tents,... then the Almighty will be thy treasure, and thou shalt have abundance of silver. For then thou shalt rejoice in the Almighty, and lift up thy face to God. If thou prayest to Him, He shall hear thee, and thou shalt pay thy vows." Nay, on Job's account God will pardon other sinners also.

JOB'S REPLY (ch. XXIII. XXIV).

The strong accusations of Eliphaz again rouse the wish on the part of Job to plead his cause before God, and to receive from Him his judgment; for he is sure that he would be acquitted: "He knows my way: let Him try me, and I shall come forth as gold. My foot has held fast to His path; I kept His way and did not swerve. Nor did I forsake the commandment of His lips; I held the words of His mouth higher than my own will."

But he feels that his desire is vain; for where can he find God? "Behold if I go eastward, He is not there; and westward, I do not perceive Him. If He works in the north, I do not behold Him; if He hides Himself in the south, I see Him not." This idea torments Job even more than all his misfortunes, and he shudders to think that he is the helpless victim of an inscrutable fate.

Then he expatiates again on the manifest impunity of the wicked, for whom the day of affliction never appears. Tyrants seize the property of the widow and the orphan, cruelly oppress the poor, and show no compassion to the helpless: cries of despair rise up to heaven, but no help or deliverance comes. Murderers and robbers infest the land; and what is their lot? Is it speedy destruction and the curse of the world? Far from it; God upholds them, watches over their safety in all dangers, and grants them an easy death in old age. And Job confidently concludes: "And if this be not so, who will contradict me, and set my words at nought?"

BILDAD'S THIRD SPEECH (ch. XXV).

The friends have exhausted their arguments; Bildad speaks indeed once more, being desirous to impress Job with the perilous presumption of appealing to God for a declaration of his innocence; but he merely repeats the remarks of Eliphaz and Zophar, and he uses almost their identical words: "Dominion and terror are with Him, He makes peace in His heights. Can His armies be numbered? and upon whom does not His light arise? How then can man be justified with God? or how can he be clean that is born of a woman? Behold even the moon, it shines not; and the stars are not pure in His sight: how much less man, a worm? and the son of man, a maggot?"

The third friend does not even attempt another address; and thus Job has gained the victory in the discussion.

JOB'S REPLY (ch. XXVI).

Job treats Bildad's meagre speech with contempt and irony; but he is indignant at his censure, and in order to prove to him that he does not require his instruction, he describes God's greatness with much more force and fulness, and shows how it manifests itself in all parts of creation, from the darkness of the lower world to the stars of the firmament: "Before Him the shadows tremble beneath the waters and their inhabitants. Hell lies open before Him, and the abyss is not covered. He stretches out the north over the empty space, and hangs the earth upon nothing. He binds up the waters in His thick mists, and the clouds are not rent under them... The pillars of heaven tremble, and are amazed at His rebuke. He stirs up the sea by His power, and by His wisdom He smites its pride." And yet all that man can say of God is but a faint shadow of His unspeakable grandeur.

JOB'S LAST ADDRESS TO HIS FRIENDS.
(ch. XXVII. XXVIII.)

The first use which Job makes of his victory, is to declare once more with the greatest solemnity that he feels entirely innocent, and that he will never acknowledge the reproaches of his friends; for if he were guilty, he could not feel so confident and hopeful in the face of imminent death. And then, having fully regained his calmness, he gives his deliberate opinion on the laws of Divine Providence, which have so long and so warmly been discussed. He admits that the wicked man can never be happy: "If his children be multiplied, it is for the sword: and his offspring are not satisfied with bread... Though he heap up silver as the dust, and acquire raiment as the clay; he may acquire them, but the just shall put them on, and the pious shall divide his silver... Terrors come over him as water, a tempest hurls him away in the night." Yet there remain many mysteries, which no human intelligence can solve. Man is indeed wonderfully endowed; he dauntlessly penetrates into the depths of the earth, and brings up the precious metals; yet he does not possess that wisdom which is necessary to fathom the intricacies of life. "But where shall wisdom be found? and where is the place of understanding? Man knows not the price thereof, it is not found in the land of the living. The depth says, It is not in me; and the sea says, It is not with me. Pure gold is not given for it, nor is silver weighed as its price." God alone possesses wisdom, and made it from the beginning the ruling principle of the universe; but to man He said, "Behold the fear of the Lord that is wisdom, and to depart from evil is understanding."

JOB'S SOLILOQUY (ch. XXIX—XXXI).

Having concluded his argument with his friends, Job calmly surveys his past and present condition, and considers the prospects that are yet left to him. His tranquillity is not the result of exhaustion, but of a clear conscience and of pious resignation. He first draws a brilliant picture of his former happiness, and shows that his house seemed to stand under God's special protection, and that he enjoyed general esteem and reverence: "The young men saw me and hid themselves, and the aged arose and stood up. The princes refrained from speaking, and laid their hands on their mouth ... To me men listened, and waited, and kept silence at my counsel ... When I chose my way among them, I sat there as chief, and dwelt as a king among a host, as one that comforts mourners." For he had ever tried to do his duty towards his fellowmen: "I delivered the oppressed that cried, and the fatherless who had no help. The blessing of the wretched came upon me, and I filled the widows' heart with joy. I put on righteousness, and it clothed me; my justice was as a robe and a diadem. I was eyes to the blind, and feet was I to the lame. I was a father to the poor, and the cause of men I knew not I searched out."

He had, therefore, hoped that his prosperity was firmly established; but how soon had it vanished, and how different is his position now! He has become a mockery and a byword, and he is insulted even by the most abject and the most despicable: "But now men younger than I deride me, men whose fathers I would have disdained to set with the dogs of my flock... They abhor me, they flee from me, and refrain not from spitting in my face." His life, once so cheerful, is consumed by grief and tears: "I go about blackened, but not by the burning sun. I stand up in the assembly and cry. I am a brother to dragons, and a companion to ostriches. My skin is black and falls off from me, and my bones are burnt with heat. Thus my harp is turned to mourning, and my flute to sounds of weeping."

And yet he feels compelled to repeat once more that he has not deserved so fearful a catastrophe; from his early youth, he says, he has watched his heart, and guarded it from every temptation; he has been truthful and sincere; just and kind to his household; charitable and considerate to the poor and the widow, to strangers and guests; he has never sought to amass wealth in order to trust to it as a protection for wrong-doing; he has acquired no property by fraud or oppression; he has worshipped neither idols nor the heavenly bodies; he has never exulted at the fall or misfortune of his enemies; and he declares that, if he has ever been guilty of any of these transgressions or crimes, he is ready to submit to the most awful punishments and calamities. He ardently wishes that God may at last appear, to pronounce judgment upon his conduct; he looks forward to the vision with joy and confidence: and while he continues his protestations of innocence, God really appears, and "answers Job out of the whirlwind" (XXXVIII. 1).

THE SPEECH OF ELIHU (ch. XXXII—XXXVII).

Here the address of a fourth friend, who is not mentioned in the introductory narrative, interrupts the development of the work, and must, for this and other apparently sufficient reasons, be regarded as the later addition of a writer who believed, that Job ought not to remain the victor in the dispute, and that he might be refuted by other and more conclusive arguments. He acknowledges indeed that trials are often sent as a punishment for sin; but he maintains that they are also intended as a means of rousing man to moral improvement. He is of opinion that Job's sceptical attacks upon the justice of God deserve even a more severe condemnation than they had received in the speeches of the three friends, and that they are contradicted both by experience and reflection. If men pray in vain, let them, he urges, examine their own hearts and lives, when they will invariably find that they are themselves in fault.

His remarks are thus introduced: "And these three men ceased to answer Job, because he was righteous in his own eyes. Then was kindled the wrath of Elihu, the son of Barachel the Buzite, of the family of Ram: against Job was his wrath kindled, because he justified himself before God. Also against his three friends was his wrath kindled, because they had found no answer, and yet had condemned Job. Now Elihu waited till Job had spoken, because they were older than he. But when Elihu saw, that there was no answer in the mouth of these three men, then his wrath was kindled." .

Elihu himself explains the reasons which induce him to join the controversy, and challenges Job to disprove his arguments. He first censures Job for his assumption of innocence, and for his complaints of unjust treatment: "Surely thou hast spoken in my hearing, and I have heard the voice of thy words, saying, I am clean without transgression, I am innocent, and there is no iniquity in me; behold, He finds enmity against me, He counts me for His adversary; He puts my feet in the stocks, He regards all my paths." He reminds Job, that God never gives an account of His deeds to mortals; that He indeed sometimes communes with them by dreams or visions, but only in order to make them conscious of their sinfulness, and to save them from further transgression; for the same ends, He occasionally sends them alarming and dangerous illness; but the sufferers are always restored, if they turn to Him in penitence; and if their supplications are not granted, it is because they are not offered up in true humility.

Elihu proceeds to brand the doubts of Job in God's justice as a fearful crime: "What man is like Job, who drinks blasphemy like water? who goes in company with the workers of iniquity, and walks with wicked men. For he has said, It profits a man nothing that he should have his delight in God. Therefore hearken to me, ye men of understanding: far be it from God that He should do wickedness, and from the Almighty that He should commit iniquity. For the work of a man He renders to him, and gives every man according to his ways. Yea, surely, God will not act wickedly, nor will the Almighty pervert judgment. Who has given Him a charge over the earth? or who has created the whole world? If He took heed of Himself only, and kept in His spirit and His breath, all flesh would perish together, and man would turn again to dust." God is gracious to the pure-minded, and sends blessings to every one according to his merits; therefore, Job will certainly be delivered, if he deserves God's favour by meekness, and is ready to acknowledge His omnipotence, which is manifest in all nature, in the clouds and the tempests, in the rolling thunder and the angry lightning, and in the terrors of winter; though man cannot explain or understand these wonders, much less can he fathom the attributes of the all-powerful and all-wise Creator.

GOD ADDRESSES JOB (ch. XXXVIII—XLII. 6).

The following speeches belong to the most beautiful and most sublime portions of the Hebrew Canon, and are alone sufficient to prove that the Book of Job was written at a very advanced period of Hebrew history. Resuming the thread of the discussion at the point where it has been interrupted by the insertion of Elihu's remarks, the author represents God as appearing to Job in a whirlwind, and calling upon him to prepare himself for that judgment which he had so often challenged: "Who is it that darkens counsel by words without knowledge? Gird up now thy loins like a man; for I will ask thee, and answer thou Me." A man, thus continues the Divine argument, who aspires fully to understand the order of the universe, and even presumes to contend with God Himself, cannot find it difficult to explain the laws of nature, the mysteries of heaven and earth, and the origin of all things and of all animated beings; and then God overwhelms him with a great number of questions in order to bring home to his mind his weakness and utter incompetence. "Where wast thou when I laid the foundations of the earth? declare, if thou hast understanding. Who has fixed its measures, if thou knowest it, or who has stretched the line upon it, . . . when the morning stars sang together, and all the sons of God shouted for joy? Or who shut up the sea with doors, when it broke forth, rushing from the depth? . . . when I said, Hitherto shalt thou come, but no further, and here shall thy proud waves be stayed? Hast thou ever in thy days commanded the morning, and assigned its place to the dayspring? . . . Have the gates of death been opened to thee? or hast thou seen the doors of the shadow of death? . . . Where is the way where light dwells? and where has darkness its place?... Thou knowest it! for then thou wast already born! and the number of thy days is so great!

"Hast thou reached the stores of snow? and hast thou seen the stores of hail?... Who has divided the torrents of rain into channels, and appointed a way for the lightning of thunder, to cause it to rain on the earth where no man is, on the wilderness wherein there is no man?... Out of whose womb does ice come? and the hoarfrost of heaven, who has engendered it? Canst thou bind the fetters of the Pleiades or loosen the bands of Orion? Canst thou bring forth the signs of the zodiac in their seasons? or guide Arcturus with his sons? Knowest thou the ordinances of heaven, or canst thou fix its dominion over the earth?... Canst thou send lightnings, that they may go, and say to thee, Here we are?...

"Wilt thou hunt the prey of the lioness? and satisfy the hunger of the young lions, when they couch in their dens, and abide in the covert to lie in wait? Who provides for the raven his food, when his young ones cry to God, and wander for lack of meat?... Who has sent out the zebra free, or who has loosened the bands of the wild ass? whose house I have made the wilderness, and the barren land his dwelling. He scorns the din of the city, and regards not the crying of the driver... Is the buffalo willing to serve thee, or to abide by thy crib? Canst thou bind the buffalo with his band in the furrow, or will he harrow the fields after thee? Wilt thou trust him, because his strength is great, or wilt thou leave thy labour to him?... The wings of the ostrich rise briskly; are they kind wings and feathers? for she leaves her eggs in the ground, and lets them be warmed in the sand, and forgets that the foot may crush them, and that the wild beast may break them... She is hard against her young ones, as though they were not hers; her labour is in vain, she is not afraid; because God has deprived her of wisdom, nor has He imparted to her understanding. Whenever she lifts up herself on high, she scorns the horse and its rider.

"Dost thou give the horse strength? dost thou clothe its neck with terror? Dost thou make it leap as a grasshopper? its neighing is glorious and fearful. It digs in the valley, and rejoices in its strength; it goes on to meet the armed men. It mocks at fear, and is not afraid; nor turns it back from the sword. The quiver rattles upon it, the glittering spear and the shield. It swallows the ground with fierceness and rage, and stands not still at the sound of the trumpet. At the trumpet it cries Ha, ha; and it smells the battle afar off, the shouting of the captains and the war-cry.

"Does the hawk fly by thy wisdom, and stretch her wings towards the south? Does the eagle arise at thy command, and make her nest on high?"

God strongly insists upon an answer to these questions: "Shall the mocker contend with the Almighty? The accuser of God, let him answer it!" Job, humbled and confounded, makes only this reply: "Behold, I am too small; what shall I answer Thee? I lay my hand upon my mouth. Once have I spoken, but I answer not; yea, twice, but I proceed no further."

Job had not merely argued with God, but had boldly denied His justice and impartial government; therefore God continues His rebukes with stern severity:

"Gird up thy loins now, like a man: I will ask thee, and thou instruct Me. Wilt thou destroy My judgment? wilt thou condemn Me, that thou mayest be righteous?" And in order to impress Job still more with His omnipotence, He finally reminds him of two marvels of His creative power, which are described with unusual fulness — the hippopotamus and the crocodile:

"Behold now the hippopotamus which I have made with thee; he eats grass as an ox. Behold his strength in his loins, and his force in the muscles of his belly!... His bones are like tubes of brass; they are like bars of iron. He is the chief of the works of God: his creator has furnished him with His sword. For the mountains bring forth his food, and there all the beasts of the fields play... Behold, the river swells up, but he flees not; he trusts, though the Jordan gush forth into his mouth. Is he taken before his eyes? is his nose pierced with fetters?

"Dost thou draw the crocodile with a hook? and dost thou put a cord through his tongue? Dost thou put a rope into his nose, or pierce his jaw with a ring?... Canst thou fill his skin with barbed irons, or his head with fish spears? Lay thy hand upon him, and think of battle no more!... None is so fierce that he dare provoke him: who then is able to stand before Me?... I will not be silent about his limbs, nor about the nature of his power, and the majesty of his armour. Who has uncovered the surface of his garment? or who has penetrated into his double row of teeth? Who has opened the doors of his face? his teeth are terrible round about. The divisions of his scales are his pride, joined together as with a close seal. They are tight to each other, that no air can come between them... His neesings make light shine forth, and his eyes are like the eyelids of the morning. Out of his mouth go torches, sparks of fire leap out. Out of his nostrils goes smoke, as out of a seething pot or cauldron. His breath kindles coals, and flames go out of his mouth. On his neck dwells strength, and before him trembles terror... His heart is cast as firm as a stone; yea, is cast as firm as a nether millstone. When he rises up, heroes are afraid, they are bewildered by terror. If the sword hits him, it does not hold, neither does the spear, nor the dart, nor the breast-plate. He regards iron as straw, and brass as rotten wood. The arrow cannot make him flee; slingstones are turned with him into stubble. The clubs are counted as stubble, he laughs at the shaking of a spear. Sharp fragments of potsherd are under him; he spreads a threshing-wain upon the mire. He causes the deep to boil like a pot; he makes the sea like a kettle of ointment. He makes a path shine after him; it might be thought that the deep were grey-haired. Upon earth there is no rule over him, who is made for dauntless courage. He looks down upon every thing that is high: he is the king over all the proud creatures."

In awe and trembling, Job now acknowledges God's unfathomable wisdom and power, and confesses his own ignorance and shortsightedness; he says that he has at last learnt from the Lord Himself and by personal experience what he had before only known through vague traditions; and he adds, "Therefore I retreat, and repent in dust and ashes."

CONCLUSION (ch. XLII. 7—17).

Though excessive grief and pain had misled Job into the utterance of rash and reckless words, his life had ever been pure and righteous; therefore God now proclaims his innocence, and severely censures his friends, who had so cruelly wronged him by their false construction of his trials, and who were only pardoned by his intercession and prayer. Job himself was fully restored to his former prosperity and happiness:

"And the Lord gave back to Job his loss when he prayed for his friends; and the Lord gave Job twice as much as he had before. Then came there to him all his brothers and all his sisters, and all who had been of his acquaintance before, and ate bread with him in his house; and they bemoaned him and comforted him over all the evil that the Lord had brought upon him; and every man gave him a kesitah, and every one a golden ring. And the Lord blessed the latter end of Job more than his beginning: for he had fourteen thousand sheep, and six thousand camels, and a thousand yoke of oxen, and a thousand she-asses. He had also seven sons and three daughters. And he called the name of the first Jemima; and the name of the second Kezia; and the name of the third Kerenhappuch. And in all the land were no women found so fair as the daughters of Job; and their father gave them inheritance among their brothers. After this lived Job a hundred and forty years, and saw his sons and his sons' sons, four generations. So Job died old and full of days."

Thus the author has achieved the object of his work; he has proved that calamity and suffering cannot always be regarded as the result of iniquity, but that they may be sent by God for inscrutable reasons, for instance, as a trial of faith and piety, as exemplified by the story of Job. The author's creed centres in the idea: "Behold, the fear of the Lord, that is wisdom, and to depart from evil is understanding." Therefore, while recommending a virtuous life, he bids men renounce the vain attempt of fathoming God's designs in the often perplexing destinies of the good and the wicked. Beyond this he did not advance; for he was unacquainted with the doctrine of immortality; had he been familiar with it, he would have pointed to an after-life for a solution of all the mysteries in the government of the world; indeed he would have hardly deemed his laborious discussions necessary; a few words giving Job the blissful promise of a happy life beyond the grave, would have sufficed to satify his doubts and silence his murmurs. This circumstance assists us in fixing the date of the Book. The prophet Ezekiel introduces the doctrine of resurrection in a manner which seems to prove that, at his time, it was fully understood and generally accepted (see p. 103). Therefore, the Book of Job was probably not written later than the Babylonian period, although the great development of the spirit world, as apparent in the introduction of Satan, shows the author's familiarity with Persian notions. The view formerly entertained, that the Book was composed in the times of the patriarchs, or by Moses, has justly been abandoned: for the tone of its moral precepts, the consummate skill it displays in the arrangement of the arguments, and above all its great freedom of philosophic enquiry, imply that the work belongs to the ripest and most finished productions of Hebrew genius.

E. ECCLESIASTES.

The didactic element, which prevails in many of the Psalms, in the Proverbs, and in the Book of Job, attains even a fuller development in the Book of Ecclesiastes. This remarkable work, which is conceived in the true spirit of philosophy, affords one of the strongest proofs that the Hebrew mind, though peculiarly gifted for prophetic oratory and lyrical composition, was by no means averse to speculative thought.

It has been shown, in the remarks on the Book of Job, that the doctrine of retribution, to which the Hebrew people had long adhered, failed to satisfy reflecting minds. And yet the only solution which is able to secure peace and comfort — the belief in immortality and in a Divine judgment after death — was not known or accepted till a very late period. In this state of confusion, scepticism and infidelity naturally grew apace, and at last the frivolous saw the highest wisdom in the giddy enjoyment of the moment, and considered pleasure the true end of life. Yet there were never wanting among the Hebrews pious and earnest men, who, though unsupported by the old doctrine, and uncheered by the new one, escaped the taint of immorality and apathy. In the midst of doubt and uncertainty, they clung to virtue as the only safe anchor of life; and amidst the fluctuation of all things, they strove to discover principles of Divine Providence, to which they might trust as permanent and imperishable. It is to one of these independent minds that we owe the Book of Ecclesiastes, the tone of which, as may be expected, is alternately despondent and hopeful, but which, as a rule, draws life with sombre rather than cheerful colours.

The Book "Koheleth" (קֹהֶלֶת), which means "the Preacher", contains indeed many maxims conveying counsel and instruction; but the "Preacher" rarely addresses his words directly to the reader. He speaks as it were to himself; he discusses his thoughts aloud as they arise in his mind, he considers their value, and he finally arrives at a conclusion, in which he acquiesces as the most satisfactory attainable by him, though he feels that even that result leaves many doubts unanswered.

Unlike Job, he is prompted to his reflections not by overwhelming misfortunes, but rather by an excess of prosperity: he has tasted every joy, and acquired every distinction that wealth and high position can bestow; yet he is unhappy and dissatisfied, and is prompted to question God's justice. In examining the chequered and perplexing lives of his fellow-men, he loses his peace of mind, and he cannot rest until he finds the clue to the mystery. But again and again he is bound to confess that man, in spite of his great endowments, is unable to unravel the riddle of life, and that he must abandon the task as hopeless.

The first sentences of the Preacher are the key-note of the Book which sounds with the melancholy burden, "Vanity of vanities, vanity of vanities, all is vanity: what advantage has man of all his labour which he takes under the sun?" This is the summary of his varied experience and reflections.

He first points out that the universal law both of nature and of human life seems to be constant but purposeless and unprofitable change — an unceasing movement in a circle without ever leading onward: "One generation passes away, and another generation comes; but the earth abides for ever. And the sun arises, and the sun goes down, and hastens to its place, and then shines again; the wind goes toward the south and turns about to the north; it whirls about continually; and the wind returns again according to the circuits. All the rivers run into the sea, yet the sea is not full, to the place whither the rivers flow, thither they flow again. The thing that has been is that which shall be; and that which is done, is that which shall be done; and there is nothing new under the sun. There are things whereof it is said, 'See this is new' — it has been already of old time which was before us."

Then the Preacher, in order to show that he is entitled to speak about the vanity of all earthly things, gives an account of his own person and pursuits. At first he sought satisfaction in knowledge and wisdom; but he soon found that they are utterly useless: "I the Preacher was king over Israel in Jerusalem. And I gave my heart to seek and search out by wisdom concerning all things that are done under heaven: this is an evil toil which God has given to the sons of man to toil therein. I have seen all the works that are done under the sun; and, behold, all is vanity and vexation of spirit. That which is crooked cannot be made straight; and all that is wanting cannot be numbered. I spoke to my own heart, saying, Behold, I have attained more and greater wisdom than all that have been before me in Jerusalem; and my heart has acquired great wisdom and knowledge. But when I gave my heart to know wisdom, and to know madness and folly, I perceived that this also is vexation of spirit. For in much wisdom is much grief; and he that increases knowledge increases sorrow."

Being thus disappointed, he next tried to find happiness in frivolity and sensual pleasure; but he soon became convinced that these are also unprofitable: "I said in my heart, Well then, I will prove thee with mirth, therefore enjoy pleasure! but, behold, this also was vanity. I said of laughter, It is mad; and of mirth, What does it?" He now attempted a combination of wisdom and worldliness, and employed his knowledge and intelligence to secure enjoyment and to increase his wealth; in these pursuits he found indeed some delight, but it was of short duration: "I sought in my heart to give myself up to wine, while my heart guided me with wisdom, and to take hold of folly, till I might see what was that good for the sons of men, which they should do under the heaven, all the days of their life. I did great things: I built for myself houses, I planted vineyards, I made gardens and orchards, and planted trees in them of all kinds of fruits; I made ponds of water, to water therewith the wood that brings forth trees; I bought servants and maidens, and I had servants born in my house; I had also large possessions of great and small cattle more than any man that was before me in Jerusalem; I gathered for myself also silver and gold, and the treasures of kings and of provinces; I acquired singers and songstresses . . . So I was great, and increased more than all that were before me in Jerusalem: also my wisdom remained with me. And whatsoever my eyes desired I kept not from them, I withheld not my heart from any joy; for my heart rejoiced in all my labour; and this was my portion of all my labour. But when I looked on all the works that my hands had wrought, and on the labour that I had laboured to do; behold, all was vanity and vexation of spirit, and there was no profit under the sun."

In this perplexity, he turned again to wisdom as his only guide, and he found that "wisdom excels folly, as far as light excels darkness"; and that "the wise man's eyes are in his head, while the fool walks in darkness": yet on closer enquiry he was pained to see that in the end the wise man and the fool meet with the same fate, that ere long both the one and the other are forgotten, and that, howsoever a man may have toiled, he must leave the fruits of his labour to others, and perhaps to worthless people: "For there is no remembrance of the wise more than of the fool for ever; seeing that all who are now shall be forgotten in the days to come. And alas! the wise man dies as the fool. Therefore I hated life; because all the work that is wrought under the sun seems grievous to me: for all is vanity and vexation of spirit. And I hated all my labour which I had wrought under the sun; because I should leave it to the man that shall be after me. And who knows, whether he shall be a wise man or a fool? yet shall he have rule over all my labour wherein I have laboured, and wherein I have shown myself wise under the sun. This is also vanity." —

This thought appeared to him so unbearable, that he gave way to an outburst of despair; he complained that he had in vain spent toilsome days and sleepless nights; and he contended that "there is nothing better for a man than that he should eat and drink, and that he should make his soul enjoy happiness in his labour." Yet not even this, he continued, man is free to do; for his liberty is chained by the relentless will of God, without whose favour man derives no pleasure from his wealth, however honestly and laboriously it may have been acquired: "this also is vanity and vexation of spirit."

Many considerations strengthened the Preacher in the view that enjoyment of life is true wisdom. He found that all things are so unalterably fixed and pre-ordained, that man has no choice and no free action: "to every thing there is a season, and a time to every purpose under the heaven"; and he believed, therefore, that it would be unavailing to attempt great works. He saw injustice, oppression, and agony everywhere, even "in the place of judgment"; and he considered, therefore, that virtue and piety are unavailing to secure a tranquil life. And lastly, he found that man is a transitory and perishable being; that, in this respect, he has no advantage over the beasts; and that after a short existence he returns to dust for ever: "For that which befalls the children of men befalls beasts; the same thing befalls them; as the one dies, so dies the other; and they have all one breath of life; so that a man has no pre-eminence over a beast: for all is vanity. All go to the same place; all are of the dust, and all turn to dust again. Who knows whether the spirit of man goes upward, and the spirit of the beasts goes downward to the earth?" And thus he was again forced to the conclusion: "Wherefore I perceived that there is nothing better, than that a man should rejoice in his works; for that is his portion; for who shall bring him to see what shall be after him?"

Reviewing again his manifold experiences, the author was more and more confirmed in the conviction that life is one long series of suffering, toil, and illusion, and he declared in bitter grief: "Wherefore I praised the dead who are dead long since, more than the living who are yet alive. But happier than both of them is he who has not lived at all, and who has not seen the evil work that is done under the sun." For tears are shed by the poor and the oppressed without hope of improvement or deliverance; jealousy embitters the days of man, and poisons the motives of his actions; indolence tempts him, and plunges him into want and misery; isolated, and deprived of his nearest relations and his dearest friends, he leads a weary and wretched life even in the midst of plenty; and he is constantly exposed to fearful vicissitudes, from which not even the king on his throne is exempted: "surely this also is vanity and vexation of spirit."

For a moment the course of the enquiry is interrupted by the insertion of some single maxims both on religious and worldly subjects, such as these: "Keep thy foot when thou goest to the House of God, and it is better to come near and to hear, than to offer the sacrifice of fools: for they care not if they do evil. Be not rash with thy mouth, and do not let thy heart be hasty to utter anything before God; for God is in heaven and thou upon earth: therefore let thy words be few ... When thou vowest a vow to God, delay not to pay it; for He has no pleasure in fools: pay that which thou hast vowed ... He who loves silver, shall not be satisfied with silver; and he that loves wealth, has no profit of it: this also is vanity. When property increases, those are increased that eat it: and what good is it to the owners, except the beholding of it with their eyes? The sleep of a labouring man is sweet, whether he eat little or much; but the surfeit of the rich will not suffer him to sleep."

But the author soon returned to his mournful theme; he pointed anew to the discord and misery which he found everywhere—the "oppression of the poor, and the violent perversion of judgment and justice"; wealth not enjoyed by the proprietor, or causing his misfortune; men dying unhonoured and unmourned after a life of unceasing drudgery, leaving the world, as they came into it, poor and naked; breathless toil undergone to satisfy ordinary wants or luxurious tastes; wisdom and piety profitless for repose and happiness; and man's perfect ignorance as regards his fate after death: therefore, he repeated his former advice, to enjoy life as long as it lasts: "Behold, that which I have seen: it is good and right for one to eat and to drink, and to enjoy the good of all his labour that he takes under the sun all the days of his life, which God gives him: for this is his portion. Also if God has given to any man riches and wealth, and gives him power to eat thereof, and to take his portion, and to rejoice in his labour; this is a gift of God." —

Finding life full of trouble and uncertainty, the author regarded it as an unmixed evil, and looked upon its end as a welcome release. This sentiment he expressed in many different ways: "A good name is better than precious ointment, and the day of death than the day of one's birth. It is better to go to the house of mourning, than to go to the house of feasting: for that is the end of all men; and the living will take it to heart. Sorrow is better than laughter; for by the sadness of the countenance the heart is made better. The heart of the wise is in the house of mourning; but the heart of fools is in the house of mirth."

And yet he could not rest satisfied with gloomy thoughts and with passive resignation; he hated folly, "for as the crackling of thorns under a pot, so is the laughter of the fool"; and he saw the great value and advantage of wisdom, which he ardently extolled: "Wisdom is as good as an inheritance, and it is a profit to those that see the sun. For wisdom is a defence, and money is a defence; but the advantage of knowledge is, that wisdom gives life to them that have it ... Wisdom makes the wise stronger than ten mighty men who are in the city ... Who is as the wise man? and who knows the interpretation of things? a man's wisdom makes his face to shine, and the boldness of his face is changed."

The Preacher inculcated fear of God and faith in His goodness, and thus described His omnipotence: "Consider the work of God; for who can make straight that which He has made crooked?" He then urged, that even misfortunes are designed by Him for beneficent purposes: "In the day of prosperity be joyful, but in the day of adversity consider that God has created the one as well as the other, to the end that man should find nothing after him." He could not indeed shut his eyes to the wrongs that met him everywhere: "There is a just man that perishes in his righteousness, and there is a wicked man that prolongs his life in his wickedness ... And so I saw the wicked buried, but those who had done right came and went away from the holy place, and were forgotten in the city; this also is vanity." Yet he clung to the belief that, in spite of apparent exceptions, the pious escape heavy afflictions, from which indeed no one can hope to be entirely free, since "there is not a just man upon earth that does good and sins not"; he cautioned the wicked not to believe that, because the punishment of crimes is often delayed, it never comes; and he confidently expressed his conviction: "Though a sinner do evil a hundred times, and his days be prolonged, yet surely I know that it shall be well with those that fear God, and who fear before Him: but it shall not be well with the wicked, nor shall he prolong his days like a shadow; because he fears not before God."

But so melancholy was the tone of his mind, and so habitually did he see the daily events in its sombre reflection, that he soon relapsed into his unhappy scepticism; he declared again that the wicked constantly reap the rewards due to the virtuous, and that the righteous suffer the misery deserved by the unjust; he insisted that giddy enjoyment of the fleeting hour was the only true boon left for mankind; and at last he gave up the problem of life as utterly unfathomable: "When I applied my heart to know wisdom, and to see the things that are done upon the earth (for man neither day nor night sees sleep with his eyes), then I beheld all the work of God that man cannot find out, the work that is done under the sun; and though a man labour to seek it out, yet he shall not find it;

and though a wise man strive to know it, yet he is not able to find it."

Believing that the fate of man is irrevocably placed in the hands of an omnipotent God, whose decrees he is unable to understand, he said despondingly: "For all this I weighed in my heart, and explored all this, that the righteous, and the wise, and their works are in the hand of God: no man knows either love or hatred; all this is before them." How then should the wicked govern their evil dispositions? how should the foolish be stimulated to strive after knowledge? Yet, in spite of all this, the wise man might try to live cheerfully amidst the comforts and embellishments which wealth can procure; but all his pleasures are embittered by the thought of death which he cannot escape, and which must bring utter dissolution and forgetfulness: "To all the living there is hope; for a living dog is better than a dead lion. For the living know that they shall die; but the dead know nothing at all, nor have they any more a reward; for their memory is forgotten. Both their love, and their hatred, and their envy, have now perished; nor have they any more a portion for ever in any thing that is done under the sun."

Therefore, as the highest relative good, though very unsatisfactory in itself, the Preacher now more emphatically than ever recommended enjoyment, recreation, and every earthly luxury: "Go thy way, eat thy bread with joy, and drink thy wine with a merry heart; for God delights in thy works. Let thy garments be always white; and let thy head lack no ointment. Live joyfully with the wife whom thou lovest all the days of the life of thy vanity, whom He has given thee under the sun all the days of thy vanity: for that is thy portion in this life, and in thy labour which thou takest under the sun. Whatsoever thy hand finds to do, do it with thy might; for there is no work, nor device, nor knowledge, nor wisdom, in the grave, whither thou goest."

But the author could not leave this healthy counsel unchallenged; and viewing it in the light of his morbid scepticism, he declared that neither talent nor industry is a guarantee of success, which depends on uncontrollable chance and an inscrutable destiny: "Again I saw under the sun, that the race is not to the swift, nor the battle to the strong, nor yet bread to the wise, nor yet riches to men of understanding, nor yet favour to men of skill; but time and chance happen to them all. For man also knows not his time: as the fishes that are taken in an evil net, and as the birds that are caught in the snare; so are the sons of men ensnared in the time of evil, when it falls suddenly upon them." Wisdom indeed sometimes achieves great things, but the wise man is despised, while the fool carries off all worldly honours and rewards.

Again a number of detached maxims are inserted. Some of them bear on the general argument of the Book — the instability and emptiness of all things: "Folly is placed in high dignity, and the rich sit in the low place. I have seen servants upon horses, and princes walking as servants on foot." Other sayings praise wisdom, to which the writer in his serener moments continually turns for support: "Wisdom is profitable for success." "The words of a wise man's mouth are gracious; but the lips of a fool destroy him." And not a few of the adages give practical instructions, or convey shrewd observations: "By much slothfulness the building decays, and through idleness of the hands the house drops through." "He that observes the wind shall not sow, and he that regards the clouds shall not reap... In the morning sow thy seed, and in the evening withhold not thy hand: for thou knowest not whether shall prosper, either this or that, or whether they both shall be alike good." "Curse not the king, not even in thy thought, and curse not the rich in thy bedchamber; for a bird of the air carries the voice, and the winged creature tells the speech."

The Preacher, resuming his general reflections, then proceeded to sum up his conclusions, which, in spite of many fluctuations, were evident from the beginning. He recommended a moderate enjoyment of life, but warned man constantly to remember the Divine judgment which weighs all deeds; he urged that life is short, and that, therefore, the fleeting years of youth should not be lost in sadness and self-castigation: "Rejoice, O young man, in thy youth, and let thy heart cheer thee in the days of thy youth, and walk in the ways of thy heart, and in the sight of thy eyes: but know thou that for all these things God will bring thee into judgment. And remove sorrow from thy heart, and keep away evil from thy body; for childhood and youth are vanity." He then drew a striking picture of the infirmities of old age, which destroy cheerfulness, hope, and comfort; and he, therefore, advised that a good use be made of the earlier and more vigorous years of life: "And remember thy Creator in the days of thy youth, before the evil days come, and the years draw nigh, of which thou shalt say, I have no pleasure in them; before the sun, and the light, and the moon, and the stars are darkened, and the clouds return after the rain. In the time when the keepers of the house [the arms] tremble, and the strong men [the feet] are bent, and the grinders cease because they are few, and those that look out of the windows are darkened, and the doors [the lips] are shut in the streets, because the sound of the mill is low, and when he [the old man] rises early at the voice of the bird, and all the daughters of music are brought low;

when they also are afraid of high places, and terrors are on the road, and the almond is despised, and the grasshopper is burdensome, and the caper-berry fails; because man goes to his eternal home, and the mourners go about the streets: and before the silver cord is severed, and the golden lamp is dashed to pieces, and the pitcher is broken at the fountain, and the wheel is dashed to pieces at the cistern. And the dust returns to the earth as it was, and the spirit returns to God who gave it."

After a few remarks on the wisdom of the Preacher and his numerous writings, the Book is brought to a close by an earnest appeal entreating the reader to flee the unsafe paths of speculation, and to adopt the following principles, which, if they throw no new light on the mysteries of human life, and cannot always secure contentment and inward happiness, must ever stimulate to pious resignation and works of righteousness: "Let us hear the conclusion of the whole matter — Fear God, and keep His commandments; for this is the whole duty of man. For God shall bring every deed into judgment, which He shall hold over every secret thing, whether it be good or whether it be evil."

There is something tragical in the hopeless struggles of a profound and God-fearing man eager to fathom the perplexities of life; at one moment he considers all human destinies as governed by chance alone; at another his better nature revolts against such a despairing view, and he seeks the directing hand of God in the apparent confusion. He is neither a narrow-minded misanthrope, nor a bitter satirist, nor a thoughtless epicurean; though he seems at times to be the one or the other, when he is struck by the perversity of men, the unjust distribution of happiness, and the poverty of human knowledge and wisdom. The Book of Ecclesiastes, which is pervaded by an intense longing for truth, concludes in a thoroughly religious spirit; and it is to this conclusion chiefly that we owe the preservation of the work, which, on account of its sceptical tendency, was in danger of being excluded from the Biblical Canon.

The author put his ideas very appropriately into the mouth of king Solomon, who, distinguished alike for wisdom and worldly prosperity, most fitly discoursed upon the value of the one and the vanity of the other; but the Book bespeaks a time estranged from simplicity of life and thought, and reflects an unhappy age of dependence and oppression; it abounds in foreign forms and phrases, and is thought to have been composed in the Persian, if not in the Macedonian period.

F. THE SONG OF SOLOMON.

The exquisite beauty and freshness which distinguish this composition, fully justify its Hebrew title of "Song of Songs" (שִׁיר הַשִּׁירִים). It is the only portion of the Bible which is of a purely secular character, and it is the only remaining specimen of a Hebrew drama: for though thoroughly moral in tone, it has no religious tendency; and though lyrical in its descriptions, it is dramatic in form and arrangement.

The subject of the poem may be briefly told. A young shepherdess from the little town of Shulem near Nazareth — and hence simply called the Shulamite — was betrothed to a shepherd, who fondly loved her. Her beauty excited admiration, and she was taken to the luxurious court of king Solomon; but she resisted all temptations and allurements; in her thoughts and in her dreams she longed for her distant bridegroom; and at last the king was compelled to send her back to her home, where the young pair were happily united in marriage.

The poet evidently desires to contrast the purity and simplicity of the rustic couple with the enervating pomp of the royal palace; he intended to hold up the mirror to the king and his courtiers, and in this sense his production has a moral object; but this tendency is veiled by lyrical language of singular exuberance and enthusiasm. We breathe throughout the atmosphere of true poetry and of idyllic peace; and we see before us nature in her brightest and most festive garb, as in this description of returning spring: "Lo the winter is past, the rain is over and gone, the flowers appear on the earth; the time of the singing of birds is come, and the voice of the turtle is heard in our land; the fig tree makes fragrant its green figs, and the vines in their blossom smell sweetly." The imagination of the poet is fervid and soaring, yet always pure and measured; and he couples depth of feeling with a gay and often playful humour. But he employs all his pathos in expatiating on his principal theme, the power of love, of which he speaks in strains like these: "Love is strong as death; affection is firm as the grave: its flames are flames of fire, a godly glow. Many waters cannot quench love, nor can floods wash it away: if a man would give all the substance of his house for love, he would be utterly rejected."

The young pair vie with each other in professions of admiration and in pledges of affection. The shepherd thus describes his bride: "Behold, thou art fair, my love; behold, thou art fair; thou hast doves' eyes behind thy veil; thy hair is as a flock of goats, which lie down on Mount Gilead. Thy teeth are like a flock of shorn sheep that come out of the water; whereof all bear twins, and none is barren among them. Thy lips are like a thread of scarlet, and thy mouth is comely: thy cheek is like the half of a pomegranate behind thy veil. Thy neck is like the tower of David built for an armoury, whereon hang a thousand bucklers, all shields of heroes ... Thou art all fair, my love; there is no fault in thee ... Thou hast taken away my heart, my sister, my bride; thou hast taken away my heart by one glance of thy eyes, by one chain of thy neck." And the maiden speaks of her bridegroom with no less fervour:

"My beloved is white and ruddy, distinguished among myriads; his head is like the finest gold; his locks are waving palm-branches, and black as a raven; his eyes are as doves by the rivers of water, bathed in milk, and fitly set; his cheeks are like a bed of spices, like sweet flowers; his lips like lilies dropping sweet-smelling myrrh; his hands are as golden rings set with chrysolith . . . His form is like the Lebanon, distinguished as the cedars; his mouth is most sweet: yea he is altogether lovely. This is my beloved, and this is my friend, O daughters of Jerusalem!"

It is indeed remarkable that a work of such a nature should have been embodied in the Biblical Canon; but the matter may be thus explained. The "Song of Songs" was probably written not long after the death of Solomon by a poet living in the northern kingdom, and it was treasured by the people as one of the finest dramatic and lyrical compositions. In the course of time, the authorship of the piece was attributed to the wise king himself, and then it was naturally believed to have a religious tendency; it was supposed to treat of the love of God towards His chosen people; in this sense the entire poem was interpreted, and was, therefore, finally incorporated in the Canon, and invested with the utmost sacredness. But it need not be remarked, that all allegorical and typical interpretations are against the tenor and spirit of the work, which is interesting because it is one of the oldest Hebrew poems preserved to us, and because it shows the power and versatility of Hebrew genius in a new and unexpected light.

G. THE WISDOM OF JESUS THE SON OF SIRACH,

or

ECCLESIASTICUS.

The literary labours of the Hebrews, so far from ceasing with the independence of their commonwealth, multiplied considerably in the Babylonian and Persian periods; and the "Preacher" declared, "Of making many books there is no end". A large number of these works, composed after the completion of the Canon, have been embodied in the Apocrypha; and among the writings thus fortunately preserved to us are two belonging to that class of didactic poetry in which the Hebrews particularly excelled — namely, the "Wisdom of Jesus the son of Sirach", and "the Wisdom of Solomon".

About 180 years before the Christian era, there lived in Jerusalem a learned man of the name of Jesus Sirach. He was probably a priest, and stood in high esteem among the eminent men of his time. Thoroughly imbued with the literature of his people, he wrote down his reflections and experiences in the popular form of proverbs and maxims. His work soon rose into high favour among his countrymen; and when, about fifty years after its publication, his grandson emigrated into Egypt during the reign of Ptolemy Euergetes or Physcon, he translated it into Greek for the benefit of the African Jews, to whom Hebrew had then already become a strange language. The original, though for centuries diffused in numerous copies, was ultimately lost; and we have, therefore, all the more reason to be grateful to the translator, who accomplished his task with the utmost care and conscientiousness.

The Book consists of a large collection of sayings, many of which, both from their purpose and their wording, remind the reader of the Proverbs of Solomon, which were evidently the author's great model. Like them, they embrace nearly everything that concerns both practical and religious life, common expediency and lofty morality. And yet the Book has a peculiar character of its own. It includes indeed many detached sentences; but for the greater part it is written in a connected form; and as kindred subjects are grouped together, a certain continuity is produced. Again, in the "Wisdom of Sirach" the moralist is more prominent than the shrewd observer of life; and in its instructions, the spiritual prevails over the worldly element. Though the later work is inferior to its prototype in pithiness and freshness, it does not yield to it in purity of sentiment and fervour of patriotism; and, though separated from it by the interval of many centuries, it propounds exactly the same moral and religious doctrines. For Jesus Sirach also proves wisdom to be identical with religion, or with that fear of God which shows itself in faithful adherence to His laws; and he also teaches the old doctrine of retribution, which limits all rewards and punishments to this life.

Reflections like the following seem almost an echo of the "Proverbs of Solomon":

"All wisdom comes from the Lord, and is with Him for ever... Wisdom has been created before all things, and the understanding of prudence from everlasting. The word of God Most High is the fountain of wisdom; and her ways are everlasting commandments... He created her, and saw her, and numbered her, and poured her out upon all His works ... The root of wisdom is to fear the Lord, and the branches thereof are long life ... If thou desire wisdom, keep the commandments, and the Lord shall give her to thee.

"I came out of the mouth of the Most High, and covered the earth as a cloud ... I alone compassed the circuit of heaven, and walked in the bottom of the deep ... So the Creator of all things gave me a commandment... He created me from the beginning before the world, and I shall never fail. In the holy Tabernacle I served before Him, and so was I established in Sion. Likewise in the beloved city He gave me rest, and in Jerusalem was my power. And I took root in an honourable people, even in the portion of the Lord's inheritance. I was exalted like a cedar in Lebanon, and as a cypress-tree upon the mountains of Hermon. I was exalted like a palm-tree in En-gaddi, and as a rose-plant in Jericho, as a fair olive-tree in a pleasant field, and grew up as a plane-tree by the water ... I am the mother of fair love, and fear, and knowledge, and holy hope: I, therefore, being eternal, am given to all my children who are named of Him ... He that obeys me shall never be confounded; and they that work by me shall never do amiss."

The diffusion of such views was the mission which the author proposed to himself, and which he pursued with the greatest zeal: "I said, I will water my best garden, and will water abundantly my garden-bed: and, lo, my brook became a river, and my river became a sea. I will yet make doctrine to shine as the morning, and will send her light afar off. I will yet pour out doctrine as prophecy, and leave it to all ages for ever. Behold that I have not laboured for myself only, but for all those that see wisdom."

The collection includes many maxims which testify to the author's noble aspirations and generous feelings. One of its principal themes is the praise of humility, and consequently the condemnation of pride and vainglorious pomp. "The fear of the Lord goes before the obtaining of authority; but haughtiness and pride cause it to be lost." "My son, glorify thy soul in meekness, and give it honour according to its dignity." "Boast not of thy clothing and raiment, and exalt not thyself in the day of honour, for the works of the Lord are wonderful, and His works among men are hidden."

The cardinal virtue of humility engenders, in the author's opinion, many other qualities, and especially moderation and gratitude. He praises a well-balanced mind, which is neither overwhelmed by trials, nor intoxicated by success; and he regrets to find that too often "in the day of prosperity there is a forgetfulness of affliction, and in the day of affliction there is no more remembrance of prosperity". And he insists that men should evince gratitude not only towards God, the Bestower of all blessings, but towards all those who have conferred some benefit upon them, or have shown their sympathy by some kindly deed; and he urges that their obligations are especially due to the physician whose care and skill bring them relief in their illness. This ready acknowledgment of the art of healing is intended to counteract that pernicious fatalism, so prevalent among eastern nations, which in times of affliction and suffering disdains human aid: "Honour a physician with the honour due to him for the uses which you may have of him: for the Lord has created him. From the Most High comes healing, and he shall receive honour of the king. The skill of the physician shall lift up his head; and in the sight of great men he shall be in admiration. The Lord has created medicines out of the earth; and he that is wise will not abhor them. Was not the water made sweet with wood, that the virtue thereof might be known? And He has given men skill, that He might be honoured in His marvellous works. With such does He heal [men], and takes away their pains ... My son, in thy sickness be not negligent; but pray to the Lord, and He will make thee whole. Leave off from sin, and order thy hands aright, and cleanse thy heart from all wickedness ... Then give place for the physician, for the Lord has created him; let him not go from thee, for thou hast need of him. There is a time when in their hands there is good success."

He often inculcates the duty of truthfulness, and dwells with great force upon the inherent power of truth: "Strive for truth unto death, and the Lord shall fight for thee." He recommends prudence and thoughtfulness as the best safeguards against failure: "Whatever thou takest in hand, remember the end, and thou shalt never do amiss." Though often exhorting his readers to a strict observance of the Mosaic precepts, he brands ceremonialism without piety of the heart as an abomination: "He that sacrifices of a thing wrongfully gotten, his offering is contemptible; and the gifts of unjust men are not accepted. The Most High is not pleased with the offerings of the wicked; nor is He appeased for sin by the multitude of sacrifices." The following sentences remind us of some of the writings of the old prophets: "He that keeps the Law brings offerings enough; he that takes heed of the commandments offers a peace-offering. He that requites a good turn, offers fine flour; and he that gives alms sacrifices a praise-offering."

Being fully aware of the weakness of the human heart, he deems indulgence to others a supreme duty, and cautions the reader against hasty censure. "Reproach not a man that turns from sin, but remember that we are all worthy of punishment." "Blame not before thou hast examined the truth; understand first, and then rebuke."

Like the Proverbs, the Wisdom of Sirach dwells with great earnestness upon the virtues which should adorn the domestic hearth, and upon the obligations which devolve upon the members of the household: the author enjoins upon all kindliness and mutual forbearance; he exhorts parents to bring up their children in the fear of God, and in the accomplishment of this duty not to shrink from wholesome severity; and he never tires to press upon children the great debt of gratitude and affection which they owe to their parents. But he declares that it is insufficient to limit our sympathies to our family circle; and with generous ardour he insists upon universal charity and brotherly love.

He extols knowledge above all other blessings, and in explaining its delights and advantages, he speaks with a certain contempt of such pursuits as agriculture and handicrafts, though he is far from underrating their utility in promoting the comforts of society. The passages in which he treats of these subjects are characteristic of a time when a new class of men, the scribes or scholars, to whom Sirach belonged, had arisen, who made the study and exposition of the Law their exclusive avocation: "The wisdom of a learned man comes by opportunity of leisure; and he that has little business shall become wise. How can he get wisdom that holds the plough, and that glories in the goad, that drives oxen, and is occupied in their labours, and whose talk is of bullocks? He gives his mind to make furrows; and is diligent to give the kine fodder. So every carpenter and workmaster that labours night and day; and they that cut and engrave seals ... All these trust to their hands, and everyone is wise in his work. Without these indeed a city cannot be inhabited; and no one can dwell therein, nor go to and fro: but they shall not be sought for in public counsel, nor sit high in the congregation; they shall not sit on the judges' seat, nor understand the sentence of judgment; they cannot declare justice and judgment; and they shall not be found where parables are spoken ... But he that gives his mind to the Law of the Most High, and is occupied in the meditation thereof, will seek out the wisdom of all the ancients, and will be occupied in prophecies. He will keep the sayings of the renowned men; and where subtle parables are, there he will be also ... Many shall commend his understanding; and so long as the world endures, it shall not be blotted out; his memorial shall not depart away, and his name shall live from generation to generation."

But the topics on which the author expatiates are almost endless, and he says himself: "Yet have I more to say which I have thought upon; for I am so filled as the moon at the full." He describes with great power and enthusiasm all nature and her phenomena — the sun "that gives light and looks upon all things", the moon "increasing wonderfully in her changing", and the stars "standing in their order, and never fainting in their watches"; the clear firmament and the beauty of the skies; the rainbow which "encompasses heaven with a glorious circle drawn by the hands of the Most High"; the flashes of lightning and the peals of thunder; winds and hurricanes; mists and dews; snow and ice that "clothes the water as with a breast plate"; hailstones and hoarfrost "poured forth upon the earth like salt"; the seas and sea-monsters: everything declares that "the Lord is terrible and very great, and marvellous is His power"; and yet He is also "full of compassion and mercy, longsuffering and full of pity, He forgives sin, and saves in time of affliction."

The Book terminates with the praise of eminent men famous in sacred history, from Enoch down to the High-priest Onias, the author's contemporary *), and the names include

---

*) See Part I. p. 577.

those of Noah and the patriarchs, Moses, Aaron, and Phinehas, Joshua and Samuel, David and Solomon, and many of the prophets; but the author seems to glorify with special fervour his own ancestor, the first High-priest Aaron: "God exalted Aaron, a holy man . . ., of the tribe of Levi. An everlasting covenant He made with him, and gave him the priesthood among the people; He beautified him with comely ornaments, and clothed him with a robe of glory. He put upon him perfect glory, and strengthened him with rich garments—with drawers, with a long robe, and the ephod. And he compassed him with pomegranates, and with many golden bells round about, so that as he went there might be a sound, and a noise made that should be heard in the Temple, for a memorial to the children of his people; with a holy garment, with gold, and blue silk, and purple, the work of the embroiderer; with a breastplate of judgment, and with Urim and Thummim; with twisted scarlet, the work of the cunning workman, with precious stones graven like seals, and set in gold, the work of the jeweller; with a writing engraven for a memorial, after the number of the tribes of Israel. He set a crown of gold upon the mitre whereon was engraven Holiness, an ornament of honour, a costly work, the desire of the eyes, goodly and beautiful. Before him there were none such, neither did ever any stranger put them on, but only his children and his children's children perpetually . . . Moses consecrated him, and anointed him with holy oil: this was appointed to him by an everlasting covenant, and to his seed so long as the heavens should remain, that they should minister to Him, and execute the office of the priesthood, and bless the people in His name. He chose him out of all men living to offer sacrifices to the Lord, incense, and a sweet savour, for a memorial, to make atonement for His people. He gave to him His commandments, and authority in the statutes of judgment, that he should teach Jacob the testimonies, and inform Israel in His laws. Strangers conspired together against him, and maligned him in the wilderness, even the men that were of Dathan's and Abiram's side, and the congregation of Korah, with fury and wrath. This the Lord saw, and it displeased Him, and in His wrathful indignation were they consumed: He did wonders upon them, to consume them with the fiery flame. But He made Aaron more honourable, and gave him a heritage, and assigned to him the firstfruits of the increase; and He especially prepared bread in abundance: for they eat of the sacrifices of the Lord, which He gave to him and his seed."

Though not forming a part of the Biblical Canon, the Wisdom of Jesus Sirach was, from early times, constantly used for public devotions, and was hence honoured with the name of Ecclesiasticus.

H. THE WISDOM OF SOLOMON.

This remarkable Book was written about a hundred years after Ecclesiasticus, to which, in many respects, it presents a striking contrast. The Wisdom of Sirach, composed in Palestine in the Hebrew language, is essentially Jewish in spirit and style; the Wisdom of Solomon, compiled in Egypt in the Greek tongue, shows that combination of Jewish and Greek elements which is characteristic of the Alexandrine school of Hebrew learning. The author of the one, who is known to us by name, clings to the traditional doctrine of retribution; while the unknown author of the other deduces his reflections and exhortations from the doctrine of immortality, and considers this life merely as a preparation for a future and more perfect existence. Thus the teaching of the Wisdom of Solomon is quite distinct from the teaching of such works as the Proverbs and Job; but it stands in even stronger opposition to the principles advocated in Ecclesiastes; for the author, so far from regarding worldly pleasures and the enjoyment of the passing hour as real boons, condemns them as the most serious obstacles to the attainment of that wisdom, which is to him the one true object of life, and the sole guarantee of happiness. To the praise of wisdom, therefore, he devotes the greatest part of his work, and he endeavours to enforce its supreme claims upon all classes, the high and the lowly, the rich and the poor. His object is essentially moral and spiritual; he hardly ever enters into the minute affairs of life, and offers but rarely practical advice. He is anxious to lead his readers to true piety through the knowledge of God; and in pursuing this task, he shows great ardour of feeling, and displays the most impressive eloquence.

He commences with an earnest appeal to the kings and rulers of the earth, who exercise so powerful an influence for good or for evil; he reminds them, that justice ought to be their chief care and their highest aim, and he declares that it can only be secured through wisdom, which is the source of all excellence: "Love righteousness, ye that are judges of the earth: think of the Lord with a pious heart, and in simplicity of mind seek Him... For into a malicious soul wisdom shall not enter, nor dwell in the body that is subject to sin. The holy spirit of discipline will flee deceit, and remove from thoughts that are without understanding... The spirit of the Lord fills the world; and that which holds together all things, has knowledge of every speech... God did not create death, nor has He pleasure in the destruction of the living. For He created all things, that they might have their being; and all things that exist in the world are wholesome; and there is no poison of destruction in them, nor has death its kingdom upon the earth."

He condemns the folly of those who see in the affairs of the world nothing but chance, and expect happiness from a giddy life of pleasure, saying: "Our days are short and miserable, and in the death of a man there is no remedy; nor was there known any man to deliver from the grave. For we are born by chance; and we shall be hereafter as though we had never been: for the breath in our nostrils is as smoke, and our mind a little spark in the pulsation of our heart, which being extinguished, our body shall be turned into ashes, and our spirit shall vanish as the thin air; and our name shall be forgotten in time, and no man shall remember our works, and our life shall pass away as the trace of a cloud, and shall be dispersed as a mist, that is driven away with the beams of the sun, and overcome with the heat thereof... Come on, therefore, and let us be merry with the good things that are at hand; and let us eagerly enjoy the world while we are young... Let none of us go without his share in our pleasures; let us leave tokens of our joyfulness in every place: for this is our portion, and our lot is this."

Who does not recognise in these words the sentiments uttered by the "Preacher" in his gloomiest moods? though in repudiating them, our author gives expression to principles never advocated by his predecessor, who, though often on the brink of despair in reflecting on the vanity of all things, ever clung to virtue as the true beacon of life: "Let us oppress the poor righteous man, let us not spare the widow, nor reverence the old gray hairs of the aged. Let our strength be the law of justice; for that which is feeble is found to be worthless. Therefore let us lay in wait for the righteous; because he is troublesome to us, and he is opposed to our doings; he upbraids us with our offending the Law, and brings disgrace upon us on account of our transgression of discipline... We are considered by him as the scum, and he keeps aloof from our ways as from filth; he pronounces the end of the just to be blessed, and boasts that God is his father. Let us see if his words be true; and let us wait what will be his end... Let us condemn him to a shameful death: for he will obtain help according to his own words!" The author strongly censures such perversity and wickedness: "These things they imagine, but they are deceived; for their own wickedness blinds them. As for the mysteries of God, they know them not; nor do they hope for the wages of righteousness, nor acknowledge the triumph of blameless souls. For God created man to be immortal, and made him an image of His own eternity. Nevertheless through envy of the devil came death into the world; and they that hold of his side find it."

He then describes in glowing colours the happiness of the virtuous, who either enjoy their reward already in this world, or will find it in the realms of immortality: "The souls of the righteous are in the hand of God, and there no torment shall touch them. In the eyes of the unwise they seemed to die, and their decease is taken for misery, and their departure from us to be utter destruction: but they are in peace. And though they be punished according to the thoughts of men, yet is their hope full of immortality. And having been a little chastised, they are greatly rewarded; for God has proved them, and found them worthy of Himself. As gold in the furnace has He tried them, and received them with favour as a burnt-offering. And in the time of their compensation they shall shine, and shall move like sparks over the stubble. They shall judge the nations, and have dominion over the people, and the Lord shall be their King for ever. Those that put their trust in Him shall understand the truth; and those that are faithful in love shall abide with Him; for grace and mercy belong to His saints, and He has care for His elect."

Nay, God often causes pious men to die young, in order to deliver them from the corruption of a sinful generation, and to let them at once participate in the glories of heaven: "But though the righteous dies early, he is in rest. For honourable age is not that which stands in length of time, nor is it measured by number of years. But wisdom is the gray hair for men, and a spotless life is old age. He pleased God, and was beloved by Him; and as he lived among sinners, he was taken away. Yea, he was removed, lest wickedness should pervert his mind, and deceit beguile his soul. For the witchery of vice obscures beautiful things; and the giddiness of desire corrupts the simple mind. He being made perfect in a short time, accomplished a long life. For his soul pleased the Lord; therefore He hastened to take him away from among the wicked." These words prove strikingly how much the views of the Hebrews had advanced since the date of the Book of Job.

On the other hand, the author draws the awful fate which awaits the wicked: "For the hope of the ungodly is like chaff that is blown away by the wind, and like dust that is driven away by the storm, and like the smoke which is dispersed by the tempest; and it passes away as the remembrance of a guest that stays but a day... Then shall well-aiming thunderbolts go abroad; and from the clouds, as from a well-drawn bow, shall they fly to the mark. And hailstones shall be cast as out of a stone bow of wrath, and the water of the sea shall rage against them, and the floods shall mercilessly drown them."

Then returning to his first theme, he reminds the kings of their high duties and their great responsibilities: "Hear, therefore, O ye kings, and understand; learn, ye judges of the ends of the earth... For power is given you of the Lord, and sovereignty from the Most High, who shall try your works, and search out your counsels... Terribly and speedily shall He come upon you; for a severe judgment shall fall upon the rulers. For mercy will be shown to the meanest from compassion; but mighty men shall be mightily punished." Their only safety lies in wisdom, which is righteousness and knowledge and love: "To you, therefore, O kings, do I speak, that you may learn wisdom, and may not stumble... Wisdom is glorious and never fading: yea, she is easily seen by those that love her, and found by those that seek her... To reflect, therefore, upon her is perfection of discretion; and he who watches for her shall soon be without care... For the very true beginning of her is a desire of instruction; but the desire of instruction is love;. and love is the keeping of her laws; and the observance of her laws is the securing of immortality; and immortality brings us near God; therefore the desire of wisdom leads to dominion. If your delight be then in thrones and sceptres, O ye kings of the people, honour wisdom, that you may reign for evermore."

In order to give more weight to the advice he offers to rulers, the author speaks in the name of king Solomon, from whose experience he attempts to show that wisdom alone leads to virtue and fame. He considers humility as the firstfruit of wisdom: "I myself also am a mortal man, like all others, and the offspring of him that was first made of the earth... And when I was born I drew in the common air, and fell upon the same earth, and the first sound which I uttered was crying, as all others do... For there is no king that has any other beginning of birth. For all men have one entrance into life, and the same departure." Then he relates how he prayed to God for wisdom as the highest earthly prize, and he extols it in the most enthusiastic terms: "Wherefore I prayed, and understanding was given me: I called upon God, and the spirit of wisdom came to me. I preferred her before sceptres and thrones, and esteemed riches nothing in comparison of her. Nor compared I to her any precious stone, because all gold is in respect of her as a little sand, and silver is counted as clay before her. I loved her above health and beauty, and preferred to possess her rather than light: for the light that comes from her is never extinguished... For she is an unfailing treasure to men, and those who use it become the friends of God... But may God grant me to speak as I would, and to think as is worthy of the things that are given me: for He is the guide to wisdom, and He directs the wise."

The king thus became familiar with the marvels of the universe and the laws of nature, with the instincts of animals and the properties of plants: "for", said he, "wisdom, which is the worker of all things, taught me: for in her is an understanding spirit, a spirit holy, simple, manifold, subtle, versatile, clear, undefiled, plain, inviolable, loving virtue, quick, unchecked, beneficent, kind, steadfast, sure, free from care, all-powerful, all-seeing, and comprehending every thing, pervading all pure and subtle spirits. For wisdom is more active than all activity; she passes and pervades through all things by reason of her purity. For she is the breath of the power of God, and a pure emanation from the glory of the Almighty: therefore no defilement can fall upon her... And though being but one, she can do all things; and though remaining the same, she makes all things new; and in all ages entering into holy souls, she makes them friends of God and prophets... For she is more beautiful than the sun, and above all the order of stars; being compared with the light, she is found superior to it. For after this comes night; but vice prevails not against wisdom."

Anxious to convince his readers still more strikingly that wisdom rules the world, the writer points out how she helped and protected the Israelites in all their dangers, and how she ever saved the pious who trusted in God. But the very opposite of wisdom is, in his eyes, the folly of idolatry; and he, therefore, shows how all idolatrous nations, however great and powerful, suffered the direst punishments, and were finally exterminated. In deriding the idols, he displays a power of irony worthy of an Isaiah. The artist makes the image "like some vile beast, overlaying it with vermilion, and colouring it red with paint... Then he finds a fit place for it, sets it up against the wall, and makes it fast with iron; and he provides that it might not fall, knowing that it is unable to help itself; for it is an image and has need of help. Then he offers up a prayer for his goods, for his wife and children, and is not ashamed to invoke that which has no life. For health he calls upon that which is weak, for life he prays to that which is dead, for aid he humbly beseeches that which has least means to help, and for a good journey he asks that which cannot set a foot forward."

The author dwells more particularly upon the forms of idolatry prevalent in Egypt, his adopted home, describes with withering sarcasm the perversity of animal worship, and sets forth the heavy chastisements which were inflicted upon the Egyptians and all other enemies of the Hebrews. He pursues this theme in a minute historical survey, and he concludes with this consolatory conviction: "In all things, O Lord, Thou hast magnified Thy people, and glorified them, nor dost Thou lightly regard them; but assistest them in every time and place."

Never has the Divine light of wisdom been more fervently praised, and never the blindness of idol worship more conclusively denounced, than by the author of our Book. His vehemence in the latter respect suggests the supposition that he had a practical object in view, and that he desired to caution his wavering co-religionists against the superstitions of their pagan neighbours. And in exhorting the kings to justice and righteousness, he apparently meant to restrain the cruelties of some contemporary despot. These two points combined lead us to the later Ptolemies, under whose reign many of the Egyptian Jews were estranged from their old faith, while those who adhered to it persistently had to suffer hardships and persecutions. The author, who shows equal culture and ability, happily blended the great fundamental truths of the

Hebrew creed with some of the beautiful conceptions of the best schools of Greek philosophy; and both in this respect and in the prominence given to the belief in the immortality of the soul, he proved, that the Jewish mind had preserved its old vigour, and was constantly extending its fields of enquiry.

END OF VOLUME II.

Leipzig: Printed by W. Drugulin.

[SEPTEMBER 1870.]

GENERAL LIST OF WORKS

PUBLISHED BY

Messrs. LONGMANS, GREEN, AND CO.

PATERNOSTER ROW, LONDON.

History, Politics, Historical Memoirs, &c.

The HISTORY of ENGLAND from the Fall of Wolsey to the Defeat of the Spanish Armada. By JAMES ANTHONY FROUDE, M.A. late Fellow of Exeter College, Oxford.
> LIBRARY EDITION, 12 VOLS. 8vo. price £8 18s.
> CABINET EDITION, now appearing, in 12 vols. crown 8vo. price 6s. each.

The HISTORY of ENGLAND from the Accession of James II. By Lord MACAULAY.
> LIBRARY EDITION, 5 vols. 8vo. £4.
> CABINET EDITION, 8 vols. post 8vo. 48s.
> PEOPLE'S EDITION, 4 vols. crown 8vo. 16s.

LORD MACAULAY'S WORKS. Complete and Uniform Library Edition. Edited by his Sister, Lady TREVELYAN. 8 vols. 8vo. with Portrait, price £5 5s. cloth, or £8 8s. bound in tree-calf by Riviere.

An ESSAY on the HISTORY of the ENGLISH GOVERNMENT and Constitution, from the Reign of Henry VII. to the Present Time. By JOHN EARL RUSSELL. Fourth Edition, revised. Crown 8vo. 6s.

SELECTIONS from SPEECHES of EARL RUSSELL, 1817 to 1841, and from Despatches, 1859 to 1865; with Introductions. 2 vols. 8vo. 28s.

VARIETIES of VICE-REGAL LIFE. By Sir WILLIAM DENISON, K.C.B. late Governor-General of the Australian Colonies, and Governor of Madras. With Two Maps. 2 vols. 8vo. 28s.

On PARLIAMENTARY GOVERNMENT in ENGLAND: Its Origin, Development, and Practical Operation. By ALPHEUS TODD, Librarian of the Legislative Assembly of Canada. 2 vols. 8vo. price £1 17s.

LAND SYSTEMS and INDUSTRIAL ECONOMY of IRELAND, ENGLAND, and CONTINENTAL COUNTRIES. By T. E. CLIFFE LESLIE, LL.B. of Lincoln's Inn, Barrister-at-Law. 8vo. 12s.

A HISTORICAL ACCOUNT of the NEUTRALITY of GREAT BRITAIN DURING the AMERICAN CIVIL WAR. By MOUNTAGUE BERNARD, M.A. Chichele Professor of International Law and Diplomacy in the University of Oxford. Royal 8vo. 16s.

The **HISTORY of ENGLAND** during the Reign of George the Third. By the Right Hon. W. N. MASSEY. Cabinet Edition. 4 vols. post 8vo. 24s.

The **CONSTITUTIONAL HISTORY of ENGLAND**, since the Accession of George III. 1760—1860. By Sir THOMAS ERSKINE MAY, C.B. Second Edition. 2 vols. 8vo. 33s.

HISTORICAL STUDIES. By HERMAN MERIVALE, M.A. 8vo. 12s. 6d.

The **OXFORD REFORMERS of 1498**—John Colet, Erasmus, and Thomas More; being a History of their Fellow-work. By FREDERIC SEEBOHM. Second Edition, enlarged. 8vo. 14s.

A **HISTORY of WALES**, derived from Authentic Sources. By JANE WILLIAMS, Ysgafell. 8vo. 14s.

LECTURES on the HISTORY of ENGLAND, from the earliest Times to the Death of King Edward II. By WILLIAM LONGMAN. With Maps and Illustrations. 8vo. 15s.

The **HISTORY of the LIFE and TIMES of EDWARD the THIRD.** By WILLIAM LONGMAN. With 9 Maps, 8 Plates, and 16 Woodcuts. 2 vols. 8vo. 28s.

HISTORY of the NORMAN KINGS of ENGLAND, from a New Collation of the Contemporary Chronicles. By THOMAS COBBE, Barrister, of the Inner Temple. 8vo. price 16s.

The **OVERTHROW of the GERMANIC CONFEDERATION** by PRUSSIA in 1866. By Sir ALEXANDER MALET, Bart. K.C.B. With 5 Maps. 8vo. 18s.

The **MILITARY RESOURCES of PRUSSIA and FRANCE**, and RECENT CHANGES in the ART of WAR. By Lieut.-Col. CHESNEY, R.E. and HENRY REEVE, D.C.L. Crown 8vo. price 7s. 6d.

WATERLOO LECTURES: a Study of the Campaign of 1815. By Colonel CHARLES C. CHESNEY, R.E. late Professor of Military Art and History in the Staff College. New Edition. 8vo. with Map, 10s. 6d.

DEMOCRACY in AMERICA. By ALEXIS DE TOCQUEVILLE. Translated by HENRY REEVE. 2 vols. 8vo. 21s.

HISTORY of the REFORMATION in EUROPE in the Time of Calvin. By J. H. MERLE D'AUBIGNÉ, D.D. VOLS. I. and II. 8vo. 28s. VOL. III. 12s. VOL. IV. 16s. VOL. V. price 16s.

HISTORY of FRANCE, from Clovis and Charlemagne to the Accession of Napoléon III. By EYRE EVANS CROWE. 5 vols. 8vo. £4 13s.

CHAPTERS from FRENCH HISTORY; St. Louis, Joan of Arc, Henri IV. with Sketches of the Intermediate Periods. By J. H. GURNEY, M.A. New Edition. Fcp. 8vo. 6s. 6d.

MEMOIR of POPE SIXTUS the FIFTH. By Baron HUBNER. Translated from the Original in French, with the Author's sanction, by HUBERT E. H. JERNINGHAM. 2 vols. 8vo. [*Nearly ready.*

IGNATIUS LOYOLA and the EARLY JESUITS. By STEWART ROSE. 8vo. with Portrait, price 16s.

The **HISTORY of GREECE.** By C. THIRLWALL, D.D. Lord Bishop of St. David's. 8 vols. fcp. 8vo. price 28s.

GREEK HISTORY from Themistocles to Alexander, in a Series of Lives from Plutarch. Revised and arranged by A. H. CLOUGH. Fcp. with 44 Woodcuts, 6s.

CRITICAL HISTORY of the LANGUAGE and LITERATURE of
Ancient Greece. By WILLIAM MURE, of Caldwell. 5 vols. 8vo. £3 9s.

The TALE of the GREAT PERSIAN WAR, from the Histories of
Herodotus. By GEORGE W. COX, M.A. New Edition. Fcp. 3s. 6d.

HISTORY of the LITERATURE of ANCIENT GREECE. By Professor K. O. MÜLLER. Translated by the Right Hon. Sir GEORGE CORNEWALL LEWIS, Bart. and by J. W. DONALDSON, D.D. 3 vols. 8vo. 21s.

HISTORY of the CITY of ROME from its Foundation to the Sixteenth Century of the Christian Era. By THOMAS H. DYER, LL.D. 8vo. with 2 Maps, 15s.

The HISTORY of ROME. By WILHELM IHNE. Translated and revised by the Author. VOLS. I. and II. 8vo. [*Nearly ready.*

HISTORY of the ROMANS under the EMPIRE. By the Very Rev. C. MERIVALE, D.C.L. Dean of Ely. 8 vols. post 8vo. 48s.

The FALL of the ROMAN REPUBLIC; a Short History of the Last Century of the Commonwealth. By the same Author. 12mo. 7s. 6d.

The STUDENT'S MANUAL of the HISTORY of INDIA, from the Earliest Period to the Present. By Colonel MEADOWS TAYLOR, M.R.A.S. M.R.I.A. Author of 'The Confessions of a Thug.' Crown 8vo. [*In the press.*

The HISTORY of INDIA, from the Earliest Period to the close of Lord Dalhousie's Administration. By JOHN CLARK MARSHMAN. 3 vols. crown 8vo. 22s. 6d.

INDIAN POLITY: a View of the System of Administration in India. By Lieutenant-Colonel GEORGE CHESNEY, Fellow of the University of Calcutta. New Edition, revised; with Map. 8vo. price 21s.

HOME POLITICS; being a consideration of the Causes of the Growth of Trade in relation to Labour, Pauperism, and Emigration. By DANIEL GRANT. 8vo. 7s.

REALITIES of IRISH LIFE. By W. STEUART TRENCH, Land Agent in Ireland to the Marquess of Lansdowne, the Marquess of Bath, and Lord Digby. Fifth Edition. Crown 8vo. price 6s.

The STUDENT'S MANUAL of the HISTORY of IRELAND. By MARY F. CUSACK, Authoress of the 'Illustrated of Ireland, from the Earliest Period to the Year of Catholic Emancipation.' Crown 8vo. price 6s.

CRITICAL and HISTORICAL ESSAYS contributed to the *Edinburgh Review.* By the Right Hon. LORD MACAULAY.
CABINET EDITION, 4 vols. post 8vo. 24s. LIBRARY EDITION, 3 vols. 8vo. 36s.
PEOPLE'S EDITION, 2 vols. crown 8vo. 8s. STUDENT'S EDITION, 1 vol. cr. 8vo. 6s.

HISTORY of EUROPEAN MORALS, from Augustus to Charlemagne. By W. E. H. LECKY, M.A. Second Edition. 2 vols. 8vo. price 28s.

HISTORY of the RISE and INFLUENCE of the SPIRIT of RATIONALISM in EUROPE. By W. E. H. LECKY, M.A. Cabinet Edition, being the Fourth. 2 vols. crown 8vo. price 16s.

GOD in HISTORY; or, the Progress of Man's Faith in the Moral Order of the World. By Baron BUNSEN. Translated by SUSANNA WINKWORTH; with a Preface by Dean STANLEY. 3 vols. 8vo. price 42s.

The **HISTORY of PHILOSOPHY**, from Thales to Comte. By GEORGE HENRY LEWES. Third Edition. 2 vols. 8vo. 30s.

The **MYTHOLOGY of the ARYAN NATIONS**. By GEORGE W. COX, M.A. late Scholar of Trinity College, Oxford, Joint-Editor, with the late Professor Brande, of the Fourth Edition of 'The Dictionary of Science, Literature, and Art,' Author of 'Tales of Ancient Greece,' &c. 2 vols. 8vo. 28s.

EGYPT'S PLACE in UNIVERSAL HISTORY; an Historical Investigation. By Baron BUNSEN, D.C.L. Translated by C. H. COTTRELL, M.A. With Additions by S. BIRCH, LL.D. 5 vols. 8vo. price £8 14s. 6d.

HISTORY of CIVILISATION in England and France, Spain and Scotland. By HENRY THOMAS BUCKLE. New Edition of the entire Work, with a complete INDEX. 3 vols. crown 8vo. 24s.

HISTORY of the CHRISTIAN CHURCH, from the Ascension of Christ to the Conversion of Constantine. By E. BURTON, D.D. late Prof. of Divinity in the Univ. of Oxford. Eighth Edition. Fcp. 3s. 6d.

SKETCH of the HISTORY of the CHURCH of ENGLAND to the Revolution of 1688. By the Right Rev. T. V. SHORT, D.D. Lord Bishop of St. Asaph. Eighth Edition. Crown 8vo. 7s. 6d.

HISTORY of the EARLY CHURCH, from the First Preaching of the Gospel to the Council of Nicæa. A.D. 325. By ELIZABETH M. SEWELL, Author of 'Amy Herbert.' New Edition, with Questions. Fcp. 4s. 6d.

The **ENGLISH REFORMATION**. By F. C. MASSINGBERD, M.A. Chancellor of Lincoln and Rector of South Ormsby. Fourth Edition, revised. Fcp. 8vo. 7s. 6d.

MAUNDER'S HISTORICAL TREASURY; comprising a General Introductory Outline of Universal History, and a series of Separate Histories. Latest Edition, revised and brought down to the Present Time by the Rev. GEORGE WILLIAM COX, M.A. Fcp. 6s. cloth, or 9s. 6d. calf.

WOODWARD'S HISTORICAL and CHRONOLOGICAL ENCYCLOPÆDIA.—The copious 'Encyclopædia of Chronology and History,' projected and left unfinished by the late B. B. WOODWARD, B.A. F.S.A. Librarian to the Queen at Windsor, is in an advanced state of preparation, and will be completed by Mr. W. L. R. CATES, Editor of the *Dictionary of General Biography*, the friend, and for ten years the collaborateur, of Mr. WOODWARD.

Biographical Works.

The **LIFE and LETTERS of FARADAY**. By Dr. BENCE JONES, Secretary of the Royal Institution. Second Edition, thoroughly revised. 2 vols. 8vo. with Portrait, and Eight Engravings on Wood, price 28s.

FARADAY as a DISCOVERER. By JOHN TYNDALL, LL.D. F.R.S. Professor of Natural Philosophy in the Royal Institution. New and Cheaper Edition, with Two Portraits. Fcp. 8vo. 3s. 6d.

The **LIFE and LETTERS of the Rev. SYDNEY SMITH**. Edited by his Daughter, Lady HOLLAND, and Mrs. AUSTIN. New Edition, complete in One Volume. Crown 8vo. price 6s.

A **MEMOIR of GEORGE EDWARD LYNCH COTTON**, D.D. late Lord Bishop of Calcutta; with Selections from his Journals and Letters. Edited by Mrs. COTTON. [*In preparation.*

The LIFE of OLIVER CROMWELL, to the Death of Charles I. By J. R. ANDREWS, Barrister-at-Law. 8vo. 14s.

DICTIONARY of GENERAL BIOGRAPHY; containing Concise Memoirs and Notices of the most Eminent Persons of all Countries, from the Earliest Ages to the Present Time. Edited by W. L. R. CATES. 8vo. 21s.

LIVES of the TUDOR PRINCESSES, including Lady Jane Grey and her Sisters. By AGNES STRICKLAND, Author of 'Lives of the Queens of England.' Post 8vo. with Portrait, &c. 12s. 6d.

LIVES of the QUEENS of ENGLAND. By AGNES STRICKLAND. Library Edition, newly revised; with Portraits of every Queen, Autographs, and Vignettes. 8 vols. post 8vo. 7s. 6d. each.

MEMOIRS of BARON BUNSEN. Drawn chiefly from Family Papers by his Widow, FRANCES Baroness BUNSEN. Second Edition, abridged; with 2 Portraits and 4 Woodcuts. 2 vols. post 8vo. 21s.

The LETTERS of the Right Hon. Sir GEORGE CORNEWALL LEWIS, Bart. to various Friends. Edited by his Brother, the Rev. Canon Sir G. F. LEWIS, Bart. 8vo. with Portrait, price 14s.

LIFE of the DUKE of WELLINGTON. By the Rev. G. R. GLEIG, M.A. Popular Edition, carefully revised; with copious Additions. Crown 8vo. with Portrait, 5s.

HISTORY of MY RELIGIOUS OPINIONS. By J. H. NEWMAN, D.D. Being the Substance of Apologia pro Vitâ Suâ. Post 8vo. 6s.

FATHER MATHEW: a Biography. By JOHN FRANCIS MAGUIRE, M.P. for Cork. Popular Edition, with Portrait. Crown 8vo. 3s. 6d.

FELIX MENDELSSOHN'S LETTERS from *Italy and Switzerland*, and *Letters from* 1833 *to* 1847, translated by Lady WALLACE. New Edition with Portrait. 2 vols. crown 8vo. 5s. each.

MEMOIRS of SIR HENRY HAVELOCK, K.C.B. By JOHN CLARK MARSHMAN. Cabinet Edition, with Portrait. Crown 8vo. price 3s. 6d.

CAPTAIN COOK'S LIFE, VOYAGES, and DISCOVERIES. 18mo. Woodcuts, 2s. 6d.

VICISSITUDES of FAMILIES. By Sir J. BERNARD BURKE, C.B. Ulster King of Arms. New Edition, remodelled and enlarged. 2 vols. crown 8vo. 21s.

THE EARLS of GRANARD: a Memoir of the Noble Family of Forbes. Written by Admiral the Hon. JOHN FORBES, and edited by GEORGE ARTHUR HASTINGS, present Earl of Granard, K.P. 8vo. 10s.

ESSAYS in ECCLESIASTICAL BIOGRAPHY. By the Right Hon. Sir J. STEPHEN, LL.D. Cabinet Edition, being the Fifth. Crown 8vo. 7s. 6d.

MAUNDER'S BIOGRAPHICAL TREASURY. Thirteenth Edition, reconstructed, thoroughly revised, and in great part rewritten; with about 1,000 additional Memoirs and Notices, by W. L. R. CATES. Fcp. 6s.

LETTERS and LIFE of FRANCIS BACON, including all his Occasional Works. Collected and edited, with a Commentary, by J. SPEDDING, Trin. Coll. Cantab. VOLS. I. and II. 8vo. 24s. VOLS. III. and IV. 24s. VOL. V. price 12s.

Criticism, Philosophy, Polity, &c.

The INSTITUTES of JUSTINIAN; with English Introduction, Translation, and Notes. By T. C. SANDARS, M.A. Barrister, late Fellow of Oriel Coll. Oxon. New Edition. 8vo. 15s.

SOCRATES and the SOCRATIC SCHOOLS. Translated from the German of Dr. E. ZELLER, with the Author's approval, by the Rev. OSWALD J. REICHEL, B.C.L. and M.A. Crown 8vo. 8s. 6d.

The STOICS, EPICUREANS, and SCEPTICS. Translated from the German of Dr. E. ZELLER, with the Author's approval, by OSWALD J. REICHEL, B.C.L. and M.A. Crown 8vo. price 14s.

The ETHICS of ARISTOTLE, illustrated with Essays and Notes. By Sir A. GRANT, Bart. M.A. LL.D. Second Edition, revised and completed. 2 vols. 8vo. price 28s.

The NICOMACHEAN ETHICS of ARISTOTLE newly translated into English. By R. WILLIAMS, B.A. Fellow and late Lecturer of Merton College, and sometime Student of Christ Church, Oxford. 8vo. 12s.

ELEMENTS of LOGIC. By R. WHATELY, D.D. late Archbishop of Dublin. New Edition. 8vo. 10s. 6d. crown 8vo. 4s. 6d.

Elements of Rhetoric. By the same Author. New Edition. 8vo. 10s. 6d. crown 8vo. 4s. 6d.

English Synonymes. By E. JANE WHATELY. Edited by Archbishop WHATELY. 5th Edition. Fcp. 3s.

BACON'S ESSAYS with ANNOTATIONS. By R. WHATELY, D.D. late Archbishop of Dublin. Sixth Edition. 8vo. 10s. 6d.

LORD BACON'S WORKS, collected and edited by J. SPEDDING, M.A. R. L. ELLIS, M.A. and D. D. HEATH. New and Cheaper Edition. 7 vols. 8vo. price £3 13s. 6d.

ENGLAND and IRELAND. By JOHN STUART MILL. Fifth Edition, vo. 1s.

The SUBJECTION of WOMEN. By JOHN STUART MILL. New Edition. Post 8vo. 5s.

On REPRESENTATIVE GOVERNMENT. By JOHN STUART MILL. Third Edition. 8vo. 9s. Crown 8vo. 2s.

On LIBERTY. By JOHN STUART MILL. Fourth Edition. Post 8vo. 7s. 6d. Crown 8vo. 1s. 4d.

Principles of Political Economy. By the same Author. Sixth Edition. 2 vols. 8vo. 30s. Or in 1 vol. crown 8vo. 5s.

A System of Logic, Ratiocinative and Inductive. By the same Author. Seventh Edition. Two vols. 8vo. 25s.

ANALYSIS of Mr. MILL'S SYSTEM of LOGIC. By W. STEBBING, M.A. Fellow of Worcester College, Oxford. New Edition. 12mo. 3s. 6d.

UTILITARIANISM. By JOHN STUART MILL. Third Edition. 8vo. 5s.

DISSERTATIONS and DISCUSSIONS, POLITICAL, PHILOSOPHI-
CAL, and HISTORICAL. By JOHN STUART MILL. Second Edition, revised.
3 vols. 8vo. 36s.

EXAMINATION of Sir W. HAMILTON'S PHILOSOPHY, and of the
Principal Philosophical Questions discussed in his Writings. By JOHN
STUART MILL. Third Edition. 8vo. 16s.

An OUTLINE of the NECESSARY LAWS of THOUGHT: a Treatise
on Pure and Applied Logic. By the Most Rev. WILLIAM, Lord Archbishop of York, D.D. F.R.S. Ninth Thousand. Crown 8vo. 5s. 6d.

The ELEMENTS of POLITICAL ECONOMY. By HENRY DUNNING
MACLEOD, M.A. Barrister-at-Law. 8vo. 16s.

A Dictionary of Political Economy; Biographical, Bibliographical,
Historical, and Practical. By the same Author. VOL. I. royal 8vo. 30s.

The ELECTION of REPRESENTATIVES, Parliamentary and Muni-
cipal; a Treatise. By THOMAS HARE, Barrister-at-Law. Third Edition,
with Additions. Crown 8vo. 6s.

SPEECHES of the RIGHT HON. LORD MACAULAY, corrected by
Himself. People's Edition, crown 8vo. 3s. 6d.

Lord Macaulay's Speeches on Parliamentary Reform in 1831 and
1832. 16mo. 1s.

INAUGURAL ADDRESS delivered to the University of St. Andrews.
By JOHN STUART MILL. 8vo. 5s. People's Edition, crown 8vo. 1s.

A DICTIONARY of the ENGLISH LANGUAGE. By R. G. LATHAM,
M.A. M.D. F.R.S. Founded on the Dictionary of Dr. SAMUEL JOHNSON, as
edited by the Rev. H. J. TODD, with numerous Emendations and Additions.
In Four Volumes, 4to. price £7.

THESAURUS of ENGLISH WORDS and PHRASES, classified and
arranged so as to facilitate the Expression of Ideas, and assist in Literary
Composition. By P. M. ROGET, M.D. New Edition. Crown 8vo. 10s. 6d.

LECTURES on the SCIENCE of LANGUAGE, delivered at the Royal
Institution. By MAX MÜLLER, M.A. Fellow of All Souls College, Oxford.
2 vols. 8vo. price 30s.

CHAPTERS on LANGUAGE. By FREDERIC W. FARRAR, F.R.S. late
Fellow of Trin. Coll. Cambridge. Crown 8vo. 8s. 6d.

WORD-GOSSIP; a Series of Familiar Essays on Words and their
Peculiarities. By the Rev. W. L. BLACKLEY, M.A. Fcp. 8vo. 5s.

A BOOK ABOUT WORDS. By G. F. GRAHAM, Author of 'English,
or the Art of Composition,' &c. Fcp. 8vo. price 3s. 6d.

The DEBATER; a Series of Complete Debates, Outlines of Debates,
and Questions for Discussion. By F. ROWTON. Fcp. 6s.

MANUAL of ENGLISH LITERATURE, Historical and Critical. By
THOMAS ARNOLD, M.A. Second Edition. Crown 8vo. price 7s. 6d.

SOUTHEY'S DOCTOR, complete in One Volume. Edited by the Rev.
J. W. WARTER, B.D. Square crown 8vo. 12s. 6d.

HISTORICAL and CRITICAL COMMENTARY on the OLD TESTA-
MENT; with a New Translation. By M. M. KALISCH, Ph.D. VOL. I.
Genesis, 8vo. 18s. or adapted for the General Reader, 12s. VOL. II. *Exodus*,
15s. or adapted for the General Reader, 12s. VOL. III. *Leviticus*, PART I.
15s. or adapted for the General Reader, 8s.

A HEBREW GRAMMAR, with **EXERCISES.** By M. M. KALISCH, Ph.D. PART I. *Outlines with Exercises,* 8vo. 12s. 6d. KEY, 5s. PART II. *Exceptional Forms and Constructions,* 12s. 6d.

A LATIN-ENGLISH DICTIONARY. By J. T. WHITE, D.D. of Corpus Christi College, and J. E. RIDDLE, M.A. of St. Edmund Hall, Oxford. Third Edition, revised. 2 vols. 4to. pp. 2,128, price 42s. cloth.

White's College Latin-English Dictionary (Intermediate Size), abridged for the use of University Students from the Parent Work (as above). Medium 8vo. pp. 1,048, price 18s. cloth.

White's Junior Student's Complete Latin-English and English-Latin Dictionary. New Edition. Square 12mo. pp. 1,058, price 12s.

Separately { The ENGLISH-LATIN DICTIONARY, price 5s. 6d.
{ The LATIN-ENGLISH DICTIONARY, price 7s. 6d.

An ENGLISH-GREEK LEXICON, containing all the Greek Words used by Writers of good authority. By C. D. YONGE, B.A. New Edition. 4to. 21s.

Mr. YONGE'S NEW LEXICON, English and Greek, abridged from his larger work (as above). Revised Edition. Square 12mo. 8s. 6d.

A GREEK-ENGLISH LEXICON. Compiled by H. G. LIDDELL, D.D. Dean of Christ Church, and R. SCOTT, D.D. Master of Balliol. Sixth Edition. Crown 4to. price 36s.

A Lexicon, Greek and English, abridged from LIDDELL and SCOTT's *Greek-English Lexicon.* Twelfth Edition. Square 12mo. 7s. 6d.

A SANSKRIT-ENGLISH DICTIONARY, the Sanskrit words printed both in the original Devanagari and in Roman Letters. Compiled by T. BENFEY, Prof. in the Univ. of Göttingen. 8vo. 52s. 6d.

WALKER'S PRONOUNCING DICTIONARY of the **ENGLISH LANGUAGE.** Thoroughly revised Editions, by B. H. SMART. 8vo. 12s. 16mo. 6s.

A PRACTICAL DICTIONARY of the **FRENCH** and **ENGLISH LANGUAGES.** By L. CONTANSEAU. Fourteenth Edition. Post 8vo. 10s. 6d.

Contanseau's Pocket Dictionary, French and English, abridged from the above by the Author. New Edition, revised. Square 18mo. 3s. 6d.

NEW PRACTICAL DICTIONARY of the **GERMAN LANGUAGE**; German-English and English-German. By the Rev. W. L. BLACKLEY, M.A. and Dr. CARL MARTIN FRIEDLÄNDER. Post 8vo. 7s. 6d.

The MASTERY of LANGUAGES; or, the Art of Speaking Foreign Tongues Idiomatically. By THOMAS PRENDERGAST, late of the Civil Service at Madras. Second Edition. 8vo. 6s.

Miscellaneous Works and *Popular Metaphysics.*

The ESSAYS and CONTRIBUTIONS of A. K. H. B., Author of ' The Recreations of a Country Parson.' Uniform Editions:—

Recreations of a Country Parson. By A. K. H. B. FIRST and SECOND SERIES, crown 8vo. 3s. 6d. each.

The Common-place Philosopher in Town and Country. By A. K. H. B. Crown 8vo. price 3s. 6d.

Leisure Hours in Town; Essays Consolatory, Æsthetical, Moral, Social, and Domestic. By A. K. H. B. Crown 8vo. 3s. 6d.

The Autumn Holidays of a Country Parson; Essays contributed to *Fraser's Magazine* and to *Good Words*. By A. K. H. B. Crown 8vo. 3s. 6d.

The Graver Thoughts of a Country Parson. By A. K. H. B. FIRST and SECOND SERIES, crown 8vo. 3s. 6d. each.

Critical Essays of a Country Parson, selected from Essays contributed to *Fraser's Magazine*. By A. K. H. B. Crown 8vo. 3s. 6d.

Sunday Afternoons at the Parish Church of a Scottish University City. By A. K. H. B. Crown 8vo. 3s. 6d.

Lessons of Middle Age; with some Account of various Cities and Men. By A. K. H. B. Crown 8vo. 3s. 6d.

Counsel and Comfort spoken from a City Pulpit. By A. K. H. B. Crown 8vo. price 3s. 6d.

Changed Aspects of Unchanged Truths; Memorials of St. Andrews Sundays. By A. K. H. B. Crown 8vo. 3s. 6d.

SHORT STUDIES on GREAT SUBJECTS. By JAMES ANTHONY FROUDE, M.A. late Fellow of Exeter Coll. Oxford. Third Edition. 8vo. 12s.

LORD MACAULAY'S MISCELLANEOUS WRITINGS:—
    LIBRARY EDITION. 2 vols. 8vo. Portrait, 21s.
    PEOPLE'S EDITION. 1 vol. crown 8vo. 4s. 6d.

The REV. SYDNEY SMITH'S MISCELLANEOUS WORKS; including his Contributions to the *Edinburgh Review*. Crown 8vo. 6s.

The Wit and Wisdom of the Rev. Sydney Smith: a Selection of the most memorable Passages in his Writings and Conversation. 16mo. 3s. 6d.

TRACES of HISTORY in the NAMES of PLACES; with a Vocabulary of the Roots out of which Names of Places in England and Wales are formed. By FLAVELL EDMUNDS. Crown 8vo. 7s. 6d.

ESSAYS selected from CONTRIBUTIONS to the *Edinburgh Review*. By HENRY ROGERS. Second Edition. 3 vols. fcp. 21s.

Reason and Faith, their Claims and Conflicts. By the same Author. New Edition, accompanied by several other Essays. Crown 8vo. 6s. 6d.

The Eclipse of Faith; or, a Visit to a Religious Sceptic. By the same Author. Twelfth Edition. Fcp. 5s.

Defence of the Eclipse of Faith, by its Author; a rejoinder to Dr. Newman's *Reply*. Third Edition. Fcp. 3s. 6d.

Selections from the Correspondence of R. E. H. Greyson. By the same Author. Third Edition. Crown 8vo. 7s. 6d.

FAMILIES of SPEECH, Four Lectures delivered at the Royal Institution of Great Britain. By the Rev. F. W. FARRAR, M.A. F.R.S. late Fellow of Trinity College, Cambridge. Post 8vo. with Two Maps, 5s. 6d.

B

CHIPS from a GERMAN WORKSHOP; being Essays on the Science of Religion, and on Mythology, Traditions, and Customs. By MAX MÜLLER, M.A. Fellow of All Souls College, Oxford. Second Edition, revised, with an Index. 2 vols. 8vo. 24s.

ANALYSIS of the PHENOMENA of the HUMAN MIND. By JAMES MILL. A New Edition, with Notes, Illustrative and Critical, by ALEXANDER BAIN, ANDREW FINDLATER, and GEORGE GROTE. Edited, with additional Notes, by JOHN STUART MILL. 2 vols. 8vo. price 28s.

An INTRODUCTION to MENTAL PHILOSOPHY, on the Inductive Method. By J. D. MORELL, M.A. LL.D. 8vo. 12s.

ELEMENTS of PSYCHOLOGY, containing the Analysis of the Intellectual Powers. By the same Author. Post 8vo. 7s. 6d.

The SECRET of HEGEL: being the Hegelian System in Origin, Principle, Form, and Matter. By J. H. STIRLING. 2 vols. 8vo. 28s.

The SENSES and the INTELLECT. By ALEXANDER BAIN, M.D. Professor of Logic in the University of Aberdeen. Third Edition. 8vo. 15s.

The EMOTIONS and the WILL. By the same Author. Second Edition. 8vo. 15s.

On the STUDY of CHARACTER, including an Estimate of Phrenology. By the same Author. 8vo. 9s.

MENTAL and MORAL SCIENCE: a Compendium of Psychology and Ethics. By the same Author. Second Edition. Crown 8vo. 10s. 6d.

LOGIC, DEDUCTIVE and INDUCTIVE. By the same Author. In TWO PARTS, crown 8vo. 10s. 6d. Each Part may be had separately:—
PART I. *Deduction*, 4s. PART II. *Induction*, 6s. 6d.

TIME and SPACE; a Metaphysical Essay. By SHADWORTH H. HODGSON. (This work covers the whole ground of Speculative Philosophy.) 8vo. price 16s.

The Theory of Practice; an Ethical Inquiry. By the same Author. (This work, in conjunction with the foregoing, completes a system of Philosophy.) 2 vols. 8vo. price 24s.

STRONG AND FREE; or, First Steps towards Social Science. By the Author of 'My Life, and What shall I do with it?' 8vo. price 10s. 6d.

The PHILOSOPHY of NECESSITY; or, Natural Law as applicable to Mental, Moral, and Social Science. By CHARLES BRAY. Second Edition. 8vo. 9s.

The Education of the Feelings and Affections. By the same Author. Third Edition. 8vo. 3s. 6d.

On Force, its Mental and Moral Correlates. By the same Author. 8vo. 5s.

CHARACTERISTICS of MEN, MANNERS, OPINIONS, TIMES. By ANTHONY, Third Earl of SHAFTESBURY. Published from the Edition of 1713, with Engravings designed by the Author; and edited, with Marginal Analysis, Notes, and Illustrations, by the Rev. W. M. HATCH, M.A. Fellow of New College, Oxford. 3 vols. 8vo. VOL. I. price 14s.

A TREATISE on HUMAN NATURE; being an Attempt to Introduce the Experimental Method of Reasoning into Moral Subjects. By DAVID HUME. Edited, with a Preliminary Dissertation and Notes, by T. H. GREEN, Fellow, and T. H. GROSE, late Scholar, of Balliol College, Oxford.
[*In the press.*

ESSAYS MORAL, POLITICAL, and LITERARY. By DAVID HUME. By the same Editors. [*In the press.*

Astronomy, Meteorology, Popular Geography, &c.

OUTLINES of ASTRONOMY. By Sir J. F. W. HERSCHEL, Bart. M.A. Tenth Edition, revised; with 9 Plates and many Woodcuts. 8vo. 18s.

OTHER WORLDS THAN OURS; the Plurality of Worlds Studied under the Light of Recent Scientific Researches. By RICHARD A. PROCTOR, B.A. F.R.A.S. With 13 Illustrations (6 of them coloured). Crown 8vo. 10s. 6d.

SATURN and its SYSTEM. By the same Author. 8vo. with 14 Plates, 14s.

CELESTIAL OBJECTS for COMMON TELESCOPES. By the Rev. T. W. WEBB, M.A. F.R.A.S. Second Edition, revised, with a large Map of the Moon, and several Woodcuts. 16mo. 7s. 6d.

NAVIGATION and NAUTICAL ASTRONOMY (Practical, Theoretical, Scientific) for the use of Students and Practical Men. By J. MERRIFIELD, F.R.A.S and H. EVERS. 8vo. 14s.

DOVE'S LAW of STORMS, considered in connexion with the Ordinary Movements of the Atmosphere. Translated by R. H. SCOTT, M.A. T.C.D. 8vo. 10s. 6d.

PHYSICAL GEOGRAPHY for SCHOOLS and GENERAL READERS. By M. F. MAURY, LL.D. Fcp. with 2 Charts, 2s. 6d.

M'CULLOCH'S DICTIONARY, Geographical, Statistical, and Historical, of the various Countries, Places, and Principal Natural Objects in the World. New Edition, with the Statistical Information brought up to the latest returns by F. MARTIN. 4 vols. 8vo. with coloured Maps, £4 4s.

A GENERAL DICTIONARY of GEOGRAPHY, Descriptive, Physical, Statistical, and Historical; forming a complete Gazetteer of the World. By A. KEITH JOHNSTON, LL.D. F.R.G.S. Revised Edition. 8vo. 31s. 6d.

A MANUAL of GEOGRAPHY, Physical, Industrial, and Political. By W. HUGHES, F.R.G.S. With 6 Maps. Fcp. 7s. 6d.

The STATES of the RIVER PLATE: their Industries and Commerce. By WILFRID LATHAM, Buenos Ayres. Second Edition, revised. 8vo. 12s.

MAUNDER'S TREASURY of GEOGRAPHY, Physical, Historical, Descriptive, and Political. Edited by W. HUGHES, F.R.G.S. Revised Edition, with 7 Maps and 16 Plates. Fcp. 6s. cloth, or 9s. 6d. bound in calf.

Natural History and Popular Science.

ELEMENTARY TREATISE on PHYSICS, Experimental and Applied. Translated and edited from GANOT's *Éléments de Physique* (with the Author's sanction) by E. ATKINSON, Ph.D. F.C.S. New Edition, revised and enlarged; with a Coloured Plate and 620 Woodcuts. Post 8vo. 15s.

The ELEMENTS of PHYSICS or NATURAL PHILOSOPHY. By NEIL ARNOTT, M.D. F.R.S. Physician Extraordinary to the Queen. Sixth Edition, rewritten and completed. Two Parts. 8vo. 21s.

SOUND: a Course of Eight Lectures delivered at the Royal Institution of Great Britain. By JOHN TYNDALL, LL.D. F.R.S. New Edition, crown 8vo. with Portrait of M. Chladni and 169 Woodcuts, price 9s.

HEAT a MODE of MOTION. By Professor JOHN TYNDALL, LL.D. F.R.S. Fourth Edition. Crown 8vo. with Woodcuts, 10s. 6d.

RESEARCHES on DIAMAGNETISM and MAGNE-CRYSTALLIC ACTION; including the Question of Diamagnetic Polarity. By the same Author. With 6 Plates and many Woodcuts. 8vo. price 14s.

NOTES of a COURSE of NINE LECTURES on LIGHT delivered at the Royal Institution of Great Britain in April–June 1869. By the same Author. Crown 8vo. price 1s. sewed, or 1s. 6d. cloth.

LIGHT: Its Influence on Life and Health. By FORBES WINSLOW, M.D. D.C.L. Oxon. (Hon.). Fcp. 8vo. 6s.

A TREATISE on ELECTRICITY, in Theory and Practice. By A. DE LA RIVE, Prof. in the Academy of Geneva. Translated by C. V. WALKER, F.R.S. 3 vols. 8vo. with Woodcuts, £3 13s.

The CORRELATION of PHYSICAL FORCES. By W. R. GROVE, Q.C. V.P.R.S. Fifth Edition, revised, and followed by a Discourse on Continuity. 8vo. 10s. 6d. The *Discourse on Continuity*, separately, 2s. 6d.

MANUAL of GEOLOGY. By S. HAUGHTON, M.D. F.R.S. Revised Edition, with 66 Woodcuts. Fcp. 7s. 6d.

A GUIDE to GEOLOGY. By J. PHILLIPS, M.A. Professor of Geology in the University of Oxford. Fifth Edition, with Plates. Fcp. 4s.

The STUDENT'S MANUAL of ZOOLOGY and COMPARATIVE PHYSIOLOGY. By J. BURNEY YEO, M.B. Resident Medical Tutor and Lecturer on Animal Physiology in King's College, London. [*Nearly ready.*

VAN DER HOEVEN'S HANDBOOK of ZOOLOGY. Translated from the Second Dutch Edition by the Rev. W. CLARK, M.D. F.R.S. 2 vols. 8vo. with 24 Plates of Figures, 60s.

Professor OWEN'S LECTURES on the COMPARATIVE ANATOMY and Physiology of the Invertebrate Animals. Second Edition, with 235 Woodcuts. 8vo. 21s.

The COMPARATIVE ANATOMY and PHYSIOLOGY of the VERTEbrate Animals. By RICHARD OWEN, F.R.S. D.C.L. With 1,472 Woodcuts. 3 vols. 8vo. £3 13s. 6d.

The ORIGIN of CIVILISATION and the PRIMITIVE CONDITION of MAN; Mental and Social Condition of Savages. By Sir JOHN LUBBOCK, Bart. M.P. F.R.S. With 25 Woodcuts. 8vo. price 16s.

The PRIMITIVE INHABITANTS of SCANDINAVIA; containing a Description of the Implements, Dwellings, Tombs, and Mode of Living of the Savages in the North of Europe during the Stone Age. By SVEN NILSSON. With 16 Plates of Figures and 3 Woodcuts. 8vo. 18s.

BIBLE ANIMALS; being a Description of every Living Creature mentioned in the Scriptures, from the Ape to the Coral. By the Rev. J. G. WOOD, M.A. F.L.S. With about 100 Vignettes on Wood, 8vo. 21s.

HOMES WITHOUT HANDS; a Description of the Habitations of Animals, classed according to their Principle of Construction. By Rev. J. G. WOOD, M.A. F.L.S. With about 140 Vignettes on Wood, 8vo. 21s.

A FAMILIAR HISTORY of BIRDS. By E. STANLEY, D.D. F.R.S. late Lord Bishop of Norwich. Seventh Edition, with Woodcuts. Fcp. 3s. 6d.

The **HARMONIES of NATURE** and **UNITY of CREATION**. By Dr. GEORGE HARTWIG. 8vo. with numerous Illustrations, 18s.

The **SEA** and its **LIVING WONDERS**. By the same Author. Third (English) Edition. 8vo. with many Illustrations, 21s.

The **TROPICAL WORLD**. By Dr. GEO. HARTWIG. With 8 Chromoxylographs and 172 Woodcuts. 8vo. 21s.

The **POLAR WORLD**; a Popular Description of Man and Nature in the Arctic and Antarctic Regions of the Globe. By Dr. GEORGE HARTWIG. With 8 Chromoxylographs, 3 Maps, and 85 Woodcuts. 8vo. 21s.

KIRBY and **SPENCE'S INTRODUCTION** to **ENTOMOLOGY**, or Elements of the Natural History of Insects. 7th Edition. Crown 8vo. 5s.

MAUNDER'S TREASURY of **NATURAL HISTORY**, or Popular Dictionary of Zoology. Revised and corrected by T. S. COBBOLD, M.D. Fcp. with 900 Woodcuts, 6s. cloth, or 9s. 6d. bound in calf.

The **TREASURY of BOTANY**, or Popular Dictionary of the Vegetable Kingdom; including a Glossary of Botanical Terms. Edited by J. LINDLEY, F.R.S. and T. MOORE, F.L.S. assisted by eminent Contributors. With 274 Woodcuts and 20 Steel Plates. Two Parts, fcp. 12s. cloth, or 19s. calf.

The **ELEMENTS of BOTANY** for **FAMILIES** and **SCHOOLS**. Tenth Edition, revised by THOMAS MOORE, F.L.S. Fcp. with 154 Woodcuts, 2s. 6d.

The **ROSE AMATEUR'S GUIDE**. By THOMAS RIVERS. Ninth Edition. Fcp. 4s.

The **BRITISH FLORA**; comprising the Phænogamous or Flowering Plants and the Ferns. By Sir W. J. HOOKER, K.H. and G. A. WALKER-ARNOTT, LL.D. 12mo. with 12 Plates, 14s.

LOUDON'S ENCYCLOPÆDIA of PLANTS; comprising the Specific Character, Description, Culture, History, &c. of all the Plants found in Great Britain. With upwards of 12,000 Woodcuts. 8vo. 42s.

MAUNDER'S SCIENTIFIC and **LITERARY TREASURY**. New Edition, thoroughly revised and in great part re-written, with above 1,000 new Articles, by J. Y. JOHNSON, Corr. M.Z.S. Fcp. 6s. cloth, or 9s. 6d. calf.

A **DICTIONARY** of **SCIENCE, LITERATURE**, and **ART**. Fourth Edition, re-edited by W. T. BRANDE (the original Author), and GEORGE W. COX, M.A. assisted by contributors of eminent Scientific and Literary Acquirements. 3 vols. medium 8vo. price 63s. cloth.

Chemistry, Medicine, Surgery, and the Allied Sciences.

A **DICTIONARY** of **CHEMISTRY** and the Allied Branches of other Sciences. By HENRY WATTS, F.R.S. assisted by eminent Contributors. Complete in 5 vols. medium 8vo. £7 3s.

ELEMENTS of CHEMISTRY, Theoretical and Practical. By W. ALLEN MILLER, M.D. &c. Prof. of Chemistry, King's Coll. London. Fourth Edition. 3 vols. 8vo. £3. PART I. CHEMICAL PHYSICS, 15s. PART II. INORGANIC CHEMISTRY, 21s. PART III. ORGANIC CHEMISTRY, 24s.

A **MANUAL of CHEMISTRY**, Descriptive and Theoretical. By WILLIAM ODLING, M.B. F.R.S. PART I. 8vo. 9s. PART II. *just ready*.

OUTLINES of CHEMISTRY; or, Brief Notes of Chemical Facts. By WILLIAM ODLING, M.B. F.R.S. Crown 8vo. 7s. 6d.

A Course of Practical Chemistry, for the use of Medical Students. By the same Author. New Edition, with 70 Woodcuts. Crown 8vo. 7s. 6d.

Lectures on Animal Chemistry, delivered at the Royal College of Physicians in 1865. By the same Author. Crown 8vo. 4s. 6d.

LECTURES on the CHEMICAL CHANGES of CARBON. Delivered at the Royal Institution of Great Britain. By WILLIAM ODLING, M.B. F.R.S. Reprinted from the *Chemical News*, with Notes by W. CROOKES, F.R.S. Crown 8vo. price 4s. 6d.

HANDBOOK of CHEMICAL ANALYSIS, adapted to the UNITARY *System* of Notation. By F. T. CONINGTON, M.A. F.C.S. Post 8vo. 7s. 6d. —CONINGTON'S *Tables of Qualitative Analysis*, price 2s. 6d.

A TREATISE on MEDICAL ELECTRICITY, THEORETICAL and PRACTICAL; and its Use in the Treatment of Paralysis, Neuralgia, and other Diseases. By JULIUS ALTHAUS, M.D. &c. Senior Physician to the Infirmary for Epilepsy and Paralysis. Second Edition, revised and partly re-written. Post 8vo. price 15s.

The DIAGNOSIS, PATHOLOGY, and TREATMENT of DISEASES of Women; including the Diagnosis of Pregnancy. By GRAILY HEWITT, M.D. Second Edition, enlarged; with 116 Woodcut Illustrations. 8vo. 24s.

LECTURES on the DISEASES of INFANCY and CHILDHOOD. By CHARLES WEST, M.D. &c. Fifth Edition, revised and enlarged. 8vo. 16s.

A SYSTEM of SURGERY, Theoretical and Practical. In Treatises by Various Authors. Edited by T. HOLMES, M.A. &c. Surgeon and Lecturer on Surgery at St. George's Hospital, and Surgeon-in-Chief to the Metropolitan Police. Second Edition, thoroughly revised, with numerous Illustrations. 5 vols. 8vo. £5 5s.

The SURGICAL TREATMENT of CHILDREN'S DISEASES. By T. HOLMES, M.A. &c. late Surgeon to the Hospital for Sick Children. Second Edition, with 9 Plates and 112 Woodcuts. 8vo. 21s.

LECTURES on the PRINCIPLES and PRACTICE of PHYSIC. By Sir THOMAS WATSON, Bart. M.D. New Edition in the press.

LECTURES on SURGICAL PATHOLOGY. By JAMES PAGET, F.R.S. Third Edition, revised and re-edited by the Author and Professor W. TURNER, M.B. 8vo. with 131 Woodcuts, 21s.

COOPER'S DICTIONARY of PRACTICAL SURGERY and Encyclopædia of Surgical Science. New Edition, brought down to the present time. By S. A. LANE, Surgeon to St. Mary's Hospital, assisted by various Eminent Surgeons. VOL. II. 8vo. completing the work. [*In the press.*

On CHRONIC BRONCHITIS, especially as connected with GOUT, EMPHYSEMA, and DISEASES of the HEART. By E. HEADLAM GREENHOW, M.D. F.R.C.P. &c. 8vo. 7s. 6d.

The CLIMATE of the SOUTH of FRANCE as SUITED to INVALIDS; with Notices of Mediterranean and other Winter Stations. By C. T. WILLIAMS, M.A. M.D. Oxon. Assistant-Physician to the Hospital for Consumption at Brompton. Second Edition, with Frontispiece and Map. Crown 8vo. 6s.

REPORTS on the PROGRESS of PRACTICAL and SCIENTIFIC MEDICINE in Different Parts of the World, from June 1868, to June 1869. Edited by HORACE DOBELL, M.D. assisted by numerous and distinguished Coadjutors. 8vo. 18s.

PULMONARY CONSUMPTION; its Nature, Treatment, and Duration exemplified by an Analysis of One Thousand Cases selected from upwards of Twenty Thousand. By C. J. B. WILLIAMS, M.D. F.R.S. Consulting Physician to the Hospital for Consumption at Brompton; and C. T. WILLIAMS, M.A. M.D. Oxon. [*Nearly ready.*

CLINICAL LECTURES on DISEASES of the LIVER, JAUNDICE, and ABDOMINAL DROPSY. By CHARLES MURCHISON, M.D. Post 8vo. with 25 Woodcuts, 10s. 6d.

ANATOMY, DESCRIPTIVE and SURGICAL. By HENRY GRAY, F.R.S. With about 400 Woodcuts from Dissections. Fifth Edition, by T. HOLMES, M.A. Cantab. with a new Introduction by the Editor. Royal 8vo. 28s.

CLINICAL NOTES on DISEASES of the LARYNX, investigated and treated with the assistance of the Laryngoscope. By W. MARCET, M.D. F.R.S. Assistant-Physician to the Hospital for Consumption and Diseases of the Chest, Brompton. Crown 8vo. with 5 Lithographs, 6s.

The THEORY of OCULAR DEFECTS and of SPECTACLES. Translated from the German of Dr. H. SCHEFFLER by R. B. CARTER, F.R.C.S. With Prefatory Notes and a Chapter of Practical Instructions. Post 8vo. price 7s. 6d.

OUTLINES of PHYSIOLOGY, Human and Comparative. By JOHN MARSHALL, F.R.C.S. Surgeon to the University College Hospital. 2 vols. crown 8vo. with 122 Woodcuts, 32s.

ESSAYS on PHYSIOLOGICAL SUBJECTS. By GILBERT W. CHILD, M.A. Second Edition, revised, with Woodcuts. Crown 8vo. 7s. 6d.

PHYSIOLOGICAL ANATOMY and PHYSIOLOGY of MAN. By the late R. B. TODD, M.D. F.R.S. and W. BOWMAN, F.R.S. of King's College. With numerous Illustrations. VOL. II. 8vo. 25s.
VOL. I. New Edition by Dr. LIONEL S. BEALE, F.R.S. in course of publication; PART I. with 8 Plates, 7s. 6d.

COPLAND'S DICTIONARY of PRACTICAL MEDICINE, abridged from the larger work and throughout brought down to the present State of Medical Science. 8vo. 36s.

REIMANN'S HANDBOOK of ANILINE and its DERIVATIVES; a Treatise on the Manufacture of Aniline and Aniline Colours. Edited by WILLIAM CROOKES, F.R.S. With 5 Woodcuts. 8vo. 10s. 6d.

A MANUAL of MATERIA MEDICA and THERAPEUTICS, abridged from Dr. PEREIRA'S *Elements* by F. J. FARRE, M.D. assisted by R. BENTLEY, M.R.C.S. and by R. WARINGTON, F.R.S. 8vo. with 90 Woodcuts, 21s.

THOMSON'S CONSPECTUS of the BRITISH PHARMACOPŒIA. 25th Edition, corrected by E. LLOYD BIRKETT, M.D. 18mo. price 6s.

MANUAL of the DOMESTIC PRACTICE of MEDICINE. By W. B. KESTEVEN, F.R.C.S.E. Third Edition, revised, with Additions. Fcp. 5s.

GYMNASTS and GYMNASTICS. By JOHN H. HOWARD, late Professor of Gymnastics, Comm. Coll. Rippouden. Second Edition, revised and enlarged, with 135 Woodcuts. Crown 8vo. 10s. 6d.

The Fine Arts, and Illustrated Editions.

IN FAIRYLAND; Pictures from the Elf-World. By RICHARD DOYLE. With a Poem by W. ALLINGHAM. With Sixteen Plates, containing Thirty-six Designs printed in Colours. Folio, 31s. 6d.

LIFE of JOHN GIBSON, R.A. SCULPTOR. Edited by Lady EASTLAKE. 8vo. 10s. 6d.

The LORD'S PRAYER ILLUSTRATED by F. R. PICKERSGILL, R.A. and HENRY ALFORD, D.D. Dean of Canterbury. Imp. 4to. price 21s. cloth.

MATERIALS for a HISTORY of OIL PAINTING. By Sir CHARLES LOCKE EASTLAKE, sometime President of the Royal Academy. 2 vols. 8vo. price 30s.

HALF-HOUR LECTURES on the HISTORY and PRACTICE of the Fine and Ornamental Arts. By WILLIAM B. SCOTT. New Edition, revised by the Author; with 50 Woodcuts. Crown 8vo. 8s. 6d.

ALBERT DURER, HIS LIFE and WORKS; including Autobiographical Papers and Complete Catalogues. By WILLIAM B. SCOTT. With Six Etchings by the Author, and other Illustrations. 8vo. 16s.

SIX LECTURES on HARMONY, delivered at the Royal Institution of Great Britain in the Year 1867. By G. A. MACFARREN. With numerous engraved Musical Examples and Specimens. 8vo. 10s. 6d.

The CHORALE BOOK for ENGLAND: the Hymns translated by Miss C. WINKWORTH; the tunes arranged by Prof. W. S. BENNETT and OTTO GOLDSCHMIDT. Fcp. 4to. 12s. 6d.

The NEW TESTAMENT, illustrated with Wood Engravings after the Early Masters, chiefly of the Italian School. Crown 4to. 63s. cloth, gilt top; or £5 5s. elegantly bound in morocco.

LYRA GERMANICA; the Christian Year. Translated by CATHERINE WINKWORTH; with 125 Illustrations on Wood drawn by J. LEIGHTON, F.S.A. 4to. 21s.

LYRA GERMANICA; the Christian Life. Translated by CATHERINE WINKWORTH; with about 200 Woodcut Illustrations by J. LEIGHTON, F.S.A. and other Artists. 4to. 21s.

The LIFE of MAN SYMBOLISED by the MONTHS of the YEAR. Text selected by R. PIGOT; Illustrations on Wood from Original Designs by J. LEIGHTON, F.S.A. 4to. 42s.

CATS' and FARLIE'S MORAL EMBLEMS; with Aphorisms, Adages, and Proverbs of all Nations. 121 Illustrations on Wood by J. LEIGHTON, F.S.A. Text selected by R. PIGOT. Imperial 8vo. 31s. 6d.

SHAKSPEARE'S MIDSUMMER-NIGHT'S DREAM, illustrated with 24 Silhouettes or Shadow-Pictures by P. KONEWKA, engraved on Wood by A. VOGEL. Folio, 31s. 6d.

SHAKSPEARE'S SENTIMENTS and SIMILES, printed in Black and Gold, and Illuminated in the Missal Style by HENRY NOEL HUMPHREYS. Square post 8vo. 21s.

SACRED and LEGENDARY ART. By Mrs. JAMESON.

Legends of the Saints and Martyrs. Fifth Edition, with 19 Etchings and 187 Woodcuts. 2 vols. square crown 8vo. 31s. 6d.

Legends of the Monastic Orders. Third Edition, with 11 Etchings and 88 Woodcuts. 1 vol. square crown 8vo. 21s.

Legends of the Madonna. Third Edition, with 27 Etchings and 165 Woodcuts. 1 vol. square crown 8vo. 21s.

The History of Our Lord, with that of his Types and Precursors. Completed by Lady EASTLAKE. Revised Edition, with 31 Etchings and 281 Woodcuts. 2 vols. square crown 8vo. 42s.

The Useful Arts, Manufactures, &c.

HISTORY of the GOTHIC REVIVAL; an Attempt to shew how far the taste for Mediæval Architecture was retained in England during the last two centuries, and has been re-developed in the present. By CHARLES L. EASTLAKE, Architect. With many Illustrations. [*Nearly ready.*

GWILT'S ENCYCLOPÆDIA of ARCHITECTURE, with above 1,100 Engravings on Wood. Fifth Edition, revised and enlarged by WYATT PAPWORTH. Additionally illustrated with nearly 400 Wood Engravings by O. Jewitt, and more than 100 other new Woodcuts. 8vo. 52s. 6d.

ITALIAN SCULPTORS; being a History of Sculpture in Northern, Southern, and Eastern Italy. By C. C. PERKINS. With 30 Etchings and 13 Wood Engravings. Imperial 8vo. 42s.

TUSCAN SCULPTORS, their Lives, Works, and Times. With 45 Etchings and 28 Woodcuts from Original Drawings and Photographs. By the same Author. 2 vols. imperial 8vo. 63s.

HINTS on HOUSEHOLD TASTE in FURNITURE, UPHOLSTERY, and other Details. By CHARLES L. EASTLAKE, Architect. Second Edition, with about 90 Illustrations. Square crown 8vo. 18s.

The ENGINEER'S HANDBOOK; explaining the Principles which should guide the Young Engineer in the Construction of Machinery. By C. S. LOWNDES. Post 8vo. 5s.

PRINCIPLES of MECHANISM, designed for the Use of Students in the Universities, and for Engineering Students generally. By R. WILLIS, M.A. F.R.S. &c. Jacksonian Professor in the University of Cambridge. A new and enlarged Edition. 8vo. [*Nearly ready.*

LATHES and TURNING, Simple, Mechanical, and ORNAMENTAL. By W. HENRY NORTHCOTT. With about 240 Illustrations on Steel and Wood. 8vo. 18s.

URE'S DICTIONARY of ARTS, MANUFACTURES, and MINES. Sixth Edition, chiefly rewritten and greatly enlarged by ROBERT HUNT, F.R.S. assisted by numerous Contributors eminent in Science and the Arts, and familiar with Manufactures. With above 2,000 Woodcuts. 3 vols. medium 8vo. price £4 14s. 6d.

HANDBOOK of PRACTICAL TELEGRAPHY, published with the sanction of the Chairman and Directors of the Electric and International Telegraph Company, and adopted by the Department of Telegraphs for India. By R. S. CULLEY. Third Edition. 8vo. 12s. 6d.

ENCYCLOPÆDIA of CIVIL ENGINEERING, Historical, Theoretical, and Practical. By E. CRESY, C.E. With above 3,000 Woodcuts. 8vo. 42s.

TREATISE on MILLS and MILLWORK. By Sir W. FAIRBAIRN, F.R.S. Second Edition, with 18 Plates and 322 Woodcuts. 2 vols. 8vo. 32s.

USEFUL INFORMATION for ENGINEERS. By the same Author. FIRST, SECOND, and THIRD SERIES, with many Plates and Woodcuts. 3 vols. crown 8vo. 10s. 6d. each.

The APPLICATION of CAST and WROUGHT IRON to Building Purposes. By the same Author. Fourth Edition, enlarged; with 6 Plates and 118 Woodcuts. 8vo. price 16s.

IRON SHIP BUILDING, its History and Progress, as comprised in a Series of Experimental Researches. By the same Author. With 4 Plates and 130 Woodcuts. 8vo. 18s.

A TREATISE on the STEAM ENGINE, in its various Applications to Mines, Mills, Steam Navigation, Railways and Agriculture. By J. BOURNE, C.E. Eighth Edition; with Portrait, 37 Plates, and 546 Woodcuts. 4to. 42s.

CATECHISM of the STEAM ENGINE, in its various Applications to Mines, Mills, Steam Navigation, Railways, and Agriculture. By the same Author. With 89 Woodcuts. Fcp. 6s.

HANDBOOK of the STEAM ENGINE. By the same Author, forming a KEY to the Catechism of the Steam Engine, with 67 Woodcuts. Fcp. 9s.

BOURNE'S RECENT IMPROVEMENTS in the STEAM ENGINE in its various applications to Mines, Mills, Steam Navigation, Railways, and Agriculture. Being a Supplement to the Author's 'Catechism of the Steam Engine.' By JOHN BOURNE, C.E. New Edition, including many New Examples; with 124 Woodcuts. Fcp. 8vo. 6s.

A TREATISE on the SCREW PROPELLER, SCREW VESSELS, and Screw Engines, as adapted for purposes of Peace and War; with Notices of other Methods of Propulsion, Tables of the Dimensions and Performance of Screw Steamers, and detailed Specifications of Ships and Engines. By J. BOURNE, C.E. New Edition, with 54 Plates and 287 Woodcuts. 4to. 63s.

EXAMPLES of MODERN STEAM, AIR, and GAS ENGINES of the most Approved Types, as employed for Pumping, for Driving Machinery, for Locomotion, and for Agriculture, minutely and practically described. By JOHN BOURNE, C.E. In course of publication in 24 Parts, price 2s. 6d. each, forming One volume 4to. with about 50 Plates and 400 Woodcuts.

A HISTORY of the MACHINE-WROUGHT HOSIERY and LACE Manufactures. By WILLIAM FELKIN, F.L.S. F.S.S. Royal 8vo. 21s.

PRACTICAL TREATISE on METALLURGY, adapted from the last German Edition of Professor KERL'S *Metallurgy* by W. CROOKES, F.R.S. &c. and E. RÖHRIG, Ph.D. M.E. In Three Volumes, 8vo. with 625 Woodcuts. VOL. I. price 31s. 6d. VOL. II. price 36s. VOL. III. price 31s. 6d.

MITCHELL'S MANUAL of PRACTICAL ASSAYING. Third Edition, for the most part re-written, with all the recent Discoveries incorporated, by W. CROOKES, F.R.S. With 188 Woodcuts. 8vo. 28s.

The ART of PERFUMERY; the History and Theory of Odours, and the Methods of Extracting the Aromas of Plants. By Dr. PIESSE, F.C.S. Third Edition, with 53 Woodcuts. Crown 8vo. 10s. 6d.

Chemical, Natural, and Physical Magic, for Juveniles during the Holidays. By the same Author. Third Edition, with 38 Woodcuts. Fcp. 6s.

LOUDON'S ENCYCLOPÆDIA of AGRICULTURE: comprising the Laying-out, Improvement, and Management of Landed Property, and the Cultivation and Economy of the Productions of Agriculture. With 1,100 Woodcuts. 8vo. 21s.

Loudon's Encyclopædia of Gardening: comprising the Theory and Practice of Horticulture, Floriculture, Arboriculture, and Landscape Gardening. With 1,000 Woodcuts. 8vo. 21s.

BAYLDON'S ART of VALUING RENTS and TILLAGES, and Claims of Tenants upon Quitting Farms, both at Michaelmas and Lady-Day. Eighth Edition, revised by J. C. MORTON. 8vo. 10s. 6d.

Religious and *Moral Works.*

CONSIDERATIONS on the REVISION of the ENGLISH NEW TESTAMENT. By C. J. ELLICOTT, D.D. Lord Bishop of Gloucester and Bristol. Post 8vo. price 5s. 6d.

An EXPOSITION of the 39 ARTICLES, Historical and Doctrinal. By E. HAROLD BROWNE, D.D. Lord Bishop of Ely. Seventh Edit. 8vo. 16s.

BISHOP COTTON'S INSTRUCTIONS in the PRINCIPLES and Practice of Christianity, intended chiefly as an introduction to Confirmation. Sixth Edition, 18mo. 2s. 6d.

The ACTS of the APOSTLES; with a Commentary, and Practical and Devotional Suggestions for Readers and Students of the English Bible. By the Rev. F. C. COOK, M.A. Canon of Exeter, &c. New Edition. 8vo. 12s. 6d.

The LIFE and EPISTLES of ST. PAUL. By the Rev. W. J. CONYBEARE, M.A., and the Very Rev. J. S. HOWSON, D.D. Dean of Chester :—
  LIBRARY EDITION, with all the Original Illustrations, Maps, Landscapes on Steel, Woodcuts, &c. 2 vols. 4to. 48s.
  INTERMEDIATE EDITION, with a Selection of Maps, Plates, and Woodcuts. 2 vols. square crown 8vo. 31s. 6d.
  STUDENT'S EDITION, revised and condensed, with 46 Illustrations and Maps. 1 vol. crown 8vo. price 9s.

The VOYAGE and SHIPWRECK of ST. PAUL; with Dissertations on the Life and Writings of St. Luke and the Ships and Navigation of the Ancients. By JAMES SMITH, F.R.S. Third Edition. Crown 8vo. 10s. 6d.

A CRITICAL and GRAMMATICAL COMMENTARY on ST. PAUL'S Epistles. By C. J. ELLICOTT, D.D. Lord Bishop of Gloucester & Bristol. 8vo.

Galatians, Fourth Edition, 8s. 6d.

Ephesians, Fourth Edition, 8s. 6d.

Pastoral Epistles, Fourth Edition, 10s. 6d.

Philippians, Colossians, and Philemon, Third Edition, 10s. 6d.

Thessalonians, Third Edition, 7s. 6d.

HISTORICAL LECTURES on the LIFE of OUR LORD JESUS CHRIST: being the Hulsean Lectures for 1859. By C. J. ELLICOTT, D.D. Lord Bishop of Gloucester and Bristol. Fifth Edition. 8vo. price 12s.

EVIDENCE of the TRUTH of the CHRISTIAN RELIGION derived from the Literal Fulfilment of Prophecy. By ALEXANDER KEITH, D.D. 37th Edition, with numerous Plates, in square 8vo. 12s. 6d.; also the 39th Edition, in post 8vo. with 5 Plates, 6s.

History and Destiny of the World and Church, according to Scripture. By the same Author. Square 8vo. with 40 Illustrations, 10s.

An INTRODUCTION to the STUDY of the NEW TESTAMENT, Critical, Exegetical, and Theological. By the Rev. S. DAVIDSON, D.D. LL.D. 2 vols. 8vo. 30s.

Rev. T. H. HORNE'S INTRODUCTION to the CRITICAL STUDY and Knowledge of the Holy Scriptures. Twelfth Edition, as last revised throughout. With 4 Maps and 22 Woodcuts and Facsimiles. 4 vols. 8vo. 42s.

Rev. T. H. Horne's Compendious Introduction to the Study of the Bible, being an Analysis of the larger work by the same Author. Re-edited by the Rev. JOHN AYRE, M.A. With Maps, &c. Post 8vo. 6s.

HISTORY of the KARAITE JEWS. By WILLIAM HARRIS RULE, D.D. Post 8vo. price 7s. 6d.

EWALD'S HISTORY of ISRAEL to the DEATH of MOSES. Translated from the German. Edited, with a Preface and an Appendix, by RUSSELL MARTINEAU, M.A. Second Edition. 2 vols. 8vo. 24s.

FIVE YEARS in a PROTESTANT SISTERHOOD and TEN YEARS in a Catholic Convent; an Autobiography. Post 8vo. 7s. 6d.

The LIFE of MARGARET MARY HALLAHAN, better known in the religious world by the name of Mother Margaret. By her RELIGIOUS CHILDREN. Second Edition. 8vo. with Portrait, 10s.

The SEE of ROME in the MIDDLE AGES. By the Rev. OSWALD J. REICHEL, B.C.L. and M.A. 8vo. price 18s.

The EVIDENCE for the PAPACY, as derived from the Holy Scriptures and from Primitive Antiquity; with an Introductory Epistle. By the Hon. COLIN LINDSAY. 8vo. price 12s. 6d.

The TREASURY of BIBLE KNOWLEDGE; being a Dictionary of the Books, Persons, Places, Events, and other matters of which mention is made in Holy Scripture. By Rev. J. AYRE, M.A. With Maps, 16 Plates, and numerous Woodcuts. Fcp. 8vo price 6s. cloth, or 9s. 6d. neatly bound in calf.

The GREEK TESTAMENT; with Notes, Grammatical and Exegetical. By the Rev. W. WEBSTER, M.A. and the Rev. W. F. WILKINSON, M.A. 2 vols. 8vo. £2 4s.

EVERY-DAY SCRIPTURE DIFFICULTIES explained and illustrated. By J. E. PRESCOTT, M.A. VOL. I. *Matthew* and *Mark*; VOL. II. *Luke* and *John*. 2 vols. 8vo. 9s. each.

The PENTATEUCH and BOOK of JOSHUA CRITICALLY EXAMINED. By the Right Rev. J. W. COLENSO, D.D. Lord Bishop of Natal. People's Edition, in 1 vol. crown 8vo. 6s. or in 5 Parts, 1s. each.

The CHURCH and the WORLD; Three Series of Essays on Questions of the Day. By Various Writers. Edited by the Rev. ORBY SHIPLEY, M.A. Three Volumes, 8vo. price 15s. each.

The FORMATION of CHRISTENDOM. By T. W. ALLIES. PARTS I. and II. 8vo. price 12s. each Part.

ENGLAND and CHRISTENDOM. By ARCHBISHOP MANNING, D.D.
Post 8vo. price 10s. 6d.

CHRISTENDOM'S DIVISIONS, PART I., a Philosophical Sketch of the Divisions of the Christian Family in East and West. By EDMUND S. FFOULKES. Post 8vo. price 7s. 6d.

Christendom's Divisions, PART II. Greeks and Latins, being a History of their Dissensions and Overtures for Peace down to the Reformation. By the same Author. Post 8vo. 15s.

The HIDDEN WISDOM of CHRIST and the KEY of KNOWLEDGE; or, History of the Apocrypha. By ERNEST DE BUNSEN. 2 vols. 8vo. 28s.

The KEYS of ST. PETER; or, the House of Rechab, connected with the History of Symbolism and Idolatry. By the same Author. 8vo. 14s.

The TYPES of GENESIS, briefly considered as Revealing the Development of Human Nature. By ANDREW JUKES. Second Edition. Crown 8vo. 7s. 6d.

The Second Death and the Restitution of All Things, with some Preliminary Remarks on the Nature and Inspiration of Holy Scripture. By the same Author. Second Edition. Crown 8vo. 3s. 6d.

A VIEW of the SCRIPTURE REVELATIONS CONCERNING a FUTURE STATE. By RICHARD WHATELY, D.D. late Archbishop of Dublin. Ninth Edition. Fcp. 8vo. 5s.

The POWER of the SOUL over the BODY. By GEORGE MOORE, M.D. M.R.C.P.L. &c. Sixth Edition. Crown 8vo. 8s. 6d.

THOUGHTS for the AGE. By ELIZABETH M. SEWELL, Author of 'Amy Herbert' &c. Fcp. 8vo. price 5s.

Passing Thoughts on Religion. By the same Author. Fcp. 8vo. 5s.

Self-Examination before Confirmation. By the same Author. 32mo. price 1s. 6d.

Readings for a Month Preparatory to Confirmation, from Writers of the Early and English Church. By the same Author. Fcp. 4s.

Readings for Every Day in Lent, compiled from the Writings of Bishop JEREMY TAYLOR. By the same Author. Fcp. 5s.

Preparation for the Holy Communion; the Devotions chiefly from the works of JEREMY TAYLOR. By the same Author. 32mo. 3s.

THOUGHTS for the HOLY WEEK for Young Persons. By the Author of 'Amy Herbert.' New Edition. Fcp. 8vo. 2s.

PRINCIPLES of EDUCATION Drawn from Nature and Revelation, and applied to Female Education in the Upper Classes. By the Author of 'Amy Herbert.' 2 vols. fcp. 12s. 6d.

The WIFE'S MANUAL; or, Prayers, Thoughts, and Songs on Several Occasions of a Matron's Life. By the Rev. W. CALVERT, M.A. Crown 8vo. price 10s. 6d.

SINGERS and SONGS of the CHURCH: being Biographical Sketches of the Hymn-Writers in all the principal Collections; with Notes on their Psalms and Hymns. By JOSIAH MILLER, M.A. Second Edition, enlarged. Post 8vo. price 10s. 6d.

LYRA GERMANICA, translated from the German by Miss C. WINKWORTH. FIRST SERIES, Hymns for the Sundays and Chief Festivals SECOND SERIES, the Christian Life. Fcp. 3s. 6d. each SERIES.

'SPIRITUAL SONGS' for the SUNDAYS and HOLIDAYS throughout the Year. By J. S. B. MONSELL, LL.D. Vicar of Egham and Rural Dean. Fourth Edition, Sixth Thousand. Fcp. 4s. 6d.

The BEATITUDES: Abasement before God; Sorrow for Sin; Meekness of Spirit; Desire for Holiness; Gentleness; Purity of Heart; the Peacemakers; Sufferings for Christ. By the same. Third Edition. Fcp. 3s. 6d.

His PRESENCE—not his MEMORY, 1855. By the same Author, in Memory of his SON. Sixth Edition. 16mo. 1s.

LYRA EUCHARISTICA; Hymns and Verses on the Holy Communion, Ancient and Modern: with other Poems. Edited by the Rev. ORBY SHIPLEY, M.A. Second Edition. Fcp. 5s.

Lyra Messianica; Hymns and Verses on the Life of Christ, Ancient and Modern; with other Poems. By the same Editor. Second Edition, altered and enlarged. Fcp. 5s.

Lyra Mystica; Hymns and Verses on Sacred Subjects, Ancient and Modern. By the same Editor. Fcp. 5s.

ENDEAVOURS after the CHRISTIAN LIFE: Discourses. By JAMES MARTINEAU. Fourth and cheaper Edition, carefully revised; the Two Series complete in One Volume. Post 8vo. 7s. 6d.

INVOCATION of SAINTS and ANGELS, for the use of Members of the English Church. Edited by the Rev. ORBY SHIPLEY. 24mo. 3s. 6d.

WHATELY'S INTRODUCTORY LESSONS on the CHRISTIAN Evidences. 18mo. 6d.

WHATELY'S INTRODUCTORY LESSONS on the HISTORY of Religious Worship. New Edition. 18mo. 2s. 6d.

BISHOP JEREMY TAYLOR'S ENTIRE WORKS. With Life by BISHOP HEBER. Revised and corrected by the Rev. C. P. EDEN, 10 vols. price £5 5s.

Travels, Voyages, &c.

NARRATIVE of a SPRING TOUR in PORTUGAL. By A. C. SMITH, M.A. Ch. Ch. Oxon. Rector of Yatesbury. Post 8vo. price 6s. 6d.

ENGLAND to DELHI; a Narrative of Indian Travel. By JOHN MATHESON, Glasgow. With Map and 82 Woodcut Illustrations. 4to. 31s. 6d.

CADORE; or, TITIAN'S COUNTRY. By JOSIAH GILBERT, one of the Authors of 'The Dolomite Mountains.' With Map, Facsimile, and 40 Illustrations. Imperial 8vo. 31s. 6d.

NARRATIVE of the EUPHRATES EXPEDITION carried on by Order of the British Government during the years 1835-1837. By General F. R. CHESNEY, F.R.S. With Maps, Plates, and Woodcuts. 8vo. 24s.

TRAVELS in the CENTRAL CAUCASUS and BASHAN. Including Visits to Ararat and Tabreez and Ascents of Kazbek and Elbruz. By D. W. FRESHFIELD. Square crown 8vo. with Maps, &c. 18s.

PICTURES in TYROL and Elsewhere. From a Family Sketch-Book. By the Authoress of 'A Voyage en Zigzag,' &c. Second Edition. Small 4to. with numerous Illustrations, 21s.

HOW WE SPENT the SUMMER; or, a Voyage en Zigzag in Switzerland and Tyrol with some Members of the ALPINE CLUB. From the Sketch-Book of one of the Party. In oblong 4to. with 300 Illustrations, 15s.

BEATEN TRACKS; or, Pen and Pencil Sketches in Italy. By the Authoress of 'A Voyage en Zigzag.' With 42 Plates, containing about 200 Sketches from Drawings made on the Spot. 8vo. 16s.

MAP of the CHAIN of MONT BLANC, from an actual Survey in 1863—1864. By A. ADAMS-REILLY, F.R.G.S. M.A.C. Published under the Authority of the Alpine Club. In Chromolithography on extra stout drawing-paper 28in. × 17in. price 10s. or mounted on canvas in a folding case, 12s. 6d.

WESTWARD by RAIL; the New Route to the East. By W. F. RAE. With Map shewing the Lines of Rail between the Atlantic and the Pacific, and Sections of the Railway. Post 8vo. price 10s. 6d.

The PARAGUAYAN WAR: with Sketches of the History of Paraguay, and of the Manners and Customs of the People; and Notes on the Military Engineering of the War. By GEORGE THOMPSON, C.E. With 8 Maps and Plans, and a Portrait of Lopez. Post 8vo. 12s. 6d.

HISTORY of DISCOVERY in our AUSTRALASIAN COLONIES, Australia, Tasmania, and New Zealand, from the Earliest Date to the Present Day. By WILLIAM HOWITT. 2 vols. 8vo. with 3 Maps, 20s.

NOTES on BURGUNDY. By CHARLES RICHARD WELD. Edited by his Widow; with Portrait and Memoir. Post 8vo. 8s. 6d.

The CAPITAL of the TYCOON; a Narrative of a Three Years' Residence in Japan. By Sir RUTHERFORD ALCOCK, K.C.B. 2 vols. 8vo. with numerous Illustrations, 42s.

The DOLOMITE MOUNTAINS; Excursions through Tyrol, Carinthia, Carniola, and Friuli, 1861-1863. By J. GILBERT and G. C. CHURCHILL, F.R.G.S. With numerous Illustrations. Square crown 8vo. 21s.

GUIDE to the PYRENEES, for the use of Mountaineers. By CHARLES PACKE. 2nd Edition, with Map and Illustrations. Cr. 8vo. 7s. 6d.

The ALPINE GUIDE. By JOHN BALL, M.R.I.A. late President of the Alpine Club. Thoroughly Revised Editions, in Three Volumes, post 8vo. with Maps and other Illustrations:—

GUIDE to the WESTERN ALPS, including Mont Blanc, Monte Rosa, Zermatt, &c. Price 6s. 6d.

GUIDE to the CENTRAL ALPS, including all the Oberland District. 7s. 6d.

GUIDE to the EASTERN ALPS, price 10s. 6d.

Introduction on Alpine Travelling in General, and on the Geology of the Alps, price 1s. Each of the Three Volumes or Parts of the *Alpine Guide* may be had with this INTRODUCTION prefixed, price 1s. extra.

The HIGH ALPS WITHOUT GUIDES. By the Rev. A. G. GIRDLESTONE, M.A. late Demy in Natural Science, Magdalen College, Oxford. With Frontispiece and 2 Maps. Square crown 8vo. price 7s. 6d.

MEMORIALS of LONDON and LONDON LIFE in the 13th, 14th, and 15th Centuries; being a Series of Extracts, Local, Social, and Political, from the Archives of the City of London, A.D. 1276-1419. Selected, translated, and edited by H. T. RILEY, M.A. Royal 8vo. 21s.

COMMENTARIES on the HISTORY, CONSTITUTION, and CHARTERED FRANCHISES of the CITY of LONDON. By GEORGE NORTON, formerly one of the Common Pleaders of the City of London. Third Edition. 8vo. 14s.

The **NORTHERN HEIGHTS of LONDON**; or, Historical Associations of Hampstead, Highgate, Muswell Hill, Hornsey, and Islington. By WILLIAM HOWITT. With about 40 Woodcuts. Square crown 8vo. 21s.

VISITS to REMARKABLE PLACES: Old Halls, Battle-Fields, and Stones Illustrative of Striking Passages in English History and Poetry. By WILLIAM HOWITT. 2 vols. square crown 8vo. with Woodcuts, 25s.

The **RURAL LIFE of ENGLAND**. By the same Author. With Woodcuts by Bewick and Williams. Medium 8vo. 12s. 6d.

ROMA SOTTERRANEA; or, an Account of the Roman Catacombs, especially of the Cemetery of San Callisto. Compiled from the Works of Commendatore G. B. DE ROSSI by the Rev. J. S. NORTHCOTE, D.D. and the Rev. W. B. BROWNLOW. With numerous Illustrations. 8vo. 31s. 6d.

PILGRIMAGES in the PYRENEES and LANDES. By DENYS SHYNE LAWLOR. Crown 8vo. with Frontispiece and Vignette, price 15s.

The **GERMAN WORKING MAN**; being an Account of the Daily Life, Amusements, and Unions for Culture and Material Progress of the Artisans of North and South Germany and Switzerland. By JAMES SAMUELSON. Crown 8vo. with Frontispiece, 3s. 6d.

Works of Fiction.

LOTHAIR. By the Right Hon. B. DISRAELI, M.P. Seventh Edition. 3 vols. post 8vo. price 31s. 6d.

Nôsse omnia hæc, salus est adolescentulis.—TERENTIUS.

NO APPEAL; a Novel. By the Author of 'Cut down like Grass.' 3 vols. post 8vo. price 31s. 6d.

The **MODERN NOVELIST'S LIBRARY.** Each Work, in crown 8vo. complete in a Single Volume:—
MELVILLE'S GLADIATORS, 2s. boards; 2s. 6d. cloth.
——— HOLMBY HOUSE, 2s. boards; 2s. 6d. cloth.
——— INTERPRETER, 2s. boards; 2s. 6d. cloth.
TROLLOPE'S WARDEN, 1s. 6d. boards; 2s. cloth.
——— BARCHESTER TOWERS, 2s. boards; 2s. 6d. cloth.
BRAMLEY-MOORE'S SIX SISTERS OF THE VALLEYS, 2s. boards; 2s. 6d. cloth.

THREE WEDDINGS. By the Author of 'Dorothy,' 'De Cressy,' &c. Fcp. 8vo. price 5s.

STORIES and TALES by ELIZABETH M. SEWELL, Author of 'Amy Herbert,' uniform Edition, each *Story* or *Tale* complete in a single Volume:

AMY HERBERT, 2s. 6d.	IVORS, 3s. 6d.
GERTRUDE, 2s. 6d.	KATHARINE ASHTON, 3s. 6d.
EARL'S DAUGHTER, 2s. 6d.	MARGARET PERCIVAL, 5s.
EXPERIENCE OF LIFE, 2s. 6d.	LANETON PARSONAGE, 4s. 6d.
CLEVE HALL, 3s. 6d.	URSULA, 4s. 6d.

A Glimpse of the World. By the Author of 'Amy Herbert.' Fcp. 7s. 6d.

The Journal of a Home Life. By the same Author. Post 8vo. 9s. 6d.

After Life; a Sequel to 'The Journal of a Home Life.' Price 10s. 6d.

UNCLE PETER'S FAIRY TALE for the XIX CENTURY. Edited by E. M. SEWELL, Author of 'Amy Herbert,' &c. Fcp. 8vo. 7s. 6d.

VIKRAM and the VAMPIRE; or, Tales of Hindu Devilry. Adapted by RICHARD F. BURTON, F.R.G.S. &c. With 33 Illustrations by Ernest Griset. Crown 8vo. 9s.

THROUGH the NIGHT; a Tale of the Times. To which is added 'Onward, or a Summer Sketch.' By WALTER SWEETMAN, B.A. 2 vols. post 8vo. 21s.

BECKER'S GALLUS; or, Roman Scenes of the Time of Augustus: with Notes and Excursuses. New Edition. Post 8vo. 7s. 6d.

BECKER'S CHARICLES; a Tale illustrative of Private Life among the Ancient Greeks: with Notes and Excursuses. New Edition. Post 8vo. 7s. 6d.

NOVELS and TALES by G. J. WHYTE MELVILLE :—
- The GLADIATORS, 5s.
- DIGBY GRAND, 5s.
- KATE COVENTRY, 5s.
- GENERAL BOUNCE, 5s.
- HOLMBY HOUSE, 5s.
- GOOD for NOTHING, 6s.
- The QUEEN'S MARIES, 6s.
- The INTERPRETER, 5s.

TALES of ANCIENT GREECE. By GEORGE W. COX, M.A. late Scholar of Trin. Coll. Oxon. Being a Collective Edition of the Author's Classical Stories and Tales, complete in One Volume. Crown 8vo. 6s. 6d.

A MANUAL of MYTHOLOGY, in the form of Question and Answer. By the same Author. Fcp. 3s.

OUR CHILDREN'S STORY, by one of their Gossips. By the Author of 'Voyage en Zigzag,' 'Pictures in Tyrol,' &c. Small 4to. with Sixty Illustrations by the Author, price 10s. 6d.

Poetry and The Drama.

THOMAS MOORE'S POETICAL WORKS, the only Editions containing the Author's last Copyright Additions :—
- CABINET EDITION, 10 vols. fcp. 8vo. price 35s.
- SHAMROCK EDITION, crown 8vo. price 3s. 6d.
- RUBY EDITION, crown 8vo. with Portrait, price 6s.
- LIBRARY EDITION, medium 8vo. Portrait and Vignette, 14s.
- PEOPLE'S EDITION, square crown 8vo. with Portrait, &c. 10s. 6d.

MOORE'S IRISH MELODIES, Maclise's Edition, with 161 Steel Plates from Original Drawings. Super-royal 8vo. 31s. 6d.

Miniature Edition of Moore's Irish Melodies with Maclise's Designs (as above) reduced in Lithography. Imp. 16mo. 10s. 6d.

MOORE'S LALLA ROOKH. Tenniel's Edition, with 68 Wood Engravings from original Drawings and other Illustrations. Fcp. 4to. 21s.

SOUTHEY'S POETICAL WORKS, with the Author's last Corrections and copyright Additions. Library Edition, in 1 vol. medium 8vo. with Portrait and Vignette, 14s.

LAYS of ANCIENT ROME; with *Ivry* and the *Armada*. By the Right Hon. LORD MACAULAY. 16mo. 4s. 6d.

Lord Macaulay's Lays of Ancient Rome. With 90 Illustrations on Wood, from the Antique, from Drawings by G. SCHARF. Fcp. 4to. 21s.

Miniature Edition of Lord Macaulay's Lays of Ancient Rome, with the Illustrations (as above) reduced in Lithography. Imp. 16mo. 10s. 6d.

GOLDSMITH'S POETICAL WORKS, with Wood Engravings from Designs by Members of the ETCHING CLUB. Imperial 16mo. 7s. 6d.

POEMS. By JEAN INGELOW. Fifteenth Edition. Fcp. 8vo. 5s.

POEMS by Jean Ingelow. With nearly 100 Illustrations by Eminent Artists, engraved on Wood by the Brothers DALZIEL. Fcp. 4to. 21s.

MOPSA the FAIRY. By JEAN INGELOW. Pp. 256, with Eight Illustrations engraved on Wood. Fcp. 8vo. 6s.

A STORY of DOOM, and other Poems. By JEAN INGELOW. Third Edition. Fcp. 5s.

POETICAL WORKS of LETITIA ELIZABETH LANDON (L.E.L.). 2 vols. 16mo. 10s.

GLAPHYRA, and OTHER POEMS By FRANCIS REYNOLDS, Author of 'Alice Rushton, and other Poems.' 16mo. price 5s.

BOWDLER'S FAMILY SHAKSPEARE, cheaper Genuine Editions: Medium 8vo. large type, with 36 Woodcuts, price 14s. Cabinet Edition, with the same ILLUSTRATIONS, 6 vols. fcp. 3s. 6d. each.

HORATII OPERA, Pocket Edition, with carefully corrected Text, Marginal References, and Introduction. Edited by the Rev. J. E. YONGE, M.A. Square 18mo. 4s. 6d.

HORATII OPERA. Library Edition, with Marginal References and English Notes. Edited by the Rev. J. E. YONGE. 8vo. 21s.

The ÆNEID of VIRGIL Translated into English Verse. By JOHN CONINGTON, M.A. New Edition. Crown 8vo. 9s.

ARUNDINES CAMI, sive Musarum Cantabrigiensium Lusus canori. Collegit atque edidit H. DRURY, M.A. Editio Sexta, curavit H. J. HODGSON, M.A. Crown 8vo. 7s. 6d.

HUNTING SONGS and MISCELLANEOUS VERSES. By R. E. EGERTON WARBURTON. Second Edition. Fcp. 8vo. 5s.

The SILVER STORE collected from Mediæval Christian and Jewish Mines. By the Rev. SABINE BARING-GOULD, M.A. Crown 8vo. 3s. 6d.

Rural Sports, &c.

ENCYCLOPÆDIA of RURAL SPORTS; a complete Account, Historical, Practical, and Descriptive, of Hunting, Shooting, Fishing, Racing, and all other Rural and Athletic Sports and Pastimes. By D. P. BLAINE. With above 600 Woodcuts (20 from Designs by JOHN LEECH). 8vo. 21s.

Col. HAWKER'S INSTRUCTIONS to YOUNG SPORTSMEN in all that relates to Guns and Shooting. Revised by the Author's SON. Square crown 8vo. with Illustrations, 18s.

The DEAD SHOT, or Sportsman's Complete Guide; a Treatise on the Use of the Gun, Dog-breaking, Pigeon-shooting, &c. By MARKSMAN. Revised Edition. Fcp. 8vo. with Plates, 5s.

The FLY-FISHER'S ENTOMOLOGY. By ALFRED RONALDS. With coloured Representations of the Natural and Artificial Insect. Sixth Edition; with 20 coloured Plates. 8vo. 14s.

A BOOK on ANGLING; a complete Treatise on the Art of Angling in every branch. By FRANCIS FRANCIS. Second Edition, with Portrait and 15 other Plates, plain and coloured. Post 8vo. 15s.

The BOOK of the ROACH. By GREVILLE FENNELL, of 'The Field.' Fcp. 8vo. price 2s. 6d.

WILCOCKS'S SEA-FISHERMAN; comprising the Chief Methods of Hook and Line Fishing in the British and other Seas, a Glance at Nets, and Remarks on Boats and Boating. Second Edition, enlarged; with 80 Woodcuts. Post 8vo. 12s. 6d.

HORSES and STABLES. By Colonel F. FITZWYGRAM, XV. the King's Hussars. With Twenty-four Plates of Illustrations, containing very numerous Figures engraved on Wood. 8vo. 15s.

The HORSE'S FOOT, and HOW to KEEP IT SOUND. By W. MILES, Esq. Ninth Edition, with Illustrations. Imperial 8vo. 12s. 6d.

A PLAIN TREATISE on HORSE-SHOEING. By the same Author. Sixth Edition. Post 8vo. with Illustrations, 2s. 6d.

STABLES and STABLE-FITTINGS. By the same. Imp. 8vo. with 13 Plates, 15s.

REMARKS on HORSES' TEETH, addressed to Purchasers. By the same. Post 8vo. 1s. 6d.

ROBBINS'S CAVALRY CATECHISM, or Instructions on Cavalry Exercise and Field Movements, Brigade Movements, Out-post Duty, Cavalry supporting Artillery, Artillery attached to Cavalry. 12mo. 5s.

BLAINE'S VETERINARY ART; a Treatise on the Anatomy, Physiology, and Curative Treatment of the Diseases of the Horse, Neat Cattle and Sheep. Seventh Edition, revised and enlarged by C. STEEL, M.R.C.V.S.L. 8vo. with Plates and Woodcuts. 18s.

The HORSE: with a Treatise on Draught. By WILLIAM YOUATT. New Edition, revised and enlarged. 8vo. with numerous Woodcuts, 12s. 6d.

The Dog. By the same Author. 8vo. with numerous Woodcuts, 6s.

The DOG in HEALTH and DISEASE. By STONEHENGE. With 70 Wood Engravings. Square crown 8vo. 10s. 6d.

The GREYHOUND. By STONEHENGE. Revised Edition, with 24 Portraits of Greyhounds. Square crown 8vo. 10s. 6d.

The OX; his Diseases and their Treatment: with an Essay on Parturition in the Cow. By J. R. DOBSON. Crown 8vo. with Illustrations. 7s. 6d.

Commerce, Navigation, and Mercantile Affairs.

The ELEMENTS of BANKING. By HENRY DUNNING MACLEOD, M.A. Barrister-at-Law. Post 8vo. [*Nearly ready.*

The THEORY and PRACTICE of BANKING. By the same Author. Second Edition, entirely remodelled. 2 vols. 8vo. 30s.

PRACTICAL GUIDE for BRITISH SHIPMASTERS to UNITED States Ports. By PIERREPONT EDWARDS. Post 8vo. 8s. 6d.

A DICTIONARY, Practical, Theoretical, and Historical, of Commerce and Commercial Navigation. By J. R. M'CULLOCH, Esq. New and thoroughly revised Edition. 8vo. price 63s. cloth, or 70s. half-bd. in russia.

The LAW of NATIONS Considered as Independent Political Communities. By Sir TRAVERS TWISS, D.C.L. 2 vols. 8vo. 30s., or separately, PART I. *Peace*, 12s. PART II. *War*, 18s.

Works of *Utility* and *General Information*.

The CABINET LAWYER; a Popular Digest of the Laws of England, Civil, Criminal, and Constitutional. Twenty-fifth Edition, brought down to the close of the Parliamentary Session of 1869. Fcp. 10s. 6d.

PEWTNER'S COMPREHENSIVE SPECIFIER; A Guide to the Practical Specification of every kind of Building-Artificers' Work; with Forms of Building Conditions and Agreements, an Appendix, Foot-Notes, and a copious Index. Edited by WILLIAM YOUNG, Architect. Crown 8vo. price 6s.

The LAW RELATING to BENEFIT BUILDING SOCIETIES; with Practical Observations on the Act and all the Cases decided thereon; also a Form of Rules and Forms of Mortgages. By W. TIDD PRATT, Barrister. Second Edition. Fcp. 3s. 6d.

COLLIERIES and COLLIERS: a Handbook of the Law and Leading Cases relating thereto. By J. C. FOWLER, of the Inner Temple, Barrister, Stipendiary Magistrate for the District of Merthyr Tydfil and Aberdare. Second Edition. Fcp. 8vo. 7s. 6d.

The MATERNAL MANAGEMENT of CHILDREN in HEALTH and Disease. By THOMAS BULL, M.D. Fcp. 5s.

HINTS to MOTHERS on the MANAGEMENT of their HEALTH during the Period of Pregnancy and in the Lying-in Room. By the late THOMAS BULL, M.D. Fcp. 5s.

NOTES on HOSPITALS. By FLORENCE NIGHTINGALE. Third Edition, enlarged; with 13 Plans. Post 4to. 18s.

The PHILOSOPHY of HEALTH; or, an Exposition of the Physiological and Sanitary Conditions conducive to Human Longevity and Happiness. By SOUTHWOOD SMITH, M.D. Eleventh Edition, revised and enlarged; with 113 Woodcuts. 8vo. 7s. 6d.

WHIST, WHAT TO LEAD. By CAM. Fourth Edition. 32mo. 1s.

CHESS OPENINGS. By F. W. LONGMAN, Balliol College, Oxford. Fcp. 8vo. 2s. 6d.

A PRACTICAL TREATISE on BREWING; with Formulæ for Public Brewers, and Instructions for Private Families. By W. BLACK. 8vo. 10s. 6d.

MODERN COOKERY for PRIVATE FAMILIES, reduced to a System of Easy Practice in a Series of carefully-tested Receipts. By ELIZA ACTON. Newly revised and enlarged Edition; with 8 Plates of Figures and 150 Woodcuts. Fcp. 6s.

ON FOOD: its Varieties, Chemical Composition, Nutritive Value, Comparative Digestibility, Physiological Functions and Uses, Preparatio , Culinary Treatment, Preservation, Adulteration, &c. By H. LETHEBY, M.B. M.A. Ph.D. &c. Crown 8vo. price 6s.

COULTHART'S DECIMAL INTEREST TABLES at 24 Different Rates not exceeding 5 per Cent. Calculated for the use of Bankers. To which are added Commission Tables at One-Eighth and One-Fourth per Cent. 8vo. price 15s.

MAUNDER'S TREASURY of KNOWLEDGE and LIBRARY of Reference: comprising an English Dictionary and Grammar, Universal Gazetteer, Classical Dictionary, Chronology, Law Dictionary, a Synopsis of the Peerage, useful Tables, &c. Revised Edition. Fcp. 8vo. price 6s.

INDEX.

Acton's Modern Cookery	28
Alcock's Residence in Japan	23
Allies on Formation of Christendom	20
Alpine Guide (The)	23
Althaus on Medical Electricity	14
Andrews's Life of Oliver Cromwell	5
Arnold's Manual of English Literature	7
Arnott's Elements of Physics	11
Arundines Cami	26
Autumn Holidays of a Country Parson	9
Ayre's Treasury of Bible Knowledge	20
Bacon's Essays, by Whately	6
——— Life and Letters, by Spedding	5
——— Works, edited by Spedding	6
Bain's Logic, Deductive and Inductive	10
——— Mental and Moral Science	10
——— on the Emotions and Will	10
——— on the Senses and Intellect	10
——— on the Study of Character	10
Ball's Alpine Guide	23
Bayldon's Rents and Tillages	19
Beaten Tracks	23
Becker's Charicles and Gallus	25
Benfey's Sanskrit Dictionary	8
Bernard on British Neutrality	1
Black's Treatise on Brewing	28
Blackley's Word-Gossip	7
——— German-English Dictionary	8
Blaine's Rural Sports	26
——— Veterinary Art	27
Bourne on Screw Propeller	18
Bourne's Catechism of the Steam Engine	18
——— Handbook of Steam Engine	18
——— Improvements in the Steam Engine	18
——— Treatise on the Steam Engine	18
——— Examples of Modern Engines	18
Bowdler's Family Shakspeare	26
Brande's Dictionary of Science, Literature, and Art	13
Bray's (C.) Education of the Feelings	10
——— Philosophy of Necessity	10
——— on Force	10
Browne's Exposition of the 39 Articles	19
Buckle's History of Civilization	4
Bull's Hints to Mothers	28
——— Maternal Management of Children	28
Bunsen's (Baron) Ancient Egypt	4
——— God in History	3
——— Memoirs	5
Bunsen (E. De) on Apocrypha	21
——— 's Keys of St. Peter	21
Burke's Vicissitudes of Families	5
Burton's Christian Church	4
——— Vikram and the Vampire	24
Cabinet Lawyer	28
Calvert's Wife's Manual	21
Cates's Biographical Dictionary	5
Cats' and Farlie's Moral Emblems	16
Changed Aspects of Unchanged Truths	9
Chesney's Euphrates Expedition	22
——— Indian Polity	3
——— Waterloo Campaign	2
——— and Reeve's Military Resources of Prussia and France, &c.	2
Child's Physiological Essays	15
Chorale Book for England	16
Clough's Lives from Plutarch	2
Colbe's Norman Kings of England	3
Colenso (Bishop) on Pentateuch and Book of Joshua	20
Commonplace Philosopher in Town and Country	9
Conington's Chemical Analysis	14
——— Translation of Virgil's Æneid	26
Contanseau's French-English Dictionaries	8
Conybeare and Howson's Work on St. Paul	19
Cook on the Acts	19
Cook's Voyages	23
Cooper's Surgical Dictionary	14
Copland's Dictionary of Practical Medicine	15
Cotton's Introduction to Confirmation	19
Coulthart's Decimal Interest Tables	28
Counsel and Comfort from a City Pulpit	9
Cox's Aryan Mythology	4
——— Manual of Mythology	5
——— Tale of the Great Persian War	3
——— Tales of Ancient Greece	25
Cresy's Encyclopædia of Civil Engineering	18
Critical Essays of a Country Parson	9
Crowe's History of France	2
Culley's Handbook of Telegraphy	17
Cusack's History of Ireland	3
D'Aubigné's History of the Reformation in the time of Calvin	2
Davidson's Introduction to New Testament	20
Dead Shot (The), by Marksman	26
De la Rive's Treatise on Electricity	12
Denison's Vice-Regal Life	1
De Tocqueville's Democracy in America	2
Disraeli's Lothair	24
Dorell's Reports on the Progress of Medicine	15
Dobson on the Ox	27
Dove on Storms	11
Doyle's Fairyland	16
Dyer's City of Rome	3
Eastlake's Hints on Household Taste	17
——— History of Oil Painting	16

EASTLAKE'S Gothic Revival.................. 17
——— Life of Gibson 16
EDMUNDS'S Names of Places 9
EDWARDS'S Shipmaster's Guide............ 27
Elements of Botany 13
ELLICOTT on the Revision of the English
 New Testament............ 19
——'s Commentary on Ephesians.... 19
——— Commentary on Galatians 19
————————————— Pastoral Epist. 19
————————————— Philippians, &c. 19
————————————— Thessalonians 19
——— Lectures on the Life of Christ.. 19
Essays and Contributions of A. K. H. B..... 8
EWALD'S History of Israel.................. 20

FAIRBAIRN on Iron Shipbuilding........... 18
——'s Applications of Iron 18
——— Information for Engineers .. 18
——— Mills and Millwork 18
FARADAY'S Life and Letters................ 4
FARRAR'S Families of Speech 9
——— Chapters on Language 7
FELKIN on Hosiery and Lace Manufactures 14
FENNELL'S Book of the Roach............. 26
FFOULKES'S Christendom's Divisions 21
FITZWYGRAM on Horses and Stables 27
Five Years in a Protestant Sisterhood 20
FORBES'S Earls of Granard 5
FOWLER'S Collieries and Colliers 24
FRANCIS'S Fishing Book................... 26
FRESHFIELD'S Travels in the Caucasus..... 22
FROUDE'S History of England.............. 1
——— Short Studies on Great Subjects.. 9

GANOT'S Elementary Physics 11
GILBERT'S Cadore, or Titian's Country 22
GILBERT and CHURCHILL'S Dolomites 23
GIRDLESTONE'S High Alps without Guides 24
GOLDSMITH'S Poems, Illustrated 25
GOULD'S Silver Store 26
GRAHAM'S Book about Words 7
GRANT'S Home Politics 3
——— Ethics of Aristotle 6
Graver Thoughts of a Country Parson..... 9
GRAY'S Anatomy 15
GREENHOW on Bronchitis 14
GROVE on Correlation of Physical Forces .. 12
GURNEY'S Chapters of French History 2
GWILT'S Encyclopædia of Architecture.... 17

HARE on Election of Representatives 7
HARTWIG'S Harmonies of Nature......... 13
——— Polar World............. 13
——— Sea and its Living Wonders .. 13
——— Tropical World 13
HAUGHTON'S Manual of Geology 12
HAWKER'S Instructions to Young Sportsmen 26
HERSCHEL'S Outlines of Astronomy....... 11
HEWITT on Diseases of Women 14
HODGSON'S Theory of Practice 10
——— Time and Space 10
HOLMES'S System of Surgery 14
——— Surgical Diseases of Infancy.. 14
HOOKER and WALKER-ARNOTT'S British
 Flora................................. 13
HORNE'S Introduction to the Scriptures.... 20
——— Compendium of ditto 20
How we Spent the Summer 22
HOWARD'S Gymnastic Exercises 15
HOWITT'S Australian Discovery........... 23
——— Northern Heights of London... 24
——— Rural Life of England........ 24
——— Visits to Remarkable Places... 24
HÜBNER'S Memoir of Sixtus V............ 2
HUGHES'S (W.) Manual of Geography 11

HUME'S Essays 10
——— Treatise on Human Nature 10
HUMPHREY'S Sentiments of Shakspeare.... 16

IHNE'S Roman History 3
INGELOW'S Poems 25
——— Story of Doom 26
——— Mopsa 26

JAMESON'S Saints and Martyrs 17
——— Legends of the Madonna......... 17
——— Monastic Orders 17
JAMESON and EASTLAKE'S History of Our
 Lord 17
JOHNSTON'S Geographical Dictionary...... 11
JUKES on Second Death 21
——— on Types of Genesis 21

KALISCH'S Commentary on the Bible 7
——— Hebrew Grammar 8
KEITH on Fulfilment of Prophecy.......... 20
——— Destiny of the World 20
KERL'S Metallurgy by CROOKES and
 RÖHRIG............................. 18
KESTEVEN'S Domestic Medicine........... 15
KIRBY and SPENCE'S Entomology......... 13

LANDON'S (L. E. L.) Poetical Works 26
LATHAM'S English Dictionary............. 7
——— River Plate 11
LAWLOR'S Pilgrimages in the Pyrenees ... 24
LECKY'S History of European Morals..... 3
——— Rationalism 3
Leisure Hours in Town 9
LESLIE on Land Systems 1
Lessons of Middle Age 9
LETHEBY on Food 28
LEWES' History of Philosophy 4
LEWIS'S Letters 5
LIDDELL and SCOTT'S Greek-English Lexi-
 con and Abridgment................. 8
Life of Man Symbolised 16
Life of Margaret M. Hallahan............ 20
LINDLEY and MOORE'S Treasury of Botany 13
LINDSAY'S Evidence for the Papacy....... 20
LONGMAN'S Edward the Third 2
——— Lectures on the History of Eng-
 land 2
——— Chess Openings 28
Lord's Prayer Illustrated 16
LOUDON'S Agriculture 19
——— Gardening 19
——— Plants 19
LOWNDES'S Engineer's Handbook 13
LUBBOCK on Origin of Civilisation........ 12
Lyra Eucharistica 22
——— Germanica 16, 21
——— Messianica 22
——— Mystica 22

MACAULAY'S (Lord) Essays 3
——— History of England .. 1
——— Lays of Ancient Rome 25
——— Miscellaneous Writings 9
——— Speeches 7
——— Complete Works 1
MACFARREN'S Lectures on Harmony 16
MACLEOD'S Elements of Political Economy 7
——— Dictionary of Political Eco-
 nomy 7
——— Elements of Banking 27
——— Theory and Practice of Banking 27
MCCULLOCH'S Dictionary of Commerce... 27
——— Geographical Dictionary .. 11
MAGUIRE'S Life of Father Mathew........ 5

MALET'S Overthrow of the Germanic Confederation by Prussia	2
MANNING'S England and Christendom	21
MARCET on the Larynx	15
MARSHALL'S Physiology	15
MARSHMAN'S Life of Havelock	5
—— History of India	3
MARTINEAU'S Endeavours after the Christian Life	22
MASSEY'S History of England	2
MASSINGBERD'S History of the Reformation	4
MATHESON'S England to Delhi	22
MAUNDER'S Biographical Treasury	5
—— Geographical Treasury	11
—— Historical Treasury	4
—— Scientific and Literary Treasury	13
—— Treasury of Knowledge	24
—— Treasury of Natural History	13
MAURY'S Physical Geography	11
MAY'S Constitutional History of England	2
MELVILLE'S Digby Grand	25
—— General Bounce	25
—— Gladiators	25
—— Good for Nothing	25
—— Holmby House	25
—— Interpreter	25
—— Kate Coventry	25
—— Queen's Maries	25
Memoir of Bishop COTTON	4
MENDELSSOHN'S Letters	5
MERIVALE'S (H.) Historical Studies	2
—— (C.) Fall of the Roman Republic	3
—— Romans under the Empire	3
MERRIFIELD and EVER'S Navigation	11
MILES on Horse's Foot and Horseshoeing	27
—— Horses' Teeth and Stables	27
MILL (J.) on the Mind	10
MILL (J. S.) on Liberty	6
—— on Representative Government	6
—— on Utilitarianism	6
MILL'S (J. S.) Dissertations and Discussions	7
—— Political Economy	6
—— System of Logic	6
—— Hamilton's Philosophy	6
—— Inaugural Address	7
—— England and Ireland	6
—— Subjection of Women	6
MILLER'S Elements of Chemistry	13
—— Hymn-Writers	21
MITCHELL'S Manual of Assaying	15
MONSELL'S Beatitudes	22
—— His Presence not his Memory	22
—— 'Spiritual Songs'	22
MOORE'S Irish Melodies	25
—— Lalla Rookh	25
—— Poetical Works	25
—— Power of the Soul over the Body	21
MORELL'S Elements of Psychology	10
—— Mental Philosophy	10
MULLER'S (MAX) Chips from a German Workshop	10
—— Lectures on the Science of Language	7
—— (K. O.) Literature of Ancient Greece	3
MURCHISON on Liver Complaints	15
MURE'S Language and Literature of Greece	3
New Testament, Illustrated Edition	16
NEWMAN'S History of his Religious Opinions	5
NIGHTINGALE'S Notes on Hospitals	24
NILSSON'S Scandinavia	12
No Appeal	24
NORTHCOTE'S Sanctuaries of the Madonna	20
NORTHCOTT'S Lathes and Turning	17
NORTON'S City of London	23

ODLING'S Animal Chemistry	14
—— Course of Practical Chemistry	14
—— Manual of Chemistry	13
—— Lectures on Carbon	14
—— Outlines of Chemistry	14
Our Children's Story	25
OWEN'S Lectures on the Invertebrate Animals	12
—— Comparative Anatomy and Physiology of Vertebrated Animals	12
PACKE'S Guide to the Pyrenees	23
PAGET'S Lectures on Surgical Pathology	14
PEREIRA'S Manual of Materia Medica	15
PERKIN'S Italian and Tuscan Sculptors	17
PEWTNER'S Comprehensive Specifier	28
PHILLIPS'S Guide to Geology	12
Pictures in Tyrol	22
PIESSE'S Art of Perfumery	18
—— Natural Magic	18
PRATT'S Law of Building Societies	28
PRENDERGAST'S Mastery of Languages	8
PRESCOTT'S Scripture Difficulties	20
PROCTOR on Plurality of Worlds	11
—— Saturn and its System	11
RAE'S Westward by Rail	23
Recreations of a Country Parson	6
REICHEL'S See of Rome	20
REILY'S Map of Mont Blanc	23
REIMANN on Aniline Dyes	15
REYNOLDS' Glaphyra, and other Poems	26
RILEY'S Memorials of London	23
RIVERS' Rose Amateur's Guide	13
ROBBIN'S Cavalry Catechism	27
ROGER'S Correspondence of Greyson	9
—— Eclipse of Faith	9
—— Defence of ditto	9
—— Essays from the *Edinburgh Review*	9
—— Reason and Faith	9
ROGET'S English Words and Phrases	7
Roma Sotterranea	24
RONALD'S Fly-Fisher's Entomology	26
ROSE'S Ignatius Loyola	2
ROWTON'S Debater	7
RULE'S Karaite Jews	20
RUSSELL'S (Earl) Speeches and Despatches	1
—— on Government and Constitution	1
SANDAR'S Justinian's Institutes	6
SAMUELSON'S German Working Man	24
SCHEFFLER on Ocular Defects and Spectacles	15
SCOTT'S Lectures on the Fine Arts	16
—— Albert Durer	16
SEEBOHM'S Oxford Reformers of 1498	2
SEWELL'S After Life	24
—— Amy Herbert	24
—— Cleve Hall	24
—— Earl's Daughter	24
—— Examination for Confirmation	21
—— Experience of Life	24
—— Gertrude	24
—— Glimpse of the World	24
—— History of the Early Church	24
—— Ivors	24
—— Journal of a Home Life	24
—— Katharine Ashton	24
—— Laneton Parsonage	24
—— Margaret Percival	24
—— Passing Thoughts on Religion	21
—— Preparations for Communion	21
—— Principles of Education	21
—— Readings for Confirmation	21
SEWELL'S Readings for Lent	21
—— Tales and Stories	24
—— Thoughts for the Age	21
—— Ursula	24

Sewell's Thoughts for the Holy Week	21
Shaftesbury's Characteristics	10
Shakespeare's Midsummer Night's Dream illustrated with Silhouettes	16
Shipley's Church and the World	20
———— Invocation of Saints	22
Short's Church History	4
Smart's Walker's Pronouncing Dictionary	8
Smith's (A. C.) Tour in Portugal	22
———— (Southwood) Philosophy of Health	28
———— (J.) Paul's Voyage and Shipwreck	19
———— (Sydney) Miscellaneous Works	9
———— Wit and Wisdom	4
———— Life and Letters	5
Southey's Doctor	7
———— Poetical Works	25
Stanley's History of British Birds	12
Stebbing's Analysis of Mill's Logic	6
Stephen's Essays in Ecclesiastical Biography	5
Stirling's Secret of Hegel	10
Stonehenge on the Dog	27
———— on the Greyhound	27
Strickland's Tudor Princesses	5
———— Queens of England	5
Strong and Free	10
Sunday Afternoons at the Parish Church of a Scottish University City (St. Andrews)	9
Sweetman's Through the Night, and Onward	24
Taylor's History of India	3
———— (Jeremy) Works, edited by Eden	22
Thirlwall's History of Greece	2
Thompson's (Archbishop) Laws of Thought	7
———— (A. T.) Conspectus	15
———— Paraguayan War	23
Three Weddings	24
Todd (A.) on Parliamentary Government	1
Todd and Bowman's Anatomy and Physiology of Man	15
Trench's Realities of Irish Life	3
Trollope's Barchester Towers	24
———— Warden	24
Twiss's Law of Nations	27
Tyndall on Diamagnetism	12
———— Heat	11
———— Sound	12

Tyndall's Faraday as a Discoverer	4
———— Lectures on Light	12
Uncle Peter's Fairy Tale	24
Ure's Dictionary of Arts, Manufactures, and Mines	17
Van Der Hoeven's Handbook of Zoology	12
Warburton's Hunting Songs	26
Watson's Principles and Practice of Physic	14
Watts's Dictionary of Chemistry	13
Webb's Objects for Common Telescopes	11
Webster and Wilkinson's Greek Testament	20
Weld's Notes on Burgundy	23
Wellington's Life, by the Rev. G. R. Gleig	5
West on Children's Diseases	14
Whately's English Synonymes	6
———— Logic	6
———— Rhetoric	6
Whately on a Future State	21
———— Religious Worship	22
———— Truth of Christianity	22
Whist, what to lead, by Cam	28
White and Riddle's Latin-English Dictionaries	8
Wilcock's Sea Fisherman	27
Williams's Aristotle's Ethics	6
———— History of Wales	2
Williams on Climate of South of France	14
———— Consumption	15
Willis's Principles of Mechanism	17
Winslow on Light	12
Wood's Bible Animals	12
———— Homes without Hands	12
Woodward's Historical and Chronological Encyclopædia	4
Yeo's Manual of Zoology	12
Yonge's English-Greek Lexicons	8
———— Editions of Horace	26
Youatt on the Dog	27
———— on the Horse	27
Zeller's Socrates	
———— Stoics, Epicureans, and Sceptics	6

LONDON: PRINTED BY
SPOTTISWOODE AND CO., NEW-STREET SQUARE
AND PARLIAMENT STREET

www.ingramcontent.com/pod-product-compliance
Lightning Source LLC
Chambersburg PA
CBHW020311240426
43673CB00039B/774